More praise for

THE

SWERVE

"The Swerve is an adventure story about scholarship that locates the foundations of modern secular, scientific thought in the brilliance and heroism of our intellectual forbears."

—Harold Varmus, Nobel Laureate in Medicine

"Greenblatt brilliantly ushers readers into this world, which is at once recognizable and wholly foreign. He has an evocative hand with description and a liquid way of introducing supporting players who soon become principals: Democritus, Epicurius, scribe monks, Thomas More, Giordano Bruno, Montaigne and Darwin, to name just a few. More wonderfully illuminating Renaissance history from a master scholar and historian."

—*Kirkus Reviews*, starred review

"[A] wondrous book."   —Nick Owchar, *Los Angeles Times*

"Whether it's the culture of medieval monasteries, Florentine humanists enthralled by ancient literature or the scandal-ridden Renaissance Papacy, Greenblatt makes the material spring to life."   —Dan Cryer, *Newsday*

"A fascinating, intelligent look at what may well be the most historically resonant book-hunt of all time."   —*Booklist*

"An intense, emotional telling of a true story. . . . A chapter in how we became what we are, how we arrived at the worldview of the present."   —John Timpane, *Philadelphia Inquirer*

"Mesmerizing. . . . Richly entertaining."   —*Newsweek*

"A wonderfully engaging book starring two often forgotten heroes of Western culture: the Roman poet Lucretius, who argued that the world was made up of atoms and that fear of death was foolish, and Poggio Bracciolini, whose rediscovery of Lucretius's great poem launched all kinds of radical intellectual inquiry into the modern world. Another triumph for Stephen Greenblatt."   —Mary Beard, professor of classics, University of Cambridge

"A love letter to books. . . . What *The Swerve* does so well is to resurrect so joyously a time when people truly loved books, and remind us what it is like to sway and swerve to the beauty of the written word."   —Jimmy So, *Daily Beast*

"Erudite and entertaining. . . . A thrilling, suspenseful tale that left this reader inspired."   —Buzzy Jackson, *Boston Globe*

"In this outstandingly constructed assessment of the birth of philosophical modernity, renowned Shakespeare scholar Greenblatt . . . deftly transports readers to the dawn of the Renaissance."   —Brian Odom Pelham, *Library Journal*, starred review

"This romantic tale of a book lover who saved a nearly extinct work of genius, which in turn might have caused a dramatic swerve into our modern world is, in Greenblatt's hands, deservedly and ably rescued." —Kimberly Marlowe Hartnett, *Seattle Times*

"*The Swerve* reveals a key moment in the history of man—the precise moment when 'humanism' in its first sense, the quest for the grammar of our ancestors, becomes 'humanism' in our sense, the quest for meaning in our pleasures. Full of weird Latin lore, vivid Renaissance characters, and startling new stories, this is truly the book that puts the epic back in Epicurean."
—Adam Gopnik, author of *The Table Comes First*

"A delightfully engaging, informative and provocative account of Bracciolini's discovery and its implications for the emergence of 'modern' culture and philosophy. Filled with spicy and surprising stories about the ancient world, the Middle Ages, and the Renaissance, *The Swerve* is an Epicurean delight."
—Glenn C. Altschuler, *San Francisco Chronicle*

"A richly imagined recreation of a forgotten history."
—Jason Gots, *Big Think*

"[Greenblatt's] story is too well imagined to recount fully here, beyond saying that the pleasures of literary detective work like his and like Poggio's often emerge from historical set pieces."
—Larry Shillock, *Bloomsbury Review*

"With his characteristic breathtaking prose, Greenblatt leads us on an amazing journey through a time when the world swerved in a new direction." —Henry L. Carrigan Jr., *BookPage*

"The strands of religion and paganism, of preservation and destruction, and the continual collision between these forces that Greenblatt does include are dexterously woven into a marvelous, protean narrative. This richly synthetic intellectual history will captivate readers." —Jaya Chatterjee, *Bookslut*

"The vivid descriptions of events and details . . . make for a suspenseful and enlightening read." —Abigail Licad, *California Literary Review*

"Stephen Greenblatt's new book lays out a banquet of learned, graceful prose. The author of the 2005 best seller *Will in the World* has once again resurrected long-dead people and ways of life to show how much they still matter." —John Repp, *Cleveland Plain Dealer*

"Greenblatt is most thrilling when he is on the trail of the intrepid book hunter rescuing great works from the engulfing darkness of time." —Mary-Liz Shaw, *Milwaukee Journal Sentinel*

"Greenblatt has written a seductive, beautiful book that will inspire wonder, reflection, and the pursuit of pleasure." —Anthony Grafton, *New York Review of Books*

"An exceptionally interesting book and Greenblatt is eloquent and erudite, the ideal guide to a moment of extraordinary change." —*Sunday Times* (London)

"Greenblatt treats the central narrative thread of *The Swerve*, his engaging retelling of Poggio's discovery of the manuscript of Lucretius, as an exemplary story of how the world became modern in the Renaissance." —David Quint, *New Republic*

"Part biography, part philosophy . . . part pop history page-turner. . . . *The Swerve* proves as approachable as it is provocative." —*Post and Courier*

THE
SWERVE

How the World Became Modern

STEPHEN
GREENBLATT

W. W. NORTON & COMPANY

New York • London

To Abigail and Alexa

Excerpt from *Giordano Bruno: Philosopher/Heretic* by Ingrid D. Rowland. Copyright © 2008 by Ingrid D. Rowland. Reprinted by permission of Farrar, Straus and Giroux, LLC. Excerpt from *The Library of the Villa dei Papiri at Herculaneum* by David Sider. © 2005 J. Paul Getty Trust. Translation from *The Epigrams of Philodemos* by David Sider. Reproduced with permission. Excerpt from Christopher Hass. *Alexandria in Late Antiquity: Topography and Social Conflict*, p. 172. © 1997 The Johns Hopkins University Press. Reprinted with permission of The Johns Hopkins University Press.

For information about permission to reproduce selections from this book,
write to Permissions, W. W. Norton & Company, Inc.,
500 Fifth Avenue, New York, NY 10110

For information about special discounts for bulk purchases,
please contact W. W. Norton Special Sales at
specialsales@wwnorton.com or 800-233-4830

Manufacturing by Courier Westford
Book design by JAMdesign
Production manager: Julia Druskin

Library of Congress Cataloging-in-Publication Data

Greenblatt, Stephen, 1943–
The swerve : how the world became modern / Stephen Greenblatt. — 1st ed.
    p. cm.
Includes bibliographical references and index.
ISBN 978-0-393-06447-6 (hardcover)
1. Lucretius Carus, Titus—Influence. 2. Lucretius Carus,
Titus. De rerum natura. 3. Renaissance. 4. Philosophy, Renaissance
5. Science, Renaissance. 6. Civilization, Modern. I. Title.
PA6484.G69 2011
940.2'1—dc23

                                        2011019765

ISBN 978-0-393-34340-3 pbk.

W. W. Norton & Company, Inc.
500 Fifth Avenue, New York, N.Y. 10110
www.wwnorton.com

W. W. Norton & Company Ltd.
Castle House, 75/76 Wells Street, London W1T 3QT

1 2 3 4 5 6 7 8 9 0

CONTENTS

THE
SWERVE

PREFACE

WHEN I WAS a student, I used to go at the end of the school year to the Yale Co-op to see what I could find to read over the summer. I had very little pocket money, but the bookstore would routinely sell its unwanted titles for ridiculously small sums. They would be jumbled together in bins through which I would rummage, with nothing much in mind, waiting for something to catch my eye. On one of my forays, I was struck by an extremely odd paperback cover, a detail from a painting by the surrealist Max Ernst. Under a crescent moon, high above the earth, two pairs of legs—the bodies were missing—were engaged in what appeared to be an act of celestial coition. The book—a prose translation of Lucretius' two-thousand-year-old poem *On the Nature of Things (De rerum natura)*—was marked down to ten cents, and I bought it, I confess, as much for the cover as for the classical account of the material universe.

Ancient physics is not a particularly promising subject for vacation reading, but sometime over the summer I idly picked up the book and began to read. I immediately encountered ample justification for the erotic cover. Lucretius begins with an ardent hymn to Venus, the goddess of love, whose coming in the spring has scattered the clouds, flooded the sky with light, and filled the entire world with frenzied sexual desire:

First, goddess, the birds of the air, pierced to the heart
with your powerful shafts, signal your entry. Next wild
creatures and cattle bound over rich pastures and swim
rushing rivers: so surely are they all captivated by your
charm, and eagerly follow your lead. Then you inject
seductive love into the heart of every creature that lives
in the seas and mountains and river torrents and bird-
haunted thickets, implanting in it the passionate urge to
reproduce its kind.

Startled by the intensity of this opening, I continued on,
past a vision of Mars asleep on Venus' lap—"vanquished by
the never-healing wound of love, throwing back his handsome
neck and gazing up at you"; a prayer for peace; a tribute to the
wisdom of the philosopher Epicurus; and a resolute condemnation of superstitious fears. When I reached the beginning
of a lengthy exposition of philosophical first principles, I fully
expected to lose interest: no one had assigned the book to me,
my only object was pleasure, and I had already gotten far more
than my ten cents' worth. But to my surprise, I continued to
find the book thrilling.

It was not Lucretius' exquisite language to which I was
responding. Later I worked through *De rerum natura* in its original Latin hexameters, and I came to understand something
of its rich verbal texture, its subtle rhythms, and the cunning
precision and poignancy of its imagery. But my first encounter
was in Martin Ferguson Smith's workmanlike English prose—
clear and unfussy, but hardly remarkable. No, it was something
else that reached me, something that lived and moved within
the sentences for more than 200 densely packed pages. I am
committed by trade to urging people to attend carefully to the
verbal surfaces of what they read. Much of the pleasure and
interest of poetry depends on such attention. But it is nonethe-

less possible to have a powerful experience of a work of art even in a modest translation, let alone a brilliant one. That is, after all, how most of the literate world has encountered Genesis or the *Iliad* or *Hamlet*, and, though it is certainly preferable to read these works in their original languages, it is misguided to insist that there is no real access to them otherwise.

I can, in any case, testify that, even in a prose translation, *On the Nature of Things* struck a very deep chord within me. Its power depended to some extent on personal circumstances— art always penetrates the particular fissures in one's psychic life. The core of Lucretius' poem is a profound, therapeutic meditation on the fear of death, and that fear dominated my entire childhood. It was not fear of my own death that so troubled me; I had the ordinary, healthy child's intimation of immortality. It was rather my mother's absolute certainty that she was destined for an early death.

My mother was not afraid of the afterlife: like most Jews she had only a vague and hazy sense of what might lie beyond the grave, and she gave it very little thought. It was death itself— simply ceasing to be—that terrified her. For as far back as I can remember, she brooded obsessively on the imminence of her end, invoking it again and again, especially at moments of parting. My life was full of extended, operatic scenes of farewell. When she went with my father from Boston to New York for the weekend, when I went off to summer camp, even—when things were especially hard for her—when I simply left the house for school, she clung tightly to me, speaking of her fragility and of the distinct possibility that I would never see her again. If we walked somewhere together, she would frequently come to a halt, as if she were about to keel over. Sometimes she would show me a vein pulsing in her neck and, taking my finger, make me feel it for myself, the sign of her heart dangerously racing.

She must have been only in her late thirties when my own memories of her fears begin, and those fears evidently went back much further in time. They seem to have taken root about a decade before my birth, when her younger sister, only sixteen years old, died of strep throat. This event—one all too familiar in the world before the introduction of penicillin—was still for my mother an open wound: she spoke of it constantly, weeping quietly, and making me read and reread the poignant letters that the teenaged girl had written through the course of her fatal illness.

I understood early on that my mother's "heart"—the palpitations that brought her and everyone around her to a halt—was a life strategy. It was a symbolic means to identify with and mourn her dead sister. It was a way to express both anger—"you see how upset you have made me"—and love—"you see how I am still doing everything for you, even though my heart is about to break." It was an acting-out, a rehearsal, of the extinction that she feared. It was above all a way to compel attention and demand love. But this understanding did not make its effect upon my childhood significantly less intense: I loved my mother and dreaded losing her. I had no resources to untangle psychological strategy and dangerous symptom. (I don't imagine that she did either.) And as a child I had no means to gauge the weirdness of this constant harping on impending death and this freighting of every farewell with finality. Only now that I have raised a family of my own do I understand how dire the compulsion must have been that led a loving parent—and she was loving—to lay such a heavy emotional burden on her children. Every day brought a renewal of the dark certainty that her end was very near.

As it turned out, my mother lived to a month shy of her ninetieth birthday. She was still only in her fifties when I encountered *On the Nature of Things* for the first time. By then my dread of her dying had become entwined with a painful perception that she had blighted much of her life—and cast a shadow on my own—in the service of her obsessive fear. Lucretius' words therefore rang out with a terrible clarity: "Death is nothing to us." To spend your existence in the grip of anxiety about death, he wrote, is mere folly. It is a sure way to let your life slip from you incomplete and unenjoyed. He gave voice as well to a thought I had not yet quite allowed myself, even inwardly, to articulate: to inflict this anxiety on others is manipulative and cruel.

Such was, in my case, the poem's personal point of entry, the immediate source of its power over me. But that power was not only a consequence of my peculiar life history. *On the Nature of Things* struck me as an astonishingly convincing account of the way things actually are. To be sure, I easily grasped that many features of this ancient account now seem absurd. What else would we expect? How accurate will our account of the universe seem two thousand years from now? Lucretius believed that the sun circled around the earth, and he argued that the sun's heat and size could hardly be much greater than are perceived by our senses. He thought that worms were spontaneously generated from the wet soil, explained lightning as seeds of fire expelled from hollow clouds, and pictured the earth as a menopausal mother exhausted by the effort of so much breeding. But at the core of the poem lay key principles of a modern understanding of the world.

The stuff of the universe, Lucretius proposed, is an infinite number of atoms moving randomly through space, like dust motes in a sunbeam, colliding, hooking together, forming complex structures, breaking apart again, in a ceaseless process of creation and destruction. There is no escape from this process. When you look up at the night sky and, feeling unaccountably moved, marvel at the numberless stars, you are not seeing the handiwork of the gods or a crystalline sphere detached from our transient world. You are seeing the same material world of which you are a part and from whose elements you are made. There is no master plan, no divine architect, no intelligent design. All things, including the species to which you belong, have evolved over vast stretches of time. The evolution is random, though in the case of living organisms it involves a principle of natural selection. That is, species that are suited to survive and to reproduce successfully endure, at least for a time; those that are not so well suited die off quickly. But nothing—from our own species to the planet on which we live to the sun that lights our days—lasts forever. Only the atoms are immortal.

In a universe so constituted, Lucretius argued, there is no reason to think that the earth or its inhabitants occupy a central place, no reason to set humans apart from all other animals, no hope of bribing or appeasing the gods, no place for religious fanaticism, no call for ascetic self-denial, no justification for dreams of limitless power or perfect security, no rationale for wars of conquest or self-aggrandizement, no possibility of triumphing over nature, no escape from the constant making and unmaking and remaking of forms. On the other side of anger at those who either peddled false visions of security or incited irrational fears of death, Lucretius offered a feeling of liberation and the power to stare down what had once seemed so menacing. What human beings can and should do, he wrote, is to conquer their fears, accept the fact that they themselves and all the things they encounter are transitory, and embrace the beauty and the pleasure of the world.

I marveled—I continue to marvel—that these perceptions were fully articulated in a work written more than two thousand years ago. The line between this work and modernity is not direct: nothing is ever so simple. There were innumerable forgettings, disappearances, recoveries, dismissals, distortions, challenges, transformations, and renewed forgettings. And yet the vital connection is there. Hidden behind the worldview I recognize as my own is an ancient poem, a poem once lost, apparently irrevocably, and then found.

It is not surprising that the philosophical tradition from which Lucretius' poem derived, so incompatible with the cult of the gods and the cult of the state, struck some, even in the tolerant culture of the classical Mediterranean, as scandalous. The adherents of this tradition were on occasion dismissed as mad or impious or simply stupid. And with the rise of Christianity, their texts were attacked, ridiculed, burned, or—most devastating— ignored and eventually forgotten. What is astonishing is that one magnificent articulation of the whole philosophy—the poem whose recovery is the subject of this book—should have survived. Apart from a few odds and ends and secondhand reports, all that was left of the whole rich tradition was contained in that single work. A random fire, an act of vandalism, a decision to snuff out the last trace of views judged to be heretical, and the course of modernity would have been different.

Of all the ancient masterpieces, this poem is one that should certainly have disappeared, finally and forever, in the company of the lost works that had inspired it. That it did not disappear, that it surfaced after many centuries and began once again to propagate its deeply subversive theses, is something one could be tempted to call a miracle. But the author of the poem in question did not believe in miracles. He thought that nothing could violate the laws of nature. He posited instead what he called a "swerve,"—Lucretius' principal Latin word for it was *clinamen*—an unexpected, unpredictable movement of matter. The reappearance of his poem was such a swerve, an unforeseen deviation from the direct trajectory—in this case, toward oblivion—on which that poem and its philosophy seemed to be traveling.

When it returned to full circulation after a millennium,

much of what the work said about a universe formed out of the clash of atoms in an infinite void seemed absurd. But those very things that first were deemed both impious and nonsensical turned out to be the basis for the contemporary rational understanding of the entire world. What is at stake is not only the startling recognition of key elements of modernity in antiquity, though it is certainly worth reminding ourselves that Greek and Roman classics, largely displaced from our curriculum, have in fact definitively shaped modern consciousness. More surprising, perhaps, is the sense, driven home by every page of *On the Nature of Things*, that the scientific vision of the world—a vision of atoms randomly moving in an infinite universe—was in its origins imbued with a poet's sense of wonder. Wonder did not depend on gods and demons and the dream of an afterlife; in Lucretius it welled up out of a recognition that we are made of the same matter as the stars and the oceans and all things else. And this recognition was the basis for the way he thought we should live our lives.

In my view, and by no means mine alone, the culture in the wake of antiquity that best epitomized the Lucretian embrace of beauty and pleasure and propelled it forward as a legitimate and worthy human pursuit was that of the Renaissance. The pursuit was not restricted to the arts. It shaped the dress and the etiquette of courtiers; the language of the liturgy; the design and decoration of everyday objects. It suffused Leonardo da Vinci's scientific and technological explorations, Galileo's vivid dialogues on astronomy, Francis Bacon's ambitious research projects, and Richard Hooker's theology. It was virtually a reflex, so that works that were seemingly far away from any aesthetic ambition at all—Machiavelli's analysis of political strategy, Walter Ralegh's description of Guiana, or Robert Burton's encyclopedic account of mental illness—were crafted in such a way as to produce the most intense pleasure. But the arts of the Renaissance—painting, sculpture, music, architecture, and literature—were the supreme manifestations of the pursuit of beauty.

My own particular love was and is for Shakespeare, but Shakespeare's achievement seemed to me only one spectacular facet of a larger cultural movement that included Alberti, Michelangelo, and Raphael, Ariosto, Montaigne, and Cervantes, along with dozens of other artists and writers. That movement had many intertwining and often conflicting aspects, but coursing through all of them there was a glorious affirmation of vitality. The affirmation extends even to those many works of Renaissance art in which death seems to triumph. Hence the grave at the close of *Romeo and Juliet* does not so much swallow up the lovers as launch them into the future as the embodiments of love. In the enraptured audiences that have flocked to the play for more than four hundred years, Juliet in effect gets her wish that after death, night should take Romeo

> and cut him out in little stars
> And he will make the face of heaven so fine
> That all the world will be in love with night.
> (III.ii.22–24)

A comparably capacious embrace of beauty and pleasure—an embrace that somehow extends to death as well as life, to dissolution as well as creation—characterizes Montaigne's restless reflections on matter in motion, Cervantes's chronicle of his mad knight, Michelangelo's depiction of flayed skin, Leonardo's sketches of whirlpools, Caravaggio's loving attention to the dirty soles of Christ's feet.

Something happened in the Renaissance, something that surged up against the constraints that centuries had constructed around curiosity, desire, individuality, sustained attention to the material world, the claims of the body. The cultural shift is notoriously difficult to define, and its significance has been fiercely contested. But it can be intuited easily enough when you look in Siena at Duccio's painting of the enthroned Virgin, the *Maestà*, and then in Florence at Botticelli's *Primavera*, a painting that, not coincidentally, was influenced by *On the Nature of Things*. In the principal panel of Duccio's magnificent altarpiece (ca. 1310), the adoration of the angels, saints, and martyrs is focused on a serene center, the heavily robed Mother of God and her child absorbed in solemn contemplation. In the *Primavera* (ca. 1482), the ancient gods of the spring appear together in a verdant wood, all intently engaged in the complex, rhythmic choreography of renewed natural fecundity evoked in Lucretius' poem; "Spring comes and Venus, preceded by Venus' winged harbinger, and mother Flora, following hard on the heels of Zephyr, prepares the way for them, strewing all their path with a profusion of exquisite hues and scents." The key to the shift lies not only in the intense, deeply informed revival of interest in the pagan deities and the rich meanings that once attached to them. It lies also in the whole vision of a world in motion, a world not rendered insignificant but made more beautiful by its transience, its erotic energy, and its ceaseless change.

Though most evident in works of art, the change from one way of perceiving and living in the world to another was not restricted to aesthetics: it helps to account for the intellectual daring of Copernicus and Vesalius, Giordano Bruno and William Harvey, Hobbes and Spinoza. The transformation was not sudden or once-for-all, but it became increasingly possible to turn away from a preoccupation with angels and demons and immaterial causes and to focus instead on things in this world; to understand that humans are made of the same stuff as everything else and are part of the natural order; to conduct experiments without fearing that one is infringing on God's jealously guarded secrets; to question authorities and challenge received doctrines; to legitimate the pursuit of pleasure and the avoidance of pain; to imagine that there are other worlds beside the one that we inhabit; to entertain the thought that the sun is only one star in an infinite universe; to live an ethical life without reference to postmortem rewards and punishments; to contemplate without trembling the death of the soul. In short, it became possible—never easy, but possible—in the poet Auden's phrase to find the mortal world enough.

There is no single explanation for the emergence of the Renaissance and the release of the forces that have shaped our own world. But I have tried in this book to tell a little known but exemplary Renaissance story, the story of Poggio Bracciolini's recovery of *On the Nature of Things*. The recovery has the virtue of being true to the term that we use to gesture toward the cultural shift at the origins of modern life and thought: a re-naissance, a rebirth, of antiquity. One poem by itself was certainly not responsible for an entire intellectual, moral, and social transformation—no single work was, let alone one that for centuries could not without danger be spoken about freely in public. But this particular ancient book, suddenly returning to view, made a difference.

This is a story then of how the world swerved in a new direction. The agent of change was not a revolution, an implacable army at the gates, or landfall on an unknown continent. For events of this magnitude, historians and artists have given the popular imagination memorable images: the fall of the Bastille, the sack of Rome, or the moment when the ragged seamen from the Spanish ships planted their flag in the New World. These emblems of world-historic change can be deceptive—the Bastille had almost no prisoners; Alaric's army quickly withdrew from the imperial capital; and, in the Americas, the truly fateful action was not the unfurling of a banner but the first time that an ill and infectious Spanish sailor, surrounded by wondering natives, sneezed or coughed. Still, we can in such cases at least cling to the vivid symbol. But the epochal change with which this book is concerned—though it has affected all of our lives—is not so easily associated with a dramatic image.

When it occurred, nearly six hundred years ago, the key moment was muffled and almost invisible, tucked away behind walls in a remote place. There were no heroic gestures, no observers keenly recording the great event for posterity, no signs in heaven or on earth that everything had changed forever. A short, genial, cannily alert man in his late thirties reached out one day, took a very old manuscript off a library shelf, saw with excitement what he had discovered, and ordered that it be copied. That was all; but it was enough.

The finder of the manuscript could not, of course, have fully grasped the implications of its vision or anticipated its influence, which took centuries to unfold. Indeed, if he had had an intimation of the forces he was unleashing, he might have thought twice about drawing so explosive a work out of the darkness in which it slept. The work that the man held in his hands had been laboriously copied by hand for centuries, but it had long rested uncirculated and perhaps uncomprehended even by the solitary souls who copied it. For many generations, no one spoke of it at all. Between the fourth and the ninth centuries, it was cited fleetingly in lists of grammatical and lexicographical examples, that is, as a quarry of correct Latin usage. In the seventh century Isidore of Seville, compiling a vast encyclopedia, used it as an authority on meteorology. It surfaced again briefly, in the time of Charlemagne, when there was a crucial burst of interest in ancient books and a scholarly Irish monk named Dungal carefully corrected a copy. But, neither debated nor disseminated, after each of these fugitive appearances it seemed to sink again beneath the waves. Then, after lying dormant and forgotten for more than a thousand years, it returned to circulation.

The person responsible for this momentous return, Poggio Bracciolini, was an avid letter writer. He penned an account of the event to a friend back in his native Italy, but the letter has been lost. Still, it is possible, on the basis of other letters, both his own and those of his circle, to reconstruct how it came about. For though this particular manuscript would turn out from our perspective to be his greatest find, it was by no means his only one, and it was no accident. Poggio Bracciolini was a book hunter, perhaps the greatest in an age obsessed with ferreting out and recovering the heritage of the ancient world.

The finding of a lost book does not ordinarily figure as a thrilling event, but behind that one moment was the arrest and imprisonment of a pope, the burning of heretics, and a great culturewide explosion of interest in pagan antiquity. The act of discovery fulfilled the life's passion of a brilliant book hunter. And that book hunter, without ever intending or realizing it, became a midwife to modernity.

CHAPTER ONE

THE BOOK HUNTER

IN THE WINTER of 1417, Poggio Bracciolini rode through the wooded hills and valleys of southern Germany toward his distant destination, a monastery reputed to have a cache of old manuscripts. As must have been immediately apparent to the villagers looking out at him from the doors of their huts, the man was a stranger. Slight of build and clean-shaven, he would probably have been modestly dressed in a well-made but simple tunic and cloak. That he was not country-bred was clear, and yet he did not resemble any of the city and court dwellers whom the locals would have been accustomed to glimpse from time to time. Unarmed and unprotected by a clanging suit of armor, he was certainly not a Teutonic knight—one stout blow from a raw-boned yokel's club would have easily felled him. Though he did not seem to be poor, he had none of the familiar signs of wealth and status: he was not a courtier, with gorgeous clothes and perfumed hair worn in long lovelocks, nor was he a nobleman out hunting and hawking. And, as was plain from his clothes and the cut of his hair, he was not a priest or a monk.

Southern Germany at the time was prosperous. The catastrophic Thirty Years' War that would ravage the countryside and shatter whole cities in the region lay far in the future, as did the horrors of our own time that destroyed much of what had survived from this period. In addition to knights, courtiers, and nobles, other men of substance busily traveled the rutted, hard-packed roads. Ravensburg, near Constance, was involved in the linen trade and had recently begun to produce paper. Ulm, on the left bank of the Danube, was a flourishing center of manu-facture and commerce, as were Heidenheim, Aalen, beautiful Rothenburg ob der Tauber, and still more beautiful Würzburg. Burghers, wool brokers, leather and cloth merchants, vintners and brewers, craftsmen and their apprentices, as well as diplo-mats, bankers, and tax collectors, all were familiar sights. But Poggio still did not fit.

There were less prosperous figures too—journeymen, tin-kers, knife-sharpeners, and others whose trades kept them on the move; pilgrims on their way to shrines where they could worship in presence of a fragment of a saint's bone or a drop of sacred blood; jugglers, fortune-tellers, hawkers, acro-bats and mimes traveling from village to village; runaways, vagabonds, and petty thieves. And there were the Jews, with the conical hats and the yellow badges that the Christian authorities forced them to wear, so that they could be easily identified as objects of contempt and hatred. Poggio was cer-tainly none of these.

To those who watched him pass, he must in fact have been a baffling figure. Most people at the time signaled their identi-ties, their place in the hierarchical social system, in visible signs that everyone could read, like the indelible stains on a dyer's hands. Poggio was barely legible. An isolated individual, con-sidered outside the structures of family and occupation, made very little sense. What mattered was what you belonged to or even whom you belonged to. The little couplet Alexander Pope mockingly wrote in the eighteenth century, to put on one of the queen's little pugs, could have applied in earnest in the world that Poggio inhabited:

> I am his Highness' dog at Kew;
> Pray tell me, sir, whose dog are you?

The household, the kinship network, the guild, the corporation —these were the building blocks of personhood. Independence and self-reliance had no cultural purchase; indeed, they could scarcely be conceived, let alone prized. Identity came with a precise, well-understood place in a chain of command and obedience.

To attempt to break the chain was folly. An impertinent gesture—a refusal to bow or kneel or uncover one's head to the appropriate person—could lead to one's nose being slit or one's neck broken. And what, after all, was the point? It was not as if there were any coherent alternatives, certainly not one articulated by the Church or the court or the town oligarchs. The best course was humbly to accept the identity to which destiny assigned you: the ploughman needed only to know how to plough, the weaver to weave, the monk to pray. It was possible, of course, to be better or worse at any of these things; the society in which Poggio found himself acknowledged and, to a considerable degree, rewarded unusual skill. But to prize a person for some ineffable individuality or for many-sidedness or for intense curiosity was virtually unheard of. Indeed, curiosity was said by the Church to be a mortal sin. To indulge it was to risk an eternity in hell.

Who was Poggio, then? Why did he not proclaim his identity on his back, the way decent folks were accustomed to do? He wore no insignia and carried no bundles of merchandise. He had the self-assured air of someone accustomed to the society of the great, but he himself was evidently a figure of no great consequence. Everyone knew what such an important person looked like, for this was a society of retainers and armed guards and liveried servants. The stranger, simply attired, rode in the company of a single companion. When they paused at inns, the companion, who appeared to be an assistant or servant, did the ordering; when the master spoke, it became clear that he knew little or no German and that his native language was Italian.

If he had tried to explain to an inquisitive person what he was up to, the mystery of his identity would only have deepened. In a culture with very limited literacy, to be interested in books was already an oddity. And how could Poggio have accounted for the still odder nature of his particular interests? He was not in search of books of hours or missals or hymnals whose exquisite illuminations and splendid bindings made manifest their value even to the illiterate. These books, some of them jewel-encrusted and edged with gold, were often locked in special boxes or chained to lecterns and shelves, so that light-fingered readers could not make off with them. But they held no special appeal for Poggio. Nor was he drawn to the theological, medical, or legal tomes that were the prestigious tools of the professional elites. Such books had a power to impress and intimidate even those who could not read them. They had a social magic, of the kind associated for the most part with unpleasant events: a lawsuit, a painful swelling in the groin, an accusation of witchcraft or heresy. An ordinary person would have grasped that volumes of this kind had teeth and claws and hence have understood why a clever person might hunt them. But here again Poggio's indifference was baffling.

The stranger was going to a monastery, but he was not a priest or a theologian or an inquisitor, and he was not looking for prayer books. He was after old manuscripts, many of them moldy, worm-eaten, and all but indecipherable even to the best-trained readers. If the sheets of parchment on which such books were written were still intact, they had a certain cash value, since they could be carefully scraped clean with knives, smoothed with talcum powder, and written over anew.

But Poggio was not in the parchment-buying business, and he actually loathed those who scratched off the old letters. He wanted to see what was written on them, even if the writing was crabbed and difficult, and he was most interested in manuscripts that were four or five hundred years old, going back then to the tenth century or even earlier.

To all but a handful of people in Germany, this quest, had Poggio tried to articulate it, would have seemed weird. And it would have seemed weirder still if Poggio had gone on to explain that he was not in fact at all interested in what was written four or five hundred years ago. He despised that time and regarded it as a sink of superstition and ignorance. What he really hoped to find were words that had nothing to do with the moment in which they were written down on the old parchment, words that were in the best possible case uncontaminated by the mental universe of the lowly scribe who copied them. That scribe, Poggio hoped, was dutifully and accurately copying a still older parchment, one made by yet another scribe whose humble life was equally of no particular consequence to the book hunter except insofar as it left behind this trace. If the nearly miraculous run of good fortune held, the earlier manuscript, long vanished into dust, was in turn a faithful copy of a more ancient manuscript, and that manuscript a copy of yet another. Now at last for Poggio the quarry became exciting, and the hunter's heart in his breast beat faster. The trail was leading him back to Rome, not the contemporary Rome of the corrupt papal court, intrigues, political debility, and periodic outbreaks of bubonic plague, but the Rome of the Forum and the Senate House and a Latin language whose crystalline beauty filled him with wonder and the longing for a lost world.

What could any of this mean to anyone who had his feet on the ground in southern Germany in 1417? Listening to Poggio, a superstitious man might have suspected a particular type of sorcery, bibliomancy; a more sophisticated man might have diagnosed a psychological obsession, bibliomania; a pious man might have wondered why any sound soul would feel a passionate attraction for the time before the Saviour brought the promise of redemption to the benighted pagans. And all would have asked the obvious question: whom does this man serve?

Poggio himself might have been hard-pressed for an answer. He had until recently served the pope, as he had served a succession of earlier Roman pontiffs. His occupation was *scriptor*, that is, a skilled writer of official documents in the papal bureaucracy, and, through adroitness and cunning, he had risen to the coveted position of apostolic secretary. He was on hand then to write down the pope's words, record his sovereign decisions, craft in elegant Latin his extensive international correspondence. In a formal court setting, in which physical proximity to the absolute ruler was a key asset, Poggio was a man of importance. He listened while the pope whispered something in his ear; he whispered something back; he knew the meaning of the pope's smiles and frowns. He had access, as the very word "secretary" suggests, to the pope's secrets. And this pope had a great many secrets.

But at the time that Poggio was riding off in search of ancient manuscripts, he was no longer apostolic secretary. He had not displeased his master, the pope, and that master was still alive. But everything had changed. The pope Poggio had served and before whom the faithful (and the less than faithful) had trembled was at that moment in the winter of 1417 sitting in an imperial prison in Heidelberg. Stripped of his title, his name, his power, and his dignity, he had been publicly disgraced, condemned by the princes of his own church. The "holy and infallible" General Council of Constance declared that by his "detestable and unseemly life" he had brought scandal on the Church and on Christendom, and that he was unfit to remain in his exalted office. Accordingly, the council released all believers from fidelity and obedience to him; indeed, it was now forbidden to call him pope or to obey him. In the long history of the Church, with its impressive share of scandals, little like this had happened before—and nothing like it has happened since.

The deposed pope was not there in person, but Poggio, his erstwhile apostolic secretary, may have been present when the archbishop of Riga handed the papal seal to a goldsmith, who solemnly broke it in pieces, along with the papal arms. All of the ex-pope's servants were formally dismissed, and his correspondence—the correspondence that Poggio had been instrumental in managing—was officially terminated. The pope who had called himself John XXIII no longer existed; the man who had borne that title was now once again what he had been christened, Baldassare Cossa. And Poggio was now a masterless man.

To be masterless in the early fifteenth century was for most men an unenviable, even dangerous state. Villages and towns looked with suspicion on itinerants; vagrants were whipped and branded; and on lonely paths in a largely unpoliced world the unprotected were exceedingly vulnerable. Of course, Poggio was hardly a vagrant. Sophisticated and highly skilled, he had long moved in the circles of the great. The armed guards at the Vatican and the Castel St. Angelo let him pass through the gates without a word of inquiry, and important suitors to the papal court tried to catch his eye. He had direct access to an absolute ruler, the wealthy and cunning master of enormous territories, who also claimed to be the spiritual master of all of Western Christendom. In the private chambers of palaces, as in the papal court itself, the apostolic secretary Poggio was a familiar presence, exchanging jokes with bejeweled cardinals, chatting with ambassadors, and drinking fine wine from cups of crystal and gold. In Florence he had been befriended by some of the most powerful figures in the Signoria, the city's ruling body, and he had a distinguished circle of friends.

But Poggio was not in Rome or Florence. He was in Germany, and the pope he had followed to the city of Constance was in prison. The enemies of John XXIII had triumphed and were now in control. Doors that had once been open to Poggio were firmly shut. And suitors eager for a favor—a dispensation, a legal ruling, a lucrative position for themselves or their relatives—who had paid court to the secretary as a means to pay court to his master were all looking elsewhere. Poggio's income abruptly ceased.

That income had been considerable. Scriptors received no fixed stipend, but they were permitted to charge fees for executing documents and obtaining what were called "concessions of grace," that is, legal favors in matters that required some technical correction or exception granted orally or in writing by the pope. And, of course, there were other, less official fees that would privately flow to someone who had the pope's ear. In the mid-fifteenth century, the income for a secretary was 250 to 300 florins annually, and an entrepreneurial spirit could make much more. At the end of a twelve-year period in this office, Poggio's colleague George of Trebizond had salted away over 4,000 florins in Roman banks, along with handsome investments in real estate.

In his letters to friends Poggio claimed throughout his life that he was neither ambitious nor greedy. He wrote a celebrated essay attacking avarice as one of the most hateful of human vices, and he excoriated the greed of hypocritical monks, unscrupulous princes, and grasping merchants. It would be foolish, of course, to take such professions at face value: there is ample evidence from later in his career, when he managed to return to the papal court, that Poggio used his office to make money hand over fist. By the 1450s, along with a family *palazzo* and a country estate, he had managed to acquire several farms, nineteen separate pieces of land, and two houses in Florence, and he had also made very large deposits in banking and business houses.

But this prosperity lay decades in the future. An official inventory (called a *catasto*) compiled in 1427 by tax officials indicated that Poggio had fairly modest means. And a decade earlier, at the time that John XXIII was deposed, he almost certainly had far less. Indeed, his later acquisitiveness may have been a reaction to the memory of those long months, stretching into several lean years, when he found himself in a strange land without a position or an income and with very few resources on which to fall back. In the winter of 1417, when he rode through the South German countryside, Poggio had little or no idea where his next florins would come from.

It is all the more striking that in this difficult period Poggio did not quickly find a new position or make haste to return to Italy. What he did instead was to go book-hunting.

CHAPTER TWO

THE MOMENT OF
DISCOVERY

I TALIANS HAD BEEN obsessed with book-hunting for the better part of a century, ever since the poet and scholar Petrarch brought glory on himself around 1330 by piecing together Livy's monumental *History of Rome* and finding forgotten masterpieces by Cicero, Propertius, and others. Petrarch's achievement had inspired others to seek out lost classics that had been lying unread, often for centuries. The recovered texts were copied, edited, commented upon, and eagerly exchanged, conferring distinction on those who had found them and forming the basis for what became known as the "study of the humanities."

The "humanists," as those who were devoted to this study were called, knew from carefully poring over the texts that had survived from classical Rome that many once famous books or parts of books were still missing. Occasionally, the ancient authors whom Poggio and his fellow humanists eagerly read gave tantalizing quotations from these books, often accompanying extravagant praise or vituperative attacks. Alongside discussions of Virgil and Ovid, for example, the Roman rhetorician Quintilian remarked that "Macer and Lucretius are certainly worth reading," and went on to discuss Varro of Atax, Cornelius Severus, Saleius Bassus, Gaius Rabirius, Albinovanus Pedo, Marcus Furius Bibaculus, Lucius Accius, Marcus Pacuvius, and others whose works he greatly admired. The humanists knew that some of these missing works were likely to have been lost forever—as it turned out, with the exception of Lucretius, all of the authors just mentioned have been lost—but they suspected that others, perhaps many others, were hidden away in dark places, not only in Italy but across the Alps. After all, Petrarch had found the manuscript of Cicero's *Pro Archia* in Liège, in Belgium, and the Propertius manuscript in Paris.

The prime hunting grounds for Poggio and his fellow book hunters were the libraries of old monasteries, and for good reason: for long centuries monasteries had been virtually the only institutions that cared about books. Even in the stable and prosperous times of the Roman Empire, literacy rates, by our standards at least, were not high. As the empire crumbled, as cities decayed, trade declined, and the increasingly anxious populace scanned the horizon for barbarian armies, the whole Roman system of elementary and higher education fell apart. What began as downsizing went on to wholesale abandonment. Schools closed, libraries and academies shut their doors, professional grammarians and teachers of rhetoric found themselves out of work. There were more important things to worry about than the fate of books.

But all monks were expected to know how to read. In a world increasingly dominated by illiterate warlords, that expectation, formulated early in the history of monasticism, was of incalculable importance. Here is the Rule from the monasteries established in Egypt and throughout the Middle East by the late fourth-century Coptic saint Pachomius. When a candidate for admission to the monastery presents himself to the elders,

> they shall give him twenty Psalms or two of the Apostles' epistles or some other part of Scripture. And if he

is illiterate he shall go at the first, third and sixth hours
to someone who can teach and has been appointed for
him. He shall stand before him and learn very studi-
ously and with all gratitude. The fundamentals of a syl-
lable, the verbs and nouns shall be written for him and
even if he does not want to, he shall be compelled to
read. (Rule 139)

"He shall be compelled to read." It was this compulsion that,
through centuries of chaos, helped to salvage the achievements
of ancient thought.

Though in the most influential of all the monastic rules,
written in the sixth century, St. Benedict did not similarly specify an explicit literacy requirement, he provided the equivalent
of one by including a period each day for reading—"prayerful
reading," as he put it—as well as manual labor. "Idleness is the
enemy of the soul," the saint wrote, and he made certain that
the hours would be filled up. Monks would be permitted to
read at certain other times as well, though such voluntary reading would have to be conducted in strict silence. (In Benedict's
time, as throughout antiquity, reading was ordinarily performed audibly.) But about the prescribed reading times there
was nothing voluntary.

The monks were to read, whether they felt like it or not, and
the Rule called for careful supervision:

Above all, one or two seniors must surely be deputed to
make the rounds of the monastery while the brothers
are reading. Their duty is to see that no brother is so
acediosus as to waste time or engage in idle talk to the
neglect of his reading, and so not only harm himself but
also distract others. (49:17–18)

Acediosus, sometimes translated as "apathetic," refers to an illness, specific to monastic communities, which had already been brilliantly diagnosed in the late fourth century by the Desert Father John Cassian. The monk in the grip of *acedia* would find it difficult or impossible to read. Looking away from his book, he might try to distract himself with gossip but would more likely glance in disgust at his surroundings and at his fellow monks. He would feel that things were better somewhere else, that he was wasting his life, that everything was stale and pointless, that he was suffocating.

> He looks about anxiously this way and that, and sighs
> that none of the brethren come to see him, and often
> goes in and out of his cell, and frequently gazes up at
> the sun, as if it was too slow in setting, and so a kind
> of unreasonable confusion of mind takes possession of
> him like some foul darkness.

Such a monk—and there were evidently many of them—had succumbed to what we would call a clinical state of depression.

Cassian called the disease "the noonday demon," and the Benedictine Rule set a careful watch, especially at reading times, to detect anyone manifesting its symptoms.

> If such a monk is found—God forbid—he should be
> reproved a first and a second time. If he does not amend,
> he must be subjected to the punishment of the rule so
> that the others may have fear.

A refusal to read at the prescribed time—whether because of distraction, boredom, or despair—would thus be visited first by public criticism and then, if the refusal continued, by blows. The symptoms of psychic pain would be driven out by physical pain. And, suitably chastened, the distressed monk would return—in principle at least—to his "prayerful reading."

There was yet another time in which the Benedictine Rule called for reading: every day at meals one of the brothers was assigned, on a weekly basis, to read aloud. Benedict was well aware that for at least certain of the monks this assignment would occasion pride, and he therefore tried to suppress the sensation as best he could: "Let the incoming reader ask all to pray for him so that God may shield him from the feeling of elation." He was aware too that for others the readings would be an occasion for mockery or simply for chat, and here too the Rule made careful provision: "Let there be complete silence. No whispering, no speaking—only the reader's voice should be heard there." But, above all, he wanted to prevent these readings from provoking discussion or debate: "No one should presume to ask a question about the reading or about anything else, lest occasion be given."

"Lest occasion be given": the phrase, in a text normally quite clear, is oddly vague. Occasion to whom or for what? Modern editors sometimes insert the phrase "to the devil" and that indeed may be what is implied here. But why should the Prince of Darkness be excited by a question about the reading? The answer must be that any question, however innocuous, could raise the prospect of a discussion, a discussion that would imply that religious doctrines were open to inquiry and argument.

Benedict did not absolutely prohibit commentary on the sacred texts that were read aloud, but he wanted to restrict its source: "The superior," the Rule allows, "may wish to say a few words of instruction." Those words were not to be questioned or contradicted, and indeed all contention was in principle to be suppressed. As the listing of punishments in the influential rule of the Irish monk Columbanus (born in the year Benedict died) makes clear, lively debate, intellectual or otherwise, was forbidden. To the monk who has dared to contradict a fellow monk with such words as "It is not as you say," there is a heavy penalty: "an imposition of silence or fifty blows." The high walls that hedged about the mental life of the monks—the imposition of silence, the prohibition of questioning, the punishing of debate with slaps or blows of the whip—were all meant to affirm unambiguously that these pious communities were the opposite of the philosophical academies of Greece or Rome, places that had thrived upon the spirit of contradiction and cultivated a restless, wide-ranging curiosity.

All the same, monastic rules did require reading, and that was enough to set in motion an extraordinary chain of consequences. Reading was not optional or desirable or recommended; in a community that took its obligations with deadly seriousness, reading was obligatory. And reading required books. Books that were opened again and again eventually fell apart, however carefully they were handled. Therefore, almost inadvertently, monastic rules necessitated that monks repeatedly purchase or acquire books. In the course of the vicious Gothic Wars of the mid-sixth century and their still more miserable aftermath, the last commercial workshops of book production folded, and the vestiges of the book market fell apart. Therefore, again almost inadvertently, monastic rules necessitated that monks carefully preserve and copy those books that they already possessed. But all trade with the papyrus makers of Egypt had long vanished, and in the absence of a commercial book market, the commercial industry for converting animal skins to writing surfaces had fallen into abeyance. Therefore, once again almost inadvertently, monastic rules necessitated that monks learn the laborious art of making parchment and salvaging existing parchment. Without wishing to emulate the pagan elites by placing books or writing at the center of society, without affirming the importance of rhetoric or grammar, without prizing either learning or debate, monks nonetheless became the principal readers, librarians, book preservers, and book producers of the Western world.

Poggio and the other humanists on the trail of lost classics knew all this. Having already sifted through many of the monastic libraries in Italy and having followed Petrarch's lead in France, they also knew that the great, uncharted territories were Switzerland and Germany. But many of those monasteries were extremely difficult to reach—their founders had built them in deliberately remote places, in order to withdraw from the temptations, distractions, and dangers of the world. And once an eager humanist, having endured the discomforts and risks of travel, managed to reach the distant monasteries, what then? The number of scholars who knew what to look for and who were competent to recognize what they had come to find, if they had the good fortune to stumble across it, was extremely small. There was, moreover, a problem of access: to get through the door a scholar would have to be able to persuade a skeptical abbot and a still more skeptical monastic librarian that he had a legitimate reason to be there. Access to the library was ordinarily denied to any outsider. Petrarch was a cleric; he could at least make his appeal from within the large institutional community of the Church. Many of the humanists by contrast were laymen and would have aroused immediate suspicion.

This daunting list did not exhaust the problems. For if a book hunter reached a monastery, got past the heavily barred door, entered the library, and actually found something interesting, he would still need to do something with the manuscript he had found.

Books were scarce and valuable. They conferred prestige

on the monastery that possessed them, and the monks were not inclined to let them out of their sight, particularly if they had any prior experience with light-fingered Italian humanists. On occasion monasteries tried to secure their possession by freighting their precious manuscripts with curses. "For him that stealeth, or borroweth and returneth not, this book from its owner," one of these curses runs,

> let it change into a serpent in his hand and rend him. Let him be struck with palsy, and all his members blasted. Let him languish in pain crying aloud for mercy, and let there be no surcease to his agony till he sing in dissolution. Let bookworms gnaw his entrails in token of the Worm that dieth not, and when at last he goeth to his final punishment, let the flames of Hell consume him forever.

Even a worldly skeptic, with a strong craving for what he had in his hands, might have hesitated before slipping such a book into his cloak.

If the monks were poor or perhaps simply venal, they could be offered some money to part with their books, but the very interest showed by a stranger would inevitably make the price soar. It was always possible to ask the abbot to allow a manuscript to be carried off, with a solemn promise that it would be shortly returned. But though exceptionally trusting or naive abbots existed, they were few and far between. There was no way to compel assent, and if the answer was no, the whole venture was a dead loss. As a last resort, one could always defy curses and try theft, of course, but monastic communities were cultures of surveillance. Visitors would be watched particularly carefully, the gates were shut and locked at night, and some of the brothers were stout churls who would not scruple to beat an apprehended thief to within an inch of his life.

Poggio was almost uniquely suited to meet these challenges. He had been exceptionally well trained in the special
skills needed to decipher old handwriting. He was a wonderfully gifted Latinist, with a particularly acute eye for the telltale
diction, rhetorical devices, and grammatical structures of classical Latin. He had read widely and attentively in the literature
of antiquity and had committed to his capacious memory the
dozens of clues that hinted at the identity of particular authors
or works that had been lost. He was not himself a monk or a
priest, but his long service in the papal curia or court had given
him intimate, inside knowledge of the institutional structures
of the Church, as well as personal acquaintance with many of
its most powerful clerics, including a succession of popes.

If even these exalted connections should prove insuffi-
cient to get him through the locked doors that led to a remote
abbey's library, Poggio also possessed considerable personal
charm. He was a marvelous raconteur, a sly gossip, and an indefatigable teller of jokes, many of them off-color. He could not,
to be sure, converse with the German monks in their native
language. Though he had lived for more than three years in a
German-speaking city, by his own account he had learned no
German. For so gifted a linguist, this ignorance seems to have
been willed: German was the language of the barbarians, and
Poggio evidently had no interest in acquiring it. In Constance
he probably cocooned himself almost entirely in a Latin- and
Italian-speaking social world.

But if a failure to speak German must have been vexing
on the road, at inns or other way stations, it would not have
posed a serious problem once Poggio had arrived at his destination. The abbot, the librarian, and many other members
of the monastic community would have spoken Latin. They
would not in all likelihood have possessed the elegant classical Latin that Poggio had painstakingly mastered but rather,
to judge from the many vigorous contemporary literary works

that survive, a vital, fluent, highly flexible Latin that could swoop effortlessly from the subtlest of scholastic distinctions to the earthiest of obscenities. If Poggio sensed that he could impress his hosts with moral seriousness, he could have discoursed eloquently about the miseries of the human condition; if he thought he could win them over by making them laugh, he could have launched into one of his tales of foolish rustics, compliant housewives, and sexually rapacious priests.

Poggio possessed one further gift that set him apart from virtually all the other book-hunting humanists. He was a superbly well-trained scribe, with exceptionally fine handwriting, great powers of concentration, and a high degree of accuracy. It is difficult for us, at this distance, to take in the significance of such qualities: our technologies for producing transcriptions, facsimiles, and copies have almost entirely erased what was once an important personal achievement. That importance began to decline, though not at all precipitously, even in Poggio's own lifetime, for by the 1430s a German entrepreneur, Johann Gutenberg, began experimenting with a new invention, movable type, which would revolutionize the reproduction and transmission of texts. By the century's end printers, especially the great Aldus in Venice, would print Latin texts in a typeface whose clarity and elegance remain unrivalled after five centuries. That typeface was based on the beautiful handwriting of Poggio and his humanist friends. What Poggio did by hand to produce a single copy would soon be done mechanically to produce hundreds.

But this achievement lay in the future, and, in any case, the printers who set the books in type still depended on accurate, readable, handwritten transcriptions, often of manuscripts that were illegible to all but a few. Poggio's talent as a transcriber struck contemporaries as uncanny, all the more so because he worked so rapidly. What this meant was that he could not

only inveigle his way into the monastery and nose out the precious manuscripts of lost works, but also that he could borrow
them, copy them quickly, and send the results back to humanists waiting eagerly at home in Italy. If borrowing proved
impossible—that is, if the librarian refused to lend a particular manuscript—Poggio could copy it on the spot, or, if necessary, could entrust the task to a scribe whom he had personally
trained up to at least a minimal level of competence.

In 1417, then, Poggio the book hunter had a near-perfect conjunction of time, skills, and desire. All that he lacked was ready
money. Traveling, even frugally, was expensive. There were
costs for renting a horse; fees for crossing rivers or riding on
toll roads; charges, little more than extortion, by surly customs officials and agents of petty lordlings; gratuities to guides
through difficult passes; and, of course, bills for food and lodging and stabling at inns. He also needed money to pay an assistant scribe, and to provide, if necessary, the incentive to induce
a reluctant monastery to lend its treasure.

Even if he had banked some funds from his years in the papal
bureaucracy, Poggio is very unlikely to have been able to pay
these costs on his own. In such circumstances, the inveterate
letter writer would have had recourse to his pen. It is probable
that he wrote to wealthy friends at home who shared his passion
and explained to them that circumstances had suddenly given
him the opportunity about which they had only dreamed. In
good health, untrammeled by work or family, obliged to no
one, at liberty to come and go as he chose, he was prepared to
embark on a serious search for the lost treasures that meant
most to them—the heritage of the ancient world.

Such support, whether it came from a single rich patron or

from a group of fellow humanists, helps to account for the fact that in January 1417, Poggio was heading toward the destination where he would make his discovery. The support must have been considerable, for this was not his only book-hunting expedition that winter. It followed directly on another trip, to the venerable monastery of St. Gall, not far from the city of Constance, and that trip was itself a return visit. The preceding year at St. Gall, in the company of two Italian friends, Poggio had made a series of important finds. Thinking that they might have overlooked other treasures, he and one of the friends went back.

Poggio and his companion, Bartolomeo de Aragazzi, had much in common. Both hailed from Tuscany, Poggio from the modest town of Terranuova near Arezzo, Bartolomeo from the beautiful hilltop city of Montepulciano. Both had gone to Rome and had acquired positions as scriptors in the papal curia. Both had come to Constance to serve as apostolic secretaries in the disastrous pontificate of John XXIII and, consequently, both found themselves, in the wake of the pope's downfall, with time on their hands. And both were ardent humanists, eager to use their skills in reading and copying to recover the lost texts of antiquity.

They were close friends, working and traveling together and sharing the same ambition, but they were also rivals, competitors in the pursuit of the fame that came with discovery. "I hate all boastful conversation, all flattery, all exaggeration," Bartolomeo wrote to an important patron in Italy; "May I be kept from taking pride in dreams of self-exaltation or vainglory." The letter, dated January 19, 1417, was written from St. Gall, and it goes on to mention a few of the notable discoveries he had made in what he calls the "prison" in which they were penned. He could not, he added, hope to describe all the volumes he had found, "for a day would hardly be sufficient to list them all." Tellingly, he does not so much as mention the name of his traveling companion, Poggio Bracciolini.

The problem was that Bartolomeo's finds were simply not very thrilling. He had dredged up a copy of a book by Flavius Vegetius Renatus on the ancient Roman army—a book, he wrote implausibly, that will "do us good, if we ever use him sometimes in camp or more gloriously on a crusade"—and a small dictionary or word list by Pompeius Festus. Not only were both books exceedingly minor but also, as Bartolomeo himself must have known, both were already available in Italy, so in fact neither was actually a discovery.

In late January, having failed to lay hands on the great treasures they had hoped to uncover and perhaps feeling the burden of their competitiveness, the friends went their separate ways. Poggio evidently headed north, probably accompanied by a German scribe whom he was training. Bartolomeo seems to have gone off by himself. "I shall set out for another monastery of the Hermits deep in the Alps," he wrote to his Italian correspondent. He planned then to go on to still more remote monasteries. The places were extremely difficult to reach, especially in winter—"the way is rough and broken, for there is no approach to them except through the precipices of the Alps and through rivers and forests"—but he reminded himself that "the path of virtue is very full of toil and peril." In these monastic libraries, rumors had it, a vast trove of ancient books was buried. "I shall try to urge this poor little body to undertake the effort of rescuing them and not to flinch at the difficulties of their location, at the discomforts and at the increasing cold of the Alps."

It is easy enough to smile at such claims of hardship—trained as a lawyer, Bartolomeo was certainly calculating a rhetorical effect—but in fact he fell ill shortly after he left St. Gall and was forced to return to Constance, where it took him months to recuperate. Poggio, on the road north, would not have known that, since Bartolomeo had dropped out of the hunt, he was now searching alone.

Poggio did not like monks. He knew several impressive ones, men of great moral seriousness and learning. But on the whole he found them superstitious, ignorant, and hopelessly lazy. Monasteries, he thought, were the dumping grounds for those deemed unfit for life in the world. Noblemen fobbed off the sons they judged to be weaklings, misfits, or good-for-nothings; merchants sent their dim-witted or paralytic children there; peasants got rid of extra mouths they could not feed. The hardiest of the inmates could at least do some productive labor in the monastery gardens and the adjacent fields, as monks in earlier, more austere times had done, but for the most part, Poggio thought, they were a pack of idlers. Behind the thick walls of the cloisters, the parasites would mumble their prayers and live off the income generated by those who farmed the monastery's extensive landholdings. The Church was a landlord, wealthier than the greatest nobles in the realm, and it possessed the worldly power to enforce its rents and all its other rights and privileges. When the newly elected bishop of Hildesheim, in the north of Germany, asked to see the diocesan library, he was brought to the armory and shown the pikes and battleaxes hanging on the walls; these, he was informed, were the books with which the rights of the bishopric had been won and must be defended. The inhabitants of wealthy monasteries might not have to call upon these weapons very frequently, but, as they sat in the dim light and contemplated their revenues, they knew—and their tenants knew—that brute force was available.

With his friends in the curia Poggio shared jokes about the

venality, stupidity, and sexual appetite of monks. And their claims to piety left him unimpressed: "I cannot find that they do anything but sing like grasshoppers," he wrote, "and I cannot help thinking they are too liberally paid for the mere exercise of their lungs." Even the hard work of monastic spiritual discipline seemed paltry to him, when set against the real hard work he observed in the fields: "They extol their labors as a kind of Herculean task, because they rise in the night to chant the praises of God. This is no doubt an extraordinary proof of merit, that they sit up to exercise themselves in psalmody. What would they say if they rose to go to the plough, like farmers, exposed to the wind and rain, with bare feet, and with their bodies thinly clad?" Their whole enterprise seemed to him an exercise in hypocrisy.

But, of course, as he approached his targeted monastery, Poggio would have buried these views in his breast. He may have despised monastic life, but he understood it well. He knew precisely where in the monastery he needed to go and what ingratiating words he had to speak to gain access to the things he most wanted to see. Above all, he knew exactly how the things he sought had been produced. Though he ridiculed what he regarded as monastic sloth, he knew that whatever he hoped to find existed only because of centuries of institutional commitment and long, painstaking human labor.

The Benedictine Rule had called for manual labor, as well as prayer and reading, and it was always assumed that this labor could include writing. The early founders of monastic orders did not regard copying manuscripts as an exalted activity; on the contrary, as they were highly aware, most of the copying in the ancient world had been done by educated slaves. The task was therefore inherently humiliating as well as tedious, a perfect combination for the ascetic project of disciplining the spirit. Poggio had no sympathy with such spiritual discipline;

competitive and ambitious, his spirit longed to shine in the light of the world, not to shrink from its gaze. For him copying manuscripts, which he did with unrivalled skill, was not an ascetic but rather an aesthetic undertaking, one by which he advanced his own personal reputation. But by virtue of that skill he was able to see at a glance—with either admiration or scorn—exactly what effort and ability had gone into the manuscript that lay before him.

Not every monk was equally adept at copying, just as not every monk was equally adept at the hard farm labor on which the survival of the early communities depended. The early regulations already envisaged a division of labor, as in the Rule of St. Ferreol (530–581), a French Benedictine: "He who does not turn up the earth with the plough ought to write the parchment with his fingers." (The reverse, of course, was also true: he who could not write parchment with his fingers was assigned to the plough.) Those who wrote unusually well—in fine, clear handwriting that the other monks could easily read and with painstaking accuracy in the transcription—came to be valued. In the "wergild" codes that in Germanic lands and in Ireland specified the payment of reparations for murder—200 shillings for killing a churl, 300 for a low-ranking cleric, 400 if the cleric was saying mass when he was attacked, and so forth—the loss of a scribe by violence was ranked equal to the loss of a bishop or an abbot.

The high price, at a time when life was cheap, suggests both how important and how difficult it was for monasteries to obtain the books that they needed in order to enforce the reading rule. Even the most celebrated monastic libraries of the Middle Ages were tiny in comparison with the libraries of antiquity or those that existed in Baghdad or Cairo. To assemble a modest number of books, in the long centuries before the invention of the printing press forever changed the equation, meant the eventual establishment of what were called *scripto-ria*, workshops where monks would be trained to sit for long hours making copies. At first the copying was probably done in an improvised setting in the cloister, where, even if the cold sometimes stiffened the fingers, at least the light would be good. But in time special rooms were designated or built for the purpose. In the greatest monasteries, increasingly eager to amass prestigious collections of books, these were large rooms equipped with clear glass windows under which the monks, as many as thirty of them, sat at individual desks, sometimes partitioned off from one another.

In charge of the scriptorium was the person on whom Poggio and the other book hunters would have focused their most seductive blandishments: the monastery's librarian. This important figure would have been accustomed to extravagant courtship, for he was responsible for providing all of the equipment that was required for the copying of the manuscripts: pens, ink, and penknives whose precise merits or defects would become overwhelmingly obvious to the laboring scribe after a few hours at the day's task. The librarian could, if he wished, make a scribe's life miserable or, alternatively, provide a favorite with particularly fine tools. Those tools also included rulers, awls (to make tiny holes for ruling the lines evenly), fine-pointed metal pens for drawing the lines, reading frames to hold the book to be copied, weights to keep the pages from turning. For manuscripts that were to be illuminated, there were still other specialized tools and materials.

Most books in the ancient world took the form of scrolls— like the Torah scrolls that Jews use in their services to this day—but by the fourth century Christians had almost completely opted for a different format, the codex, from which our familiar books derive. The codex has the huge advantage of being far easier for readers to find their way about in: the text can be conveniently paginated and indexed, and the pages can be turned quickly to the desired place. Not until the invention of the computer, with its superior search functions, could a serious challenge be mounted to the codex's magnificently simple and flexible format. Only now have we begun once again to speak of "scrolling" through a text.

Since papyrus was no longer available and paper did not come into general use until the fourteenth century, for more than a thousand years the chief writing material used for books was made from the skins of animals—cows, sheep, goats, and occasionally deer. These surfaces needed to be made smooth, and hence another tool that the monastic librarian distributed was pumice stone, to rub away the remaining animal hair along with any bumps or imperfections. The scribe to whom a poor-quality parchment had been given was in for a very disagreeable task, and in the margins of surviving monastic manuscripts there are occasional outbursts of distress: "The parchment is hairy" . . . "Thin ink, bad parchment, difficult text" . . . "Thank God, it will soon be dark." "Let the copyist be permitted to put an end to his labor," a weary monk wrote beneath his name, the date, and the place where he worked; "Now I've written the whole thing," wrote another. "For Christ's sake give me a drink."

The finest parchment, the one that made life easier for scribes and must have figured in their sweetest dreams, was made of calfskin and called vellum. And the best of the lot was uterine vellum, from the skins of aborted calves. Brilliantly white, smooth, and durable, these skins were reserved for the most precious books, ones graced with elaborate, gemlike miniatures and occasionally encased in covers encrusted with actual gems. The libraries of the world still preserve a reasonable number of these remarkable objects, the achievement of scribes who lived seven or eight hundred years ago and labored for untold hours to create something beautiful.

Good scribes were exempted from certain times of collective prayer, in order to maximize the hours of daylight in the scriptorium. And they did not have to work at night: because of an entirely justifiable fear of fire, all candlelight was forbidden. But for the time—about six hours a day—that they actually spent at their desks, their lives belonged entirely to their books. It was possible, in certain monasteries at least, to hope that monks would understand what they were copying: "Vouchsafe, O Lord, to bless this workroom of Thy servants," declared the dedication of one scriptorium, "that all which they write therein may be comprehended by their intelligence and realized in their works." But the actual interest of the scribes in the books they copied (or their distaste for those books) was strictly irrelevant. Indeed, insofar as the copying was a form of discipline—an exercise in humility and a willing embrace of pain—distaste or simple incomprehension might be preferable to engagement. Curiosity was to be avoided at all costs.

The complete subordination of the monastic scribe to the text—the erasure, in the interest of crushing the monk's spirit, of his intellect and sensibility—could not have been further from Poggio's own avid curiosity and egotism. But he understood that his passionate hope of recovering reasonably accurate traces of the ancient past depended heavily on this subordination. An engaged reader, Poggio knew, was prone to alter his text in order to get it to make sense, but such alterations, over centuries, inevitably led to wholesale corruptions. It was better that monastic scribes had been forced to copy everything exactly at it appeared before their eyes, even those things that made no sense at all.

A sheet with a cutout window generally covered the page of

the manuscript being copied, so that the monk had to focus on one line at a time. And monks were strictly forbidden to change what they thought were mistakes in the texts they were copying. They could correct only their own slips of the pen by carefully scraping off the ink with a razor and repairing the spot with a mixture of milk, cheese, and lime, the medieval version of our own product for whiting out mistakes. There was no crumpling up the page and starting afresh. Though the skins of sheep and goats were plentiful, the process of producing parchment from them was laborious. Good parchment was far too valuable and scarce to be discarded. This value helps to account for the fact that monasteries collected ancient manuscripts in the first place and did not consign them to the rubbish.

To be sure, there were a certain number of abbots and of monastic librarians who treasured not only the parchment but also the pagan works written on them. Steeped in classical literature, some believed that they could rifle its treasures without contamination, the way the ancient Hebrews had been permitted by God to steal the riches of the Egyptians. But over the generations, as a substantial Christian literature was created, it became less easy to make such an argument. Fewer and fewer monks were inclined, in any case, to make it. Between the sixth century and the middle of the eighth century, Greek and Latin classics virtually ceased to be copied at all. What had begun as an active campaign to forget—a pious attack on pagan ideas—had evolved into actual forgetting. The ancient poems, philosophical treatises, and political speeches, at one time so threatening and so alluring, were no longer in anyone's mind, let alone on anyone's lips. They had been reduced to the condition of mute things, sheets of parchment, stitched together, covered with unread words.

Only the remarkable durability of the parchment used in these codices kept the ideas of the ancients alive at all, and, as the humanist book hunters knew, even strong material was no guarantee of survival. Working with knives, brushes, and rags, monks often carefully washed away the old writings— Virgil, Ovid, Cicero, Seneca, Lucretius—and wrote in their place the texts that they were instructed by their superiors to copy. The task must have been a tiresome one, and, for the very rare scribe who actually cared about the work he was erasing, an excruciating one.

If the original ink proved tenacious, it could still be possible to make out the traces of the texts that were written over: a unique fourth-century copy of Cicero's *On the Republic* remained visible beneath a seventh-century copy of St. Augustine's meditation on the Psalms; the sole surviving copy of Seneca's book on friendship was deciphered beneath an Old Testament inscribed in the late sixth century. These strange, layered manuscripts—called *palimpsests*; from the Greek for "scraped again"—have served as the source of several major works from the ancient past that would not otherwise be known. But no medieval monk would have been encouraged to read, as it were, between the lines.

The monastery was a place of rules, but in the scriptorium there were rules within rules. Access was denied to all nonscribes. Absolute silence reigned. Scribes were not allowed to choose the particular books that they copied or to break the dead silence by requesting aloud from the librarian such books as they might wish to consult in order to complete the task that had been assigned them. An elaborate gestural language was invented in order to facilitate such requests as were permitted. If a scribe wanted to consult a psalter, he made the general sign for a book—extending his hands and turning over imaginary pages—and then, by putting his hands on his head in the shape of a crown, the specific sign for the psalms of King David. If he was asking for a pagan book, he began, after making the general sign, to scratch behind his ear, like a dog scratching his fleas. And if he wished to have what the Church regarded as a particularly offensive or dangerous pagan book, he could put two fingers into his mouth, as if he were gagging.

Poggio was a layman, part of a very different world. His precise destination in 1417, after he parted ways with Bartolomeo, is not known—perhaps like a prospector hiding the location of his mine, he deliberately withheld its name from his letters. There were dozens of monasteries to which he might have gone in the hope of turning up something remarkable, but many scholars have long thought that the likeliest candidate is the Benedictine Abbey of Fulda. That abbey, in a strategic area of central Germany, between the Rhön and the Vogelsberg Mountains, had the features that most excited the interest of a book hunter: it was ancient, it was rich, it had once possessed a great tradition of learning, and it was now in decline.

If it was Fulda that he approached, Poggio could not afford to seem overbearing. Founded in the eighth century by a disciple of the Apostle of Germany, St. Boniface, the abbey was unusually independent. Its abbot was a prince of the Holy Roman Empire: when he walked in procession, an armor-clad knight carried the imperial banner before him, and he had the privilege of sitting at the left hand of the emperor himself. Many of the monks were German nobles—men who would have had a very clear sense of the respect that was due to them. If the monastery had lost some of the prestige it once enjoyed and had been forced in the not too distant past to part with some of its immense territories, it nonetheless was a force to reckon with. With his modest birth and very limited means, Poggio, the former apostolic secretary of a disgraced and deposed pope, had few cards to play.

Rehearsing in his mind his little speech of introduction, Poggio would have dismounted and walked up the tree-lined avenue toward the abbey's single, heavy gate. From the outside Fulda resembled a fortress; indeed, in the preceding century, in a bitter dispute with the burghers of the adjacent city, it had been violently attacked. Inside, like most monasteries, it was strikingly self-sufficient. By January the extensive vegetable, flower, and botanical gardens were in their winter sleep, but the monks would have carefully harvested what they could store for the long, dark months, taking special care to gather the medicinal herbs that would be used in the infirmary and the communal bath. The granaries at this point in the winter would have still been reasonably full, and there would have been ample straw and oats for the horses and donkeys in the stables. Looking around, Poggio would have taken in the chicken coops, the covered yard for sheep, the cowshed with its smell of manure and fresh milk, and the large pigsties. He might have felt a pang for the olives and the wine of Tuscany, but he knew that he would not go hungry. Past the mills and the oil press, past the great basilica and its adjacent cloister, past the houses for the novices, the dormitory, the servants' quarters, and the pilgrims' hospice where he and his assistant would be lodged, Poggio would have been led to the abbot's house to meet the ruler of this little kingdom.

In 1417, if Fulda was indeed Poggio's destination, that ruler was Johann von Merlau. After greeting him humbly, explaining something about himself, and presenting a letter of recommendation from a well-known cardinal, Poggio would almost certainly have begun by expressing his interest in glimpsing the precious relics of St. Boniface and saying a prayer in their holy presence. His life, after all, was full of such observances: bureaucrats in the papal court routinely began and ended their days with prayers. And if nothing in his letters suggests a par-

ticular interest in relics or the intervention of saints or the ritu-
als employed to reduce the soul's painful time in Purgatory,
Poggio nonetheless would have known upon what possessions
Fulda most prided itself.

The visitor would then as a special favor have been led into
the basilica. If he had not already taken it in, Poggio would
certainly have realized, as he entered the transept and walked
down the stairs into the dark, vaulted crypt, that Fulda's pilgrimage church seemed strangely familiar: it was directly modeled after Rome's fourth-century Basilica of St. Peter's. (The vast
St. Peter's in Rome today was built long after Poggio's death.)
There by candlelight, enshrined in a rich setting of gold, crystal, and jewels, he would have seen the bones of the saint, mas-
sacred in 754 by the Frisians he was struggling to convert.

When he and his hosts emerged once again into the light
and when he deemed that he had reached the appropriate
moment, Poggio would have nudged the conversation toward
his actual purpose in coming. He could have done so by initiat-
ing a discussion of one of Fulda's most celebrated figures, Rabanus Maurus, who had served as abbot for two decades, from
822 to 842. Rabanus Maurus was a prolific author of biblical
commentaries, doctrinal treatises, pedagogical guides, scholarly compendia, and a series of fantastically beautiful poems
in cipher. Most of these works Poggio could easily have seen in
the Vatican Library, along with the vast tome for which Rabanus was best known: a work of stupefying erudition and dull-
ness that attempted to bring together in its twenty-two books
all of human knowledge. Its title was De rerum naturis—"On the
Natures of Things"—but contemporaries, acknowledging the
scope of its ambition, called it "On the Universe."

The works of the ninth-century monk epitomized the heavy,
plodding style that Poggio and his fellow humanists despised.
But he also recognized that Rabanus Maurus was an immensely

learned man, steeped in pagan as well as Christian literature, and that he had transformed Fulda's monastic school into the most important in Germany. As all schools do, the one at Fulda needed books, and Rabanus had met the need by greatly enriching the monastic library. Rabanus, who as a young man had studied with Alcuin, the greatest scholar of the age of Charlemagne, knew where to get his hands on important manuscripts. He had them brought to Fulda, where he trained a large cohort of scribes to copy them. And so he had built what was for the time a stupendous collection.

That time, some six hundred years before Poggio, was from the book hunter's perspective highly propitious. It was far enough into the past to hold out the possibility of a link to a more distant past. And the gradual decline over the centuries in the monastery's intellectual seriousness only intensified the excitement. Who knew what was sitting on those shelves, untouched perhaps for centuries? Tattered manuscripts that had chanced to survive the long nightmare of chaos and destruction, in the wake of the fall of the Roman Empire, might well have found their way to remote Fulda. Rabanus's monks could have made the scratching or gagging sign for pagan books to copy, and those copies, having fallen into oblivion, would be awaiting the humanist's revivifying touch.

Such, in any case, was Poggio's ardent hope, in Fulda or wherever he found himself, and his pulse must have quickened when at last he would have been led by the monastery's chief librarian into a large vaulted room and shown a volume attached by a chain to the librarian's own desk. The volume was a catalogue, and as he pored over its pages, Poggio pointed—for the rule of silence in the library was strictly observed—to the books he wanted to see.

Genuine interest, as well as a sense of discretion, might have dictated that Poggio request first to see unfamiliar works by one of the greatest Church Fathers, Tertullian. Then, as the manuscripts were brought to his desk, he plunged, with what must have been increasing excitement, into a series of ancient Roman authors whose works were utterly unknown to him and to any of his fellow humanists. Though Poggio did not reveal precisely where he went, he did reveal—indeed, he trumpeted—what he had found. For what all book hunters dreamed of was actually happening.

He opened an epic poem in some 14,000 lines on the wars between Rome and Carthage. Poggio might have recognized the name of the author, Silius Italicus, though until this moment none of his works had surfaced. A canny politician and a wily, unscrupulous orator, who served as a tool in a succession of show trials, Silius had managed to survive the murderous reigns of Caligula, Nero, and Domitian. In retirement, the younger Pliny had written with urbane irony, he "obliterated by the praiseworthy use he made of leisure the stain he had incurred through his active exertions in former days." Now Poggio and his friends would be able to savor one of the fruits of this leisure.

He opened another long poem, this one by an author, Manilius, whose name the book hunter would certainly not have recognized, for it is not mentioned by any surviving ancient author. Poggio saw at once that it was a learned work on astronomy, and he would have been able to tell from the style and from the poet's own allusions that it had been written at the very beginning of the empire, during the reigns of Augustus and Tiberius.

More ghosts surged up from the Roman past. An ancient literary critic who had flourished during Nero's reign and had written notes and glosses on classical authors; another critic who quoted extensively from lost epics written in imitation of

Homer; a grammarian who wrote a treatise on spelling that Poggio knew his Latin-obsessed friends in Florence would find thrilling. Yet another manuscript was a discovery whose thrill might have been tinged for him with melancholy: a large fragment of a hitherto unknown history of the Roman Empire written by a high-ranking officer in the imperial army, Ammianus Marcellinus. The melancholy would have arisen not only from the fact that the first thirteen of the original thirty-one books were missing from the manuscript Poggio copied by hand—and these lost books have never been found—but also from the fact that the work was written on the eve of the empire's collapse. A clearheaded, thoughtful, and unusually impartial historian, Ammianus seems to have sensed the impending end. His description of a world exhausted by crushing taxes, the financial ruin of large segments of the population, and the dangerous decline in the army's morale vividly conjured up the conditions that made it possible, some twenty years after his death, for the Goths to sack Rome.

Even the smallest of the finds that Poggio was making was highly significant—for anything at all to surface after so long seemed miraculous—but they were all eclipsed, from our own perspective if not immediately, by the discovery of a work still more ancient than any of the others that he had found. One of the manuscripts consisted of a long text written around 50 BCE by a poet and philosopher named Titus Lucretius Carus. The text's title, *De rerum natura*—*On the Nature of Things*—was strikingly similar to the title of Rabanus Maurus's celebrated encyclopedia, *De rerum naturis*. But where the monk's work was dull and conventional, Lucretius' work was dangerously radical.

Poggio would almost certainly have recognized the name Lucretius from Ovid, Cicero, and other ancient sources he had painstakingly pored over, in the company of his humanist friends, but neither he nor anyone in his circle had encountered more than a scrap or two of his actual writing, which had, as far as anyone knew, been lost forever.

Poggio may not have had time, in the gathering darkness of the monastic library, and under the wary eyes of the abbot or his librarian, to do more than read the opening lines. But he would have seen immediately that Lucretius' Latin verses were astonishingly beautiful. Ordering his scribe to make a copy, he hurried to liberate it from the monastery. What is not clear is whether he had any intimation at all that he was releasing a book that would help in time to dismantle his entire world.

CHAPTER THREE

IN SEARCH OF LUCRETIUS

S OME FOURTEEN HUNDRED and fifty years before Poggio set out to see what he could find, Lucretius' contemporaries had read his poem, and it continued to be read for several centuries after its publication. Italian humanists, on the lookout for clues to lost ancient works, would have been alert to even fleeting references in the works of those celebrated authors whose writings had survived in significant quantities. Thus, though he strongly disagreed with its philosophical principles, Cicero—Poggio's favorite Latin writer—conceded the marvelous power of *On the Nature of Things*. "The poetry of Lucretius," he wrote to his brother Quintus on February 11, 54 BCE, "is, as you say in your letter, rich in brilliant genius, yet highly artistic." Cicero's turn of phrase—especially that slightly odd word "yet"—registers his surprise: he was evidently struck by something unusual. He had encountered a poem that conjoined "brilliant genius" in philosophy and science with unusual poetic power. The conjunction was as rare then as it is now.

Cicero and his brother were not alone in grasping that Lucretius had accomplished a near-perfect integration of intellectual distinction and aesthetic mastery. The greatest Roman poet, Virgil, about fifteen years old when Lucretius died, was under the spell of *On the Nature of Things*. "Blessed is he who has succeeded in finding out the causes of things," Virgil wrote in the *Georgics*, "and has trampled underfoot all fears and inexorable fate and the roar of greedy Acheron." Assuming that this is a subtle allusion to the title of Lucretius' poem, the older poet in this account is a culture hero, someone who has heard the menacing roar of the underworld and triumphed over the superstitious fears that threaten to sap the human spirit. But Virgil did not mention his hero by name, and, though he had certainly read the *Georgics*, Poggio was unlikely to have picked up the allusion before he had actually read Lucretius. Still less would Poggio have been able to grasp the extent to which Virgil's great epic, the *Aeneid*, was a sustained attempt to construct an alternative to *On the Nature of Things*: pious, where Lucretius was skeptical; militantly patriotic, where Lucretius counseled pacifism; soberly renunciatory, where Lucretius embraced the pursuit of pleasure.

What Poggio and other Italian humanists probably did notice, however, were the words of Ovid, words that were enough to send any book hunter scurrying through the catalogs of monastic libraries: "The verses of sublime Lucretius are destined to perish only when a single day will consign the world to destruction."

It is all the more striking then that Lucretius' verses did almost perish—the survival of his work hung by slenderest of threads—and that virtually nothing about his actual identity is reliably known. Many of the major poets and philosophers of ancient Rome had been celebrities in their own time, the objects of gossip which eager book hunters centuries later pored over for clues. But in the case of Lucretius there were almost no biographical traces. The poet must have been a very private person, living his life in the shadows, and he does not seem to have written anything apart from his one great work. That work, difficult and challenging, was hardly the kind of

popular success that got diffused in so many copies that significant fragments of it were assured of surviving into the Middle
Ages. Looking back from this distance, with Lucretius' masterpiece securely in hand, modern scholars have been able to identify a network of early medieval signs of the text's existence—a
citation here, a catalogue entry there—but most of these would
have been invisible to the early fifteenth-century book hunters.
They were groping in the dark, sensing perhaps a tiny gossa-
mer filament but unable to track it to its source. And following
in their wake, after almost six hundred years of work by clas-
sicists, historians, and archaeologists, we know almost nothing
more than they did about the identity of the author.

The Lucretii were an old, distinguished Roman clan—as
Poggio may have known—but since slaves, when freed, often
took the name of the family that had owned them, the author
was not necessarily an aristocrat. Still, an aristocratic lineage
was plausible, for the simple reason that Lucretius addressed
his poem, in terms of easy intimacy, to a nobleman, Gaius
Memmius. That name Poggio might have encountered in his
wide reading, for Memmius had a relatively successful political
career, was a patron of celebrated writers, including the love
poet Catullus, and was himself reputed to be a poet (an obscene
one, according to Ovid). He was also an orator, as Cicero noted
somewhat grudgingly, "of the subtle, ingenious type." But the
question remained, who was Lucretius?

The answer, for Poggio and his circle, would have come almost
completely from a brief biographical sketch that the great Church
Father St. Jerome (c. 340–420 CE) added to an earlier chronicle. In
the entry for 94 BCE, Jerome noted that "Titus Lucretius, poet, is
born. After a love-philtre had turned him mad, and he had written, in the intervals of his insanity, several books which Cicero
revised, he killed himself by his own hand in the forty-fourth
year of his age." These lurid details have shaped all subsequent

representations of Lucretius, including a celebrated Victorian poem in which Tennyson imagined the voice of the mad, suicidal philosopher tormented by erotic fantasies.

Modern classical scholarship suggests that every one of Jerome's biographical claims should be taken with a heavy dose of skepticism. They were recorded—or invented—centuries after Lucretius' death by a Christian polemicist who had an interest in telling cautionary tales about pagan philosophers. However, since no good fifteenth-century Christian would have been likely to doubt the saint's account, Poggio must have thought that the poem that he had found and was returning to circulation was tainted by its pagan author's madness and suicide. But the humanist book hunter was part of a generation passionately eager to unearth ancient texts, even by those whose lives epitomized moral confusion and mortal sin. And the thought that Cicero himself had revised the books would have sufficed to quiet any lingering reservations.

In the more than sixteen hundred years that have elapsed since the fourth-century chronicle entry, no further biographical information has turned up, either to confirm or disprove Jerome's story of the love potion and its tragic aftermath. As a person, Lucretius remains almost as little known as he was when Poggio recovered his poem in 1417. Given the extravagance of Ovid's praise of "the verse of sublime Lucretius" and the other signs of the poem's influence, it remains a mystery that so little was said directly about him by his contemporaries and near contemporaries. But archaeological disoveries, made long after Poggio's death, have helped us to get eerily close to the world in which *On the Nature of Things* was first read, and perhaps to the poet himself.

The discoveries were made possible by a famous ancient disaster. On August 24, 79 CE, the massive eruption of Mount Vesuvius completely destroyed not only Pompeii but also the small seaside resort of Herculaneum on the Bay of Naples. Buried under some sixty-five feet of volcanic debris hardened to the density of concrete, this site, where wealthy Romans had once vacationed in their elegant, colonnaded villas, was forgotten until the early eighteenth century, when workmen, digging a well, uncovered some marble statues. An Austrian officer— for Naples at the time was under the control of Austria—took over, and excavators began digging shafts through the thick crust.

The explorations, which continued when Naples passed into Bourbon hands, were extremely crude, less an archaeological investigation than a prolonged smash-and-grab. The official in charge for more than a decade was a Spanish army engineer, Roque Joaquin de Alcubierre, who seemed to treat the site as an ossified garbage dump in which loot had unaccountably been buried. ("This man," remarked a contemporary, dismayed at the wanton damage, "knew as much of antiquities as the moon does of lobsters.") The diggers burrowed away in search of statues, gems, precious marbles, and other more or less familiar treasures, which they found in abundance and delivered in jumbled heaps to their royal masters.

In 1750, under a new director, the explorers became somewhat more careful about what they were doing. Three years later, tunneling through the remains of one of the villas, they came across something baffling: the ruins of a room graced with a mosaic floor and filled with innumerable objects "about half a palm long, and round," as one of them wrote, "which appeared like roots of wood, all black, and seeming to be only of one piece." At first they thought they had come on a cache of charcoal briquettes, some of which they burned to dissipate the early morning chill. Others thought that the peculiar fragments might have been rolls of burned cloth or fishing nets. Then one of these objects, chancing to fall on the ground, broke open.

The unexpected sight of letters inside what had looked like a charred root made the explorers realize what they were looking at: books. They had stumbled on the remains of a private library.

The volumes that Romans piled up in their libraries were smaller than most modern books: they were for the most part written on scrolls of papyrus. (The word "volume" comes from *volumen,* the Latin word for a thing that is rolled or wound up.) Rolls of papyrus—the plant from which we get our word "paper"—were produced from tall reeds that grew in the marshy delta region of the Nile in Lower Egypt. The reeds were harvested; their stalks cut open and sliced into very thin strips. The strips were laid side by side, slightly overlapping one another; another layer was placed on top, at right angles to the one below; and then the sheet was gently pounded with a mallet. The natural sap that was released allowed the fibers to adhere smoothly to each other, and the individual sheets were then glued into rolls. (The first sheet, on which the contents of the roll could be noted, was called in Greek the *protokol-lon,* literally, "first glued"—the origin of our word "protocol.") Wooden sticks, attached to one or both of the ends of the roll and slightly projecting from the top and bottom edges, made it easier to scroll through as one read along: to read a book in the ancient world was to unwind it. The Romans called such a stick the *umbilicus,* and to read a book cover-to-cover was "to unroll to the umbilicus."

At first white and flexible, the papyrus would over time gradually get brittle and discolored—nothing lasts forever— but it was lightweight, convenient, relatively inexpensive, and surprisingly durable. Small landowners in Egypt had long realized that they could write their tax receipts on a scrap of papyrus and be reasonably confident that the record would be perfectly legible for years and even generations to come.

Priests could use this medium to record the precise language for supplicating the gods; poets could lay claim to the symbolic immortality they dreamed of in their art; philosophers could convey their thoughts to disciples yet unborn. Romans, like the Greeks before them, easily grasped that this was the best writing material available, and they imported it in bulk from Egypt to meet their growing desire for record keeping, official documents, personal letters, and books. A roll of papyrus might last three hundred years.

The room unearthed in Herculaneum had once been lined with inlaid wooden shelves; at its center were the traces of what had been a large, freestanding, rectangular bookcase. Scattered about were the carbonized remains—so fragile that they fell apart at the touch—of the erasable waxed tablets on which readers once took notes (a bit like the Mystic Writing Pads with which children play today). The shelves had been piled high with papyrus rolls. Some of the rolls, perhaps the more valuable ones, were wrapped about with tree bark and covered with pieces of wood at each end. In another part of the villa, other rolls, now fused into a single mass by the volcanic ash, seemed to have been hastily bundled together in a wooden box, as if someone on the terrible August day had for a brief, wild moment thought to carry some particularly valued books away from the holocaust. Altogether—even with the irrevocable loss of the many that were trashed before it was understood what they were—some eleven hundred books were eventually recovered.

Many of the rolls in what became known as the Villa of the Papyri had been crushed by falling debris and the weight of the heavy mud; all had been carbonized by the volcanic lava, ash, and gas. But what had blackened these books had also preserved them from further decay. For centuries they had in effect been sealed in an airtight container. (Even today only one small segment of the villa has been exposed to view, and a substantial portion remains unexcavated.) The discoverers, however, were disappointed: they could barely make out anything written on the charcoal-like rolls. And when again and again they tried to unwind them, the rolls inevitably crumbled into fragments.

Dozens, perhaps hundreds, of books were destroyed in these attempts. But eventually a number of the rolls that had been cut open were found to contain near the center some readable portions. At this point—after two years of more or less destructive and fruitless effort—a learned Neapolitan priest who had been working in the Vatican Library in Rome, Father Antonio Piaggio, was called in. Taking issue with the prevailing method of investigation—simply scraping off the charred outer layers of the rolls until some words could be discerned—he invented an ingenious device, a machine that would delicately and slowly unroll the carbonized papyrus scrolls, disclosing much more readable material than anyone had imagined to have survived.

Those who read the recovered texts, carefully flattened and glued onto strips, found that the villa's library (or at least the portion of it that they had found) was a specialized one, many of the rolls being tracts in Greek by a philosopher named Philodemus. The researchers were disappointed—they had been hoping to find lost works by the likes of Sophocles and Virgil—but what they had so implausibly snatched from oblivion has an important bearing on the discovery made centuries earlier by Poggio. For Philodemus, who taught in Rome from about 75 to about 40 BCE, was Lucretius' exact contemporary and a follower of the school of thought most perfectly represented in *On the Nature of Things*.

Why were the works of a minor Greek philosopher in the library of the elegant seaside retreat? And why, for that matter, did a vacation house have an extensive library at all? Philodemus, a pedagogue paid to give lessons and deliver lectures, was certainly not the master of the Villa of the Papyri. But the pres-

ence of a substantial selection of his works probably provides a
clue to the owner's interests and illuminates the moment that
brought forth Lucretius' poem. That moment was the culmi-
nation of a lengthy process that braided together Greek and
Roman high culture.

The two cultures had not always been comfortably inter-
twined. Among the Greeks, Romans had long held the reputation of tough, disciplined people, with a gift for survival
and a hunger for conquest. But they were also regarded as
barbarians—"refined barbarians," in the moderate view of the
Alexandrian scientist Eratosthenes, crude and dangerous barbarians in the view of many others. When their independent
city-states were still flourishing, Greek intellectuals collected
some arcane lore about the Romans, as they did about the
Carthaginians and Indians, but they did not find anything in
Roman cultural life worthy of their notice.

The Romans of the early republic might not altogether have
disagreed with this assessment. Rome had traditionally been
wary of poets and philosophers. It prided itself on being a city
of virtue and action, not of flowery words, intellectual speculation, and books. But even as Rome's legions steadily established
military dominance over Greece, Greek culture just as steadily
began to colonize the minds of the conquerors. Skeptical as ever
of effete intellectuals and priding themselves on their practical
intelligence, Romans nonetheless acknowledged with growing
enthusiasm the achievements of Greek philosophers, scientists,
writers, and artists. They made fun of what they took to be
the defects of the Greek character, mocking what they saw as
its loquaciousness, its taste for philosophizing, and its foppish-
ness. But ambitious Roman families sent their sons to study at
the philosophical academies for which Athens was famous, and
Greek intellectuals like Philodemus were brought to Rome and
paid handsome salaries to teach.

It was never quite respectable for a Roman aristocrat to

admit to a boundlessly ardent Hellenism. Sophisticated Romans found it desirable to downplay a mastery of Greek language and a connoisseur's grasp of Greek art. Yet Roman temples and public spaces were graced with splendid statues stolen from the conquered cities of the Greek mainland and the Peloponnese, while battle-hardened Roman generals adorned their villas with precious Greek vases and sculptures.

The survival of stone and fired clay makes it easy for us to register the pervasive presence in Rome of Greek artifacts, but it was books that carried the full weight of cultural influence. In keeping with the city's martial character, the first great collections were brought there as spoils of war. In 167 BCE the Roman general Aemilius Paulus routed King Perseus of Macedon and put an end to a dynasty that had descended from Alexander the Great and his father Philip. Perseus and his three sons were sent in chains to be paraded through the streets of Rome behind the triumphal chariot. In the tradition of national kleptocracy, Aemilius Paulus shipped back enormous plunder to deposit in the Roman treasury. But for himself and his children the conqueror reserved only a single prize: the captive monarch's library. The gesture was evidence, of course, of the aristocratic general's personal fortune, but it was also a spectacular signal of the value of Greek books and the culture these books embodied.

Others followed in Aemilius Paulus' wake. It became increasingly fashionable for wealthy Romans to amass large private libraries in their town houses and country villas. (There were no bookshops in the early years in Rome, but, in addition to the collections seized as booty, books could be purchased from dealers in southern Italy and Sicily where the Greeks had founded such cities as Naples, Tarentum, and Syracuse.) The grammarian Tyrannion is reputed to have had 30,000 volumes; Serenus Sammonicus, a physician who was an expert on the use of the magical formula "Abracadabra" to ward off illness, had more than 60,000. Rome had caught the Greek fever for books.

Lucretius lived his life in a culture of wealthy private book collectors, and the society into which he launched his poem was poised to expand the circle of reading to a larger public. In 40 BCE, a decade after Lucretius' death, Rome's first public library was established by a friend of the poet Virgil, Asinius Pollio. The idea seems to have originated with Julius Caesar, who admired the public libraries he had seen in Greece, Asia Minor, and Egypt, and determined to bestow such an institution upon the Roman people. But Caesar was assassinated before he could carry out the plan, and it took Pollio, who had sided with Caesar against Pompey and then with Mark Antony against Brutus, to do so. A skillful military commander, canny (or extremely lucky) in his choice of allies, Pollio was also a man of broad literary interests. Apart from a few fragments of his speeches, all of his writings are now lost, but he composed tragedies—worthy of Sophocles, according to Virgil—histories, and literary criticism, and he was one of the first Roman authors to recite his writings to an audience of his friends.

The library established by Pollio was built on the Aventine Hill and paid for, in the typical Roman way, by wealth seized from the conquered—in this case, from a people on the Adriatic coast who had made the mistake of backing Brutus against Antony. Shortly afterwards, the emperor Augustus founded two more public libraries, and many subsequent emperors followed in his wake. (Altogether, by the fourth century CE, there were twenty-eight public libraries in Rome.) The structures, all of which have been destroyed, evidently followed the same general pattern, one that would be familiar to us. There was a large reading room adjoining smaller rooms in which the collections were stored in numbered bookcases. The reading room, either rectangular or semicircular in shape and sometimes lit through a circular opening in the roof, was adorned with busts or life-sized statues of celebrated writers: Homer, Plato, Aristotle, Epicurus, among others. The statues functioned, as they do for us, as an honorific, a gesture toward the canon of writers whom every civilized person should know. But in Rome they may have had an additional significance, akin to the masks of ancestors that Romans traditionally kept in their houses and that they donned on commemorative occasions. That is, they were signs of access to the spirits of the dead, symbols of the spirits that the books enabled readers to conjure up.

Many other cities of the ancient world came to boast public collections, endowed by tax revenues or by the gifts of wealthy, civic-minded donors. Greek libraries had had few amenities, but throughout their territories the Romans designed comfortable chairs and tables where readers could sit and slowly unfold the papyrus, the left hand rolling up each column after it was read. The great architect Vitruvius—one of the ancient writers whose work Poggio recovered—advised that libraries should face toward the east, to catch the morning light and reduce the humidity that might damage books. Excavations at Pompeii and elsewhere have uncovered the plaques honoring the donors, along with statuary, writing tables, shelves to store papyrus rolls, numbered bookcases to hold the bound parchment volumes or codices that gradually began to supplement the rolls, and even graffiti scribbled on the walls. The resemblance to the design of public libraries in our own society is no accident: our sense that a library is a public good and our idea of what such a place should look like derive precisely from a model created in Rome several thousand years ago.

Through the massive extent of the Roman world, whether on the banks of the Rhône in Gaul or near the grove and Temple of Daphne in the province of Syria, on the island of Cos, near Rhodes, or in Dyrrhkhion in what is now Albania, the houses of cultivated men and women had rooms set aside for quiet reading. Papyrus rolls were carefully indexed, labeled (with a protruding tag called in Greek a *sillybos*), and stacked on shelves or stored in leather baskets. Even in the elaborate bath complexes that Romans loved, reading rooms, decorated with busts of Greek and Latin authors, were carefully designed to make it possible for educated Romans to combine care for the body with care for the mind. By the first century CE there were distinctive signs of the emergence of what we think of as a "literary culture." At the games in the Colosseum one day, the historian Tacitus had a conversation on literature with a perfect stranger who turned out to have read his works. Culture was no longer located in close-knit circles of friends and acquaintances; Tacitus was encountering his "public" in the form of someone who had bought his book at a stall in the Forum or read it in a library. This broad commitment to reading, with its roots in the everyday lives of the Roman elite over many generations, explains why a pleasure palace like the Villa of the Papyri had a well-stocked library.

In the 1980s, modern archaeologists resumed serious work on the buried villa, in the hopes of gaining a better understanding of the whole style of life expressed in its design, a design vividly evoked in the architecture of the Getty Museum in Malibu, California, where some of the statues and other treasures found at Herculaneum now reside. The bulk of the marble and bronze masterpieces—images of gods and goddesses, portrait busts of philosophers, orators, poets, and playwrights; a graceful young athlete; a wild boar in mid-leap; a drunken satyr; a sleeping satyr; and a startlingly obscene Pan and goat *in flagrante delicto*—are now in the National Museum in Naples.

The renewed exploration got off to a slow start: the rich volcanic soil covering the site was used to grow carnations, and the owners were understandably reluctant to permit excavators to disrupt their business. But after lengthy negotiations, researchers were permitted to descend the shafts and approach the villa in small gondolalike craft that could glide safely through tunnels that had been bored through the ruins. In these eerie conditions, they succeeded in mapping the villa's layout more accurately than ever before, charting the precise dimensions of the atrium, the square and rectangular peristyles, and other structures, and locating as they did so such features as a large mosaic floor and an unusual double column. Traces of vine shoots and leaves enabled them to determine the precise site of the garden where some two thousand years ago the wealthy proprietor and his cultivated friends once came together.

It is, of course, impossible at this great distance in time to know exactly what these particular people talked about, during the long sunlit afternoons in the colonnaded garden at Herculaneum, but an intriguing further clue turned up, also in the 1980s. Scholars, this time above ground, were at work once again on the blackened papyri that had been discovered by the eighteenth-century treasure hunters. These scrolls, hardened into lumps, had resisted the early attempts to open them and had sat for more than two centuries in the National Library of Naples. In 1987, using new techniques, Tommaso Starace managed to open two badly preserved papyri. He mounted the legible fragments from these books—unread since the ancient volcanic eruption—on Japanese paper, micro-photographed them, and undertook to decipher the contents. Two years later Knut Kleve, a distinguished Norwegian papyrologist (as those who specialize in deciphering papyri are called), made an announcement: *"De rerum natura* has been rediscovered in Herculaneum, 235 years after the papyri were found."

The world at large understandably took this announcement

in stride—that is, ignored it altogether—and even scholars interested in ancient culture may be forgiven for giving the news,
buried in volume 19 of the massive Italian *Chronicles of Herculaneum,* little or no attention. What Kleve and his colleagues
had found were only sixteen minuscule fragments—little more
than words or parts of words—that, under close analysis, could
be shown to come from books 1, 3, 4, and 5 of the six-book-long
Latin poem. Forlorn pieces from an enormous jigsaw puzzle,
the fragments by themselves are virtually meaningless. But
their range suggests that the whole of *De rerum natura* was in
the library, and the presence of that poem in the Villa of the
Papyri is tantalizing.

The discoveries at Herculaneum enable us to glimpse the
social circles where the poem that Poggio found in the monastic library had originally circulated. In the monastic library,
among the missals, confessional manuals, and theological
tomes, Lucretius' work was an uncanny stranger, a relic that
had floated ashore from distant shipwreck. In Herculaneum,
it was a native. The contents of the surviving rolls suggest that
the villa's collection focused precisely on the school of thought
of which *De rerum natura* is the most remarkable surviving
expression.

Though the identity of the villa's owner during Lucretius'
lifetime is unknown, the strongest candidate is Lucius Calpur-
nius Piso. This powerful politician, who had served for a time
as governor of the province of Macedonia and was, among
other things, Julius Caesar's father-in-law, had an interest in
Greek philosophy. Cicero, a political enemy, pictured Piso singing obscene ditties and lolling naked "amid his tipsy and mal-
odorous Greeks"; but, judging from the contents of the library,
the guests during the afternoons in Herculaneum were likely
to have been devoted to more refined pursuits.

Piso is known to have had a personal acquaintance with

Philodemus. In an epigram discovered in one of his books in
the charred library, the philosopher invites Piso to join him in
his own modest home to celebrate a "Twentieth"—a monthly
feast observed in honor of Epicurus, born on the twentieth of
the Greek month of Gamelion:

> Tomorrow, friend Piso, your musical comrade drags you
>   to his modest
>   digs at three in the afternoon,
> feeding you at your annual visit to the Twentieth. If you
>   will miss udders
>   and Bromian wine *mis en bouteilles* in Chios,
> yet you will see faithful comrades, yet you will hear
>   things far sweeter
>   than the land of the Phaeacians.
> And if you ever turn your eye our way too, Piso, instead
>   of a modest
>   Twentieth we shall lead a richer one.

The closing lines morph into an appeal for money or perhaps express the hope that Philodemus will himself be invited
to an afternoon of philosophical conversation and expensive
wine at Piso's grand villa. Half-reclining on couches, under the
shade of trellised vines and silken canopies, the privileged men
and women who were Piso's guests—for it is entirely possible
that some women participated in the conversation as well—
had much to think about. Rome had been afflicted for years by
political and social unrest, culminating in several vicious civil
wars, and though the violence had abated, the threats to peace
and stability were by no means safely past. Ambitious generals
relentlessly jockeyed for position; murmuring troops had to be
paid in cash and land; the provinces were restive, and rumors of
trouble in Egypt had already caused grain prices to soar.

But cosseted by slaves, in the comfort and security of the elegant villa, the proprietor and his guests had the temporary luxury of regarding these menaces as relatively remote, remote enough at least to allow them to pursue civilized conversations. Staring up idly at the plumes of smoke rising from nearby Vesuvius, they may well have felt some queasiness about the future, but they were an elite, living at the center of the world's greatest power, and one of their most cherished privileges was the cultivation of the life of the mind.

Romans of the late republic were remarkably tenacious about this privilege, which they clung to in circumstances that would have made others quail and run for cover. For them it seemed to function as a sign that their world was still intact or at least that they were secure in their innermost lives. Like a man who, hearing the distant sound of sirens in the street, sits down at the Bechstein to play a Beethoven sonata, the men and women in the garden affirmed their urbane security by immersing themselves in speculative dialogue.

In the years leading up to the assassination of Julius Caesar, philosophical speculation was hardly the only available response to social stress. Religious cults originating in far-off places like Persia, Syria, and Palestine began to make their way to the capital, where they aroused wild fears and expectations, particularly among the plebs. A handful of the elite—those more insecure or simply curious—may have attended with something other than contempt to the prophecies from the east, prophecies of a saviour born of obscure parentage who would be brought low, suffer terribly, and yet ultimately triumph. But most would have regarded such tales as the overheated fantasies of a sect of stiff-necked Jews.

Those of a pious disposition would far more likely have gone as supplicants to the temples and chapels to the gods that dotted the fertile landscape. It was, in any case, a world in which nature seemed saturated with the presence of the divine, on mountaintops and springs, in the thermal vents that spewed smoke from a mysterious realm under the earth, in ancient groves of trees on whose branches the faithful hung colorful cloths. But though the villa in Herculaneum was in close proximity to this intense religious life, it is unlikely that many of those with the sophisticated intellectual tastes reflected in the library joined processions of pious supplicants. Judging from the contents of the charred papyrus scrolls, the villa's inhabitants seem to have turned not to ritual but to conversation about the meaning of life.

Ancient Greeks and Romans did not share our idealization of isolated geniuses, working alone to think through the knottiest problems. Such scenes—Descartes in his secret retreat, calling everything into question, or the excommunicated Spinoza quietly reasoning to himself while grinding lenses—would eventually become our dominant emblem of the life of the mind. But this vision of proper intellectual pursuits rested on a profound shift in cultural prestige, one that began with the early Christian hermits who deliberately withdrew from whatever it was that pagans valued: St. Anthony (250–356) in the desert or St. Symeon Stylites (390–459) perched on his column. Such figures, modern scholars have shown, characteristically had in fact bands of followers, and though they lived apart, they often played a significant role in the life of large communities. But the dominant cultural image that they fashioned—or that came to be fashioned around them—was of radical isolation.

Not so the Greeks and Romans. As thinking and writing generally require quiet and a minimum of distraction, their poets and philosophers must have periodically pulled away from the noise and business of the world in order to accomplish what they did. But the image that they projected was social. Poets depicted themselves as shepherds singing to other shep-

herds; philosophers depicted themselves engaged in long conversations, often stretching out over several days. The pulling
away from the distractions of the everyday world was figured
not as a retreat to the solitary cell but as a quiet exchange of
words among friends in a garden.

Humans, Aristotle wrote, are social animals: to realize one's
nature as a human then was to participate in a group activity.
And the activity of choice, for cultivated Romans, as for the
Greeks before them, was discourse. There is, Cicero remarked
at the beginning of a typical philosophical work, a wide diversity of opinion about the most important religious questions.
"This has often struck me," Cicero wrote,

> but it did so with especial force on one occasion, when
> the topic of the immortal gods was made the subject of
> a very searching and thorough discussion at the house
> of my friend Gaius Cotta.
>
> It was the Latin Festival, and I had come at Cotta's
> express invitation to pay him a visit. I found him sitting
> in an alcove, engaged in debate with Gaius Velleius, a
> Member of the Senate, accounted by the Epicureans as
> their chief Roman adherent at the time. With them was
> Quintus Lucilius Balbus, who was so accomplished a
> student of Stoicism as to rank with the leading Greek
> exponents of that system.

Cicero does not want to present his thoughts to his readers as
a tract composed after solitary reflection; he wants to present
them as an exchange of views among social and intellectual
equals, a conversation in which he himself plays only a small
part and in which there will be no clear victor.

The end of this dialogue—a long work that would have filled
several sizable papyrus rolls—is characteristically inconclusive:

"Here the conversation ended, and we parted, Velleius think-ing Cotta's discourse to be the truer, while I felt that that of Balbus approximated more nearly to a semblance of the truth." The inconclusiveness is not intellectual modesty—Cicero was not a modest man—but a strategy of civilized openness among friends. The exchange itself, not its final conclusions, carries much of the meaning. The discussion itself is what most mat-ters, the fact that we can reason together easily, with a blend of wit and seriousness, never descending into gossip or slan-der and always allowing room for alternative views. "The one who engages in conversation," Cicero wrote, "should not debar others from participating in it, as if he were entering upon a private monopoly; but, as in other things, so in a general conver-sation he should think it not unfair for each to have his turn."

The dialogues Cicero and others wrote were not transcrip-tions of real exchanges, though the characters in them were real, but they were idealized versions of conversations that undoubtedly occurred in places like the villa in Herculaneum. The conversations in that particular setting, to judge from the topics of the charred books found in the buried library, touched on music, painting, poetry, the art of public speaking, and other subjects of perennial interest to cultivated Greeks and Romans. They are likely to have turned as well to more troubling scien-tific, ethical, and philosophical questions: What is the cause of thunder or earthquakes or eclipses—are they signs from the gods, as some claim, or do they have an origin in nature? How can we understand the world we inhabit? What goals should we be pursuing in our lives? Does it make sense to devote one's life to the pursuit of power? How are good and evil to be defined? What happens to us when we die?

That the villa's powerful owner and his friends took plea-sure in grappling with such questions and were willing to devote significant periods of their very busy lives to teasing out possible answers reflects their conception of an existence appropriate for people of their education, class, and status. It reflects as well something extraordinary about the mental or spiritual world they inhabited, something noted in one of his letters by the French novelist Gustave Flaubert: "Just when the gods had ceased to be, and the Christ had not yet come, there was a unique moment in history, between Cicero and Marcus Aurelius, when man stood alone." No doubt one could quibble with this claim. For many Romans at least, the gods had not actually ceased to be—even the Epicureans, sometimes reputed to be atheists, thought that gods existed, though at a far remove from the affairs of mortals—and the "unique moment" to which Flaubert gestures, from Cicero (106–43 BCE) to Marcus Aurelius (121–180 CE), may have been longer or shorter than the time frame he suggests. But the core perception is eloquently borne out by Cicero's dialogues and by the works found in the library of Herculaneum. Many of the early readers of those works evidently lacked a fixed repertory of beliefs and practices reinforced by what was said to be the divine will. They were men and women whose lives were unusually free of the dictates of the gods (or their priests). Standing alone, as Flaubert puts it, they found themselves in the peculiar position of choosing among sharply divergent visions of the nature of things and competing strategies for living.

The charred fragments in the library give us a glimpse of how the villa's residents made this choice, whom they wished to read, what they are likely to have discussed, whom they might have summoned to enter into the conversation. And here the Norwegian papyrologist's tiny fragments become deeply resonant. Lucretius was a contemporary of Philodemus and, more important, of Philodemus' patron, who may, when he invited friends to join him for an afternoon on the verdant slopes of the volcano, have shared with them passages from *On the Nature of*

Things. Indeed, the wealthy patron with philosophical interests could have wished to meet the author in person. It would have been a small matter to send a few slaves and a litter to carry Lucretius to Herculaneum to join the guests. And therefore it is even remotely possible that, reclining on a couch, Lucretius himself read aloud from the very manuscript whose fragments survive.

If Lucretius had participated in the conversations at the villa, it is clear enough what he would have said. His own conclusions would not have been inconclusive or tinged with skepticism, in the manner of Cicero. The answers to all of their questions, he passionately argued, were to be found in the work of a man whose portrait bust and writings graced the villa's library, the philosopher Epicurus.

It was only Epicurus, Lucretius wrote, who could cure the miserable condition of the man who, bored to death at home, rushes off frantically to his country villa only to find that he is just as oppressed in spirit. Indeed, in Lucretius' view, Epicurus, who had died more than two centuries earlier, was nothing less than the saviour. When "human life lay groveling igno-miniously in the dust, crushed beneath the grinding weight of superstition," Lucretius wrote, one supremely brave man arose and became "the first who ventured to confront it boldly." (1.62ff.) This hero—one strikingly at odds with a Roman culture that traditionally prided itself on toughness, pragmatism, and military virtue—was a Greek who triumphed not through the force of arms but through the power of intellect.

On the Nature of Things is the work of a disciple who is transmitting ideas that had been developed centuries earlier. Epicurus, Lucretius' philosophical messiah, was born toward the end of

342 BCE on the Aegean island of Samos where his father, a poor Athenian schoolmaster, had gone as a colonist. Many Greek philosophers, including Plato and Aristotle, came from wealthy families and prided themselves on their distinguished ancestry. Epicurus decidedly had no comparable claims. His philosophical enemies, basking in their social superiority, made much of the modesty of his background. He assisted his father in his school for a pittance, they sneered, and used to go round with his mother to cottages to read charms. One of his brothers, they added, was a pander and lived with a prostitute. This was not a philosopher with whom respectable people should associate themselves.

That Lucretius and many others did more than simply associate themselves with Epicurus—that they celebrated him as godlike in his wisdom and courage—depended not on his social credentials but upon what they took to be the saving power of his vision. The core of this vision may be traced back to a single incandescent idea: that everything that has ever existed and everything that will ever exist is put together out of indestructible building blocks, irreducibly small in size, unimaginably vast in number. The Greeks had a word for these invisible building blocks, things that, as they conceived them, could not be divided any further: atoms.

The notion of atoms, which originated in the fifth century BCE with Leucippus of Abdera and his prize student Democritus, was only a dazzling speculation; there was no way to get any empirical proof and wouldn't be for more than two thousand years. Other philosophers had competing theories: the core matter of the universe, they argued, was fire or water or air or earth, or some combination of these. Others suggested that if you could perceive the smallest particle of a man, you would find an infinitesimally tiny man; and similarly for a horse, a droplet of water, or a blade of grass. Others again proposed that the intricate order in the universe was evidence of an invisible mind or spirit that carefully put the pieces together according to a preconceived plan. Democritus' conception of an infinite number of atoms that have no qualities except size, figure, and weight—particles then that are not miniature versions of what we see but rather form what we see by combining with each other in an inexhaustible variety of shapes—was a fantastically daring solution to a problem that engaged the great intellects of his world.

It took many generations to think through the implications of this solution. (We have by no means yet thought through them all.) Epicurus began his efforts to do so at the age of twelve, when to his disgust his teachers could not explain to him the meaning of chaos. Democritus' old idea of atoms seemed to him the most promising clue, and he set to work to follow it wherever it would take him. By the age of thirty-two he was ready to found a school. There, in a garden in Athens, Epicurus constructed a whole account of the universe and a philosophy of human life.

In constant motion, atoms collide with each other, Epicurus reasoned, and in certain circumstances, they form larger and larger bodies. The largest observable bodies—the sun and the moon—are made of atoms, just as are human beings and water-flies and grains of sand. There are no supercategories of matter; no hierarchy of elements. Heavenly bodies are not divine beings who shape our destiny for good or ill, nor do they move through the void under the guidance of gods: they are simply part of the natural order, enormous structures of atoms subject to the same principles of creation and destruction that govern everything that exists. And if the natural order is unimaginably vast and complex, it is nonetheless possible to understand something of its basic constitutive elements and its universal laws. Indeed, such understanding is one of human life's deepest pleasures.

This pleasure is perhaps the key to comprehending the powerful impact of Epicurus' philosophy; it was as if he unlocked for his followers an inexhaustible source of gratification hidden within Democritus' atoms. For us, the impact is rather difficult to grasp. For one thing, the pleasure seems too intellectual to reach more than a tiny number of specialists; for another, we have come to associate atoms far more with fear than with gratification. But though ancient philosophy was hardly a mass movement, Epicurus was offering something more than caviar to a handful of particle physicists. Indeed, eschewing the self-enclosed, specialized language of an inner circle of adepts, he insisted on using ordinary language, on addressing the widest circle of listeners, even on proselytizing. And the enlightenment he offered did not require sustained scientific inquiry. You did not need a detailed grasp of the actual laws of the physical universe; you needed only to comprehend that there is a hidden natural explanation for everything that alarms or eludes you. That explanation will inevitably lead you back to atoms. If you can hold on to and repeat to yourself the simplest fact of existence—atoms and void and nothing else, atoms and void and nothing else, atoms and void and nothing else—your life will change. You will no longer fear Jove's wrath, whenever you hear a peal of thunder, or suspect that someone has offended Apollo, whenever there is an outbreak of influenza. And you will be freed from a terrible affliction—what Hamlet, many centuries later, described as "the dread of something after death,/The undiscovered country from whose bourn/No traveller returns."

The affliction—the fear of some horrendous punishment waiting for one in a realm beyond the grave—no longer weighs heavily on most modern men and women, but it evidently did in the ancient Athens of Epicurus and the ancient Rome of Lucretius, and it did as well in the Christian world inhabited by Poggio. Certainly Poggio would have seen images of such horrors, lovingly carved on the tympanum above the doors to churches or painted on their inner walls. And those horrors were in turn modeled on accounts of the afterlife fashioned in the pagan imagination. To be sure, not everyone in any of these periods, pagan or Christian, believed in such accounts. Aren't you terrified, one of the characters in a dialogue by Cicero asks, by the underworld, with its terrible three-headed dog, its black river, its hideous punishments? "Do you suppose me so crazy as to believe such tales?" his companion replies. Fear of death is not about the fate of Sisyphus and Tantalus: "Where is the crone so silly as to be afraid" of such scare stories? It is about the dread of suffering and the dread of perishing, and it is difficult to understand, Cicero wrote, why the Epicureans think that they are offering any palliative. To be told that one perishes completely and forever, soul as well as body, is hardly a robust consolation.

Followers of Epicurus responded by recalling the last days of the master, dying from an excruciating obstruction of the bladder but achieving serenity of spirit by recalling all of the pleasures he had experienced in his life. It is not clear that this model was easily imitable—"Who can hold a fire in his hand/ By thinking on the frosty Caucasus?" as one of Shakespeare's characters asks—but then it is not clear that any of the available alternatives, in a world without Demerol or morphine, was more successful at dealing with death agonies. What the Greek philosopher offered was not help in dying but help in living. Liberated from superstition, Epicurus taught, you would be free to pursue pleasure.

Epicurus' enemies seized upon his celebration of pleasure and invented malicious stories of his debauchery, stories heightened by his unusual inclusion of women as well as men among his followers. He "vomited twice a day from over-indulgence," went one of these stories, and spent a fortune on his feasting.

In reality, the philosopher seems to have lived a conspicuously simple and frugal life. "Send me a pot of cheese," he wrote once to a friend, "that, when I like, I may fare sumptuously." So much for the alleged abundance of his table. And he urged a comparable frugality on his students. The motto carved over the door to Epicurus' garden urged the stranger to linger, for "here our highest good is pleasure." But according to the philosopher Seneca, who quotes these words in a famous letter that Poggio and his friends knew and admired, the passerby who entered would be served a simple meal of barley gruel and water. "When we say, then, that pleasure is the goal," Epicurus wrote in one of his few surviving letters, "we do not mean the pleasures of the prodigal or the pleasures of sensuality." The feverish attempt to satisfy certain appetites—"an unbroken succession of drinking bouts and of revelry . . . sexual love . . . the enjoyment of the fish and other delicacies of a luxurious table"—cannot lead to the peace of mind that is the key to enduring pleasure.

"Men suffer the worst evils for the sake of the most alien desires," wrote his disciple Philodemus, in one of the books found in the library at Herculaneum, and "they neglect the most necessary appetites as if they were the most alien to nature." What are these necessary appetites that lead to pleasure? It is impossible to live pleasurably, Philodemus continued, "without living prudently and honourably and justly, and also without living courageously and temperately and magnanimously, and without making friends, and without being philanthropic."

This is the voice of an authentic follower of Epicurus, a voice recovered in modern times from a volcano-blackened papyrus roll. But it is hardly the voice that anyone familiar with the term "Epicureanism" would ever expect. In one of his memorable satirical grotesques, Shakespeare's contemporary Ben Jonson perfectly depicted the spirit in which Epicurus' philosophy was for long centuries widely understood. "I'll have all my beds blown up, not stuffed," Jonson's character declares. "Down is too hard."

> My meat shall all come in in Indian shells,
> Dishes of agate, set in gold, and studded,
> With emeralds, sapphires, hyacinths, and rubies. . . .
> My foot-boy shall eat pheasants, calvered salmons,
> Knots, godwits, lampreys. I myself will have
> The beards of barbels served instead of salads;
> Oiled mushrooms; and the swelling unctuous paps
> Of a fat pregnant sow, newly cut off,
> Drest with an exquisite and poignant sauce;
> For which, I'll say unto my cook, "There's gold,
> Go forth and be a knight."

The name Jonson gave to this mad pleasure seeker is Sir Epicure Mammon.

A philosophical claim that life's ultimate goal is pleasure—even if that pleasure was defined in the most restrained and responsible terms—was a scandal, both for pagans and for their adversaries, the Jews and later the Christians. Pleasure as the highest good? What about worshipping the gods and ancestors? Serving the family, the city, and the state? Scrupulously observing the laws and commandments? Pursuing virtue or a vision of the divine? These competing claims inevitably entailed forms of ascetic self-denial, self-sacrifice, even self-loathing. None was compatible with the pursuit of pleasure as the highest good. Two thousand years after Epicurus lived and taught, the sense of scandal was still felt intensely enough to generate the manic energy in travesties like Jonson's.

Behind such travesties lay a half-hidden fear that to maximize pleasure and to avoid pain were in fact appealing goals and might plausibly serve as the rational organizing principles of human life. If they succeeded in doing so, a whole set of time-honored alternative principles—sacrifice, ambition, social status, discipline, piety—would be challenged, along with the institutions that such principles served. To push the Epicurean pursuit of pleasure toward grotesque sensual self-indulgence—depicted as the single-minded pursuit of sex or power or money or even (as in Jonson) extravagant, absurdly expensive food—helped to ward off the challenge.

In his secluded garden in Athens, the real Epicurus, dining on cheese, bread, and water, lived a quiet life. Indeed, one of the more legitimate charges against him was that his life was *too* quiet: he counseled his followers against a full, robust engagement in the affairs of the city. "Some men have sought to become famous and renowned," he wrote, "thinking that thus they would make themselves secure against their fellowmen." If security actually came with fame and renown, then the person who sought them attained a "natural good." But if fame actually brought heightened insecurity, as it did in most cases, then such an achievement was not worth pursuing. From this perspective, Epicurus' critics observed, it would be difficult to justify most of the restless striving and risk taking that leads to a city's greatness.

Such a criticism of Epicurean quietism may well have been voiced in the sun-drenched garden of Herculaneum: the guests at the Villa of the Papyri, after all, would probably have included their share of those who sought fame and renown at the center of the greatest city in the Western world. But perhaps Julius Caesar's father-in-law—if Piso was indeed the villa's owner—and some in his circle of friends were drawn to this philosophical school precisely because it offered an alternative to their stressful endeavors. Rome's enemies were falling before the might of its legions, but it did not take prophetic powers to perceive ominous signs for the future of the republic. And even for those most safely situated, it was difficult to gainsay one of Epicurus' celebrated aphorisms: "Against other things it is possible to obtain security, but when it comes to death we human beings all live in an unwalled city." The key point, as Epicurus' disciple Lucretius wrote in verses of unrivalled beauty, was to abandon the anxious and doomed attempt to build higher and higher walls and to turn instead toward the cultivation of pleasure.

CHAPTER FOUR

THE TEETH OF TIME

A PART FROM THE charred papyrus fragments recovered in Herculaneum and another cache of fragments discovered in rubbish mounds in the ancient Egyptian city of Oxyrhynchus, there are no surviving contemporary manuscripts from the ancient Greek and Roman world. Everything that has reached us is a copy, most often very far removed in time, place, and culture from the original. And these copies represent only a small portion of the works even of the most celebrated writers of antiquity. Of Aeschylus' eighty or ninety plays and the roughly one hundred twenty by Sophocles, only seven each have survived; Euripides and Aristophanes did slightly better: eighteen of ninety-two plays by the former have come down to us; eleven of forty-three by the latter.

These are the great success stories. Virtually the entire output of many other writers, famous in antiquity, has disappeared without a trace. Scientists, historians, mathematicians, philosophers, and statesmen have left behind some of their achievements—the invention of trigonometry, for example, or the calculation of position by reference to latitude and longitude, or the rational analysis of political power—but their books are gone. The indefatigable scholar Didymus of Alexandria earned the nickname Bronze-Ass (literally, "Brazen-Bowelled") for having what it took to write more than 3,500 books; apart from a few fragments, all have vanished. At the end of the fifth century CE an ambitious literary editor known as Stobaeus compiled an anthology of prose and poetry by the ancient world's best authors: out of 1,430 quotations, 1,115 are from works that are now lost.

In this general vanishing, all the works of the brilliant founders of atomism, Leucippus and Democritus, and most of the works of their intellectual heir Epicurus, disappeared. Epicurus had been extraordinarily prolific. He and his principal philosophical opponent, the Stoic Chrysippus, wrote between them, it was said, more than a thousand books. Even if this figure is exaggerated or if it counts as books what we would regard as essays and letters, the written record was clearly massive. That record no longer exists. Apart from three letters quoted by an ancient historian of philosophy, Diogenes Laertius, along with a list of forty maxims, almost nothing by Epicurus has survived. Modern scholarship, since the nineteenth century, has only been able to add some fragments. Some of these were culled from the blackened papyrus rolls found at Herculaneum; others were painstakingly recovered from the broken pieces of an ancient wall. On that wall, discovered in the town of Oenoanda, in the rugged mountains in southwest Turkey, an old man, in the early years of the second century CE, had had his distinctly Epicurean philosophy of life—"a fine anthem to celebrate the fullness of pleasure"—chiseled in stone. But where did all the books go?

The actual material disappearance of the books was largely the effect of climate and pests. Though papyrus and parchment were impressively long-lived (far more so than either our cheap paper or computerized data), books inevitably deteriorated over the centuries, even if they managed to escape the ravages of fire and flood. The ink was a mixture of soot (from burnt lamp wicks), water, and tree gum: that made it cheap and agreeably easy to read, but also water-soluble. (A scribe who made a mistake could erase it with a sponge.) A spilled glass of wine or a heavy downpour, and the text disappeared. And that was only the most common threat. Rolling and unrolling the scrolls or poring over the codices, touching them, dropping them, coughing on them, allowing them to be scorched by fire from the candles, or simply reading them over and over eventually destroyed them.

Carefully sequestering books from excessive use was of little help, for they then became the objects not of intellectual hunger but of a more literal appetite. Tiny animals, Aristotle noted, may be detected in such things as clothes, woolen blankets, and cream cheese. "Others are found," he observed, "in books, some of them similar to those found in clothes, others like tailless scorpions, very small indeed." Almost two thousand years later in *Micrographia* (1655), the scientist Robert Hooke reported with fascination what he saw when he examined one of these creatures under that remarkable new invention, the microscope:

> a small white silver-shining Worm or Moth, which I found much conversant among books and papers, and is supposed to be that which corrodes and eats holes through the leaves and covers. Its head appears big and blunt, and its body tapers from it towards the tail, smaller and smaller, being shaped almost like a carrot. . . . It has two long horns before, which are straight, and tapering towards the top, curiously ringed or knobbed. . . . The hinder part is terminated with three tails, in every particular resembling the two longer horns that grow out of the head. The legs are scaled and haired. This animal probably feeds upon the paper and covers of books, and perforates in them several small round holes.

The bookworm—"one of the teeth of time," as Hooke put it—is no longer familiar to ordinary readers, but the ancients knew it very well. In exile, the Roman poet Ovid likened the "constant gnawing of sorrow" at his heart to the gnawing of the bookworm—"as the book when laid away is nibbled by the worm's teeth." His contemporary Horace feared that his book will eventually become "food for vandal moths." And for the Greek poet Evenus, the bookworm was the symbolic enemy of human culture: "Page-eater, the Muses' bitterest foe, lurking destroyer, ever feeding on thy thefts from learning, why, black bookworm, dost thou lie concealed among the sacred utterances, producing the image of envy?" Some protective measures, such as sprinkling cedar oil on the pages, were discovered to be effective in warding off damage, but it was widely recognized that the best way to preserve books from being eaten into oblivion was simply to use them and, when they finally wore out, to make more copies.

Though the book trade in the ancient world was entirely about copying, little information has survived about how the enterprise was organized. There were scribes in Athens, as in other cities of the Greek and Hellenistic world, but it is not clear whether they received training in special schools or were apprenticed to master scribes or simply set up on their own. Some were evidently paid for the beauty of their calligraphy; others were paid by the total number of lines written (there are line numbers recorded at the end of some surviving manuscripts). In neither case is the payment likely to have gone directly to the scribe: many, perhaps most, Greek scribes must have been slaves working for a publisher who owned or rented them. (An inventory of the property of a wealthy Roman citizen with an estate in Egypt lists, among his fifty-nine slaves, five notaries, two amanuenses, one scribe, and a book repairer, along with a cook and a barber.) But we do not know whether these scribes generally sat in large groups, writing from dictation, or worked individually from a master copy. And if the author of the work was alive, we do not know if he was involved in checking or correcting the finished copy.

Somewhat more is known about the Roman book trade, where a distinction evolved between copyists (*librarii*) and scribes (*scribae*). The *librarii* generally were slaves or paid laborers who worked for booksellers. The booksellers set up advertisements on pillars and sold their wares in shops located in the Roman Forum. The *scribae* were free citizens; they worked as archivists, government bureaucrats, and personal secretaries. (Julius Caesar had seven scribes who followed him around taking dictation.) Wealthy Romans employed (or owned as slaves) personal librarians and clerks who copied books borrowed from the libraries of their friends. "I have received the book," Cicero wrote to his friend Atticus, who had lent him a copy of a geographical work in verse by Alexander of Ephesus. "He's incompetent as a poet and he knows nothing; however, he's of some use. I'm having it copied and I'll return it."

Authors made nothing from the sale of their books; their profits derived from the wealthy patron to whom the work was dedicated. (The arrangement—which helps to account for the fulsome flattery of dedicatory epistles—seems odd to us, but it had an impressive stability, remaining in place until the invention of copyright in the eighteenth century.) Publishers had to contend, as we have seen, with the widespread copying of books among friends, but the business of producing and marketing books must have been a profitable one: there were bookshops not only in Rome but also in Brindisi, Carthage, Lyons, Reims, and other cities in the empire.

Large numbers of men and women—for there are records of female as well as male copyists—spent their lives bent over paper, with an inkwell, ruler, and hard split-reed pen, satisfying the demand for books. The invention of movable type in the fifteenth century changed the scale of production exponentially, but the book in the ancient world was not a rare commodity: a well-trained slave reading a manuscript aloud to a roomful of well-trained scribes could produce masses of text. Over the course of centuries, tens of thousands of books, hundreds of thousands of copies, were made and sold.

There was a time in the ancient world—a very long time—in which the central cultural problem must have seemed an inexhaustible outpouring of books. Where to put them all? How to organize them on the groaning shelves? How to hold the profusion of knowledge in one's head? The loss of this plenitude would have been virtually inconceivable to anyone living in its midst.

Then, not all at once but with the cumulative force of a mass extinction, the whole enterprise came to an end. What looked stable turned out to be fragile, and what had seemed for all time was only for the time being.

The scribes must have been among the first to notice: they had less and less to do. Most of the copying stopped. The slow rains, dripping through the holes in the decaying roofs, washed away the letters in books that the flames had spared, and the worms, those "teeth of time," set to work on what was left. But worms were only the lowliest agents of the Great Vanishing. Other forces were at work to hasten the disappearance of the books, and the crumbling of the shelves themselves into dust and ashes. Poggio and his fellow book hunters were lucky to find anything at all.

———

The fate of the books in all their vast numbers is epitomized in the fate of the greatest library in the ancient world, a library located not in Italy but in Alexandria, the capital of Egypt and the commercial hub of the eastern Mediterranean. The city had many tourist attractions, including an impressive theater and red-light district, but visitors always took note of something quite exceptional: in the center of the city, at a lavish site known as the Museum, most of the intellectual inheritance of Greek, Latin, Babylonian, Egyptian, and Jewish cultures had been assembled at enormous cost and carefully archived for research. Starting as early as 300 BCE, the Ptolemaic kings who ruled Alexandria had the inspired idea of luring leading scholars, scientists, and poets to their city by offering them life appointments at the Museum, with handsome salaries, tax exemptions, free food and lodging, and the almost limitless resources of the library.

The recipients of this largesse established remarkably high intellectual standards. Euclid developed his geometry in Alexandria; Archimedes discovered pi and laid the foundation for calculus; Eratosthenes posited that the earth was round and calculated its circumference to within 1 percent; Galen revolutionized medicine. Alexandrian astronomers postulated a heliocentric universe; geometers deduced that the length of a year was 365¼ days and proposed adding a "leap day" every fourth year; geographers speculated that it would be possible to reach India by sailing west from Spain; engineers developed hydraulics and pneumatics; anatomists first understood clearly that the brain and the nervous system were a unit, studied the function of the heart and the digestive system, and conducted experiments in nutrition. The level of achievement was staggering.

The Alexandrian library was not associated with a particular doctrine or philosophical school; its scope was the entire range of intellectual inquiry. It represented a global cosmopolitanism, a determination to assemble the accumulated knowledge of the whole world and to perfect and add to this knowledge. Fantastic efforts were made not only to amass vast numbers of books but also to acquire or establish definitive editions. Alexandrian scholars were famously obsessed with the pursuit of textual accuracy. How was it possible to strip away the corruptions that inevitably seeped into books copied and recopied, for the most part by slaves, for centuries? Generations of dedicated scholars developed elaborate techniques of comparative analysis and painstaking commentary in pursuit of the master texts. They pursued as well access to the knowledge that lay beyond the boundaries of the Greek-speaking world. It is for this reason that an Alexandrian ruler, Ptolomey Philadelphus, is said to have undertaken the expensive and ambitious project of commissioning some seventy scholars to translate the Hebrew Bible into Greek. The result—known as the Septuagint (after the Latin for "seventy")—was for many early Christians their principal access to what they came to call the Old Testament.

At its height the Museum contained at least a half-million papyrus rolls systematically organized, labeled, and shelved according to a clever new system that its first director, a Homer scholar named Zenodotus, seems to have invented: the system was alphabetical order. The institution extended beyond the Museum's enormous holdings to a second collection, housed in one of the architectural marvels of the age, the Serapeon, the Temple of Jupiter Serapis. Adorned with elegant, colonnaded courtyards, lecture halls, "almost breathing statues," and many other precious works of art, the Serapeon, in the words of Ammianus Marcellinus, the fourth-century historian rediscovered by Poggio, was second in magnificence only to the Capitol in Rome.

The forces that destroyed this institution help us understand how it came about that the Lucretius manuscript recovered in

1417 was almost all that remained of a school of thought that was once eagerly debated in thousands of books. The first blow came as a consequence of war. A part of the library's collection—possibly only scrolls kept in warehouses near the harbor—was accidentally burned in 48 BCE when Julius Caesar struggled to maintain control of the city. But there were greater threats than military action alone, threats bound up with an institution that was part of a temple complex, replete with statues of gods and goddesses, altars, and other paraphernalia of pagan worship. The Museum was, as its name implies, a shrine dedicated to the Muses, the nine goddesses who embodied human creative achievement. The Serapeon, where the secondary collection was located, housed a colossal statue of the god Serapis—a masterpiece fashioned in ivory and gold by the famous Greek sculptor Bryaxis—combining the cult of the Roman deity Jupiter with the cult of the Egyptian deities Osiris and Apis.

The Jews and Christians who lived in large numbers in Alexandria were intensely uneasy with this polytheism. They did not doubt that other gods existed, but those gods were without exception demons, fiendishly bent on luring gullible humanity away from the sole and universal truth. All other revelations and prayers recorded in those mountains of papyrus rolls were lies. Salvation lay in the Scriptures, which Christians opted to read in a new format: not the old-fashioned scroll (used by Jews and pagans alike) but the compact, convenient, easily portable codex.

Centuries of religious pluralism under paganism—three faiths living side by side in a spirit of mingled rivalry and absorptive tolerance—were coming to an end. In the early fourth century the emperor Constantine began the process whereby Rome's official religion became Christianity. It was only a matter of time before a zealous successor—Theodosius the Great, beginning in 391 CE—issued edicts forbidding public sacrifices and closing major cultic sites. The state had embarked on the destruction of paganism.

In Alexandria, the spiritual leader of the Christian community, the patriarch Theophilus, heeded the edicts with a vengeance. At once contentious and ruthless, Theophilus unleashed mobs of Christian zealots who roamed through the streets insulting pagans. The pagans responded with predictable shock and anxiety, and tensions between the two communities rose. All that was needed was an appropriately charged incident for matters to be brought to a head, and the incident was not long in coming. Workmen renovating a Christian basilica found an underground sanctuary that still contained pagan cult objects (such a sanctuary—a shrine to Mithras—may be seen today in Rome, deep below the Basilica of S. Clemente). Seeing a chance to expose the secret symbols of pagan "mysteries" to public mockery, Theophilus ordered that the cult objects be paraded through the streets.

Pious pagans erupted in anger: "as though," a contemporary Christian observer wryly noted, "they had drunk a chalice of serpents." The enraged pagans violently attacked Christians and then withdrew behind the locked doors of the Serapeon. Armed with axes and hammers, a comparably frenzied Christian crowd burst into the shrine, overwhelmed its defenders, and smashed the celebrated marble, ivory, and gold statue of the god. Pieces were taken to different parts of the city to be destroyed; the headless, limbless trunk was dragged to the theater and publicly burned. Theophilus ordered monks to move into the precincts of the pagan temple, whose beautiful buildings would be converted into churches. Where the statue of Serapis had stood, the triumphant Christians would erect reliquaries holding the precious remains of Elijah and John the Baptist.

After the downfall of the Serapeon, a pagan poet, Palladas, expressed his mood of devastation:

> Is it not true that we are dead, and living only in
>   appearance,
> We Hellenes, fallen on disaster,
> Likening life to a dream, since we remain alive while
> Our way of life is dead and gone?

The significance of the destruction, as Palladas understood, extended beyond the loss of the single cult image. Whether on this occasion mayhem reached the library is unknown. But libraries, museums, and schools are fragile institutions; they cannot long survive violent assaults. A way of life was dying.

A few years later, Theophilus' successor as Christian patriarch, his nephew Cyril, expanded the scope of the attacks, directing pious wrath this time upon the Jews. Violent skirmishes broke out at the theater, in the streets, and in front of churches and synagogues. Jews taunted and threw stones at Christians; Christians broke into and plundered Jewish shops and homes. Emboldened by the arrival from the desert of five hundred monks who joined the already formidable Christian street mobs, Cyril demanded the expulsion of the city's large Jewish population. Alexandria's governor Orestes, a moderate Christian, refused, and this refusal was supported by the city's pagan intellectual elite whose most distinguished representative was the influential and immensely learned Hypatia.

Hypatia was the daughter of a mathematician, one of the Museum's famous scholars-in-residence. Legendarily beautiful as a young woman, she had become famous for her attainments in astronomy, music, mathematics, and philosophy. Students came from great distances to study the works of Plato and Aristotle under her tutelage. Such was her authority that other philosophers wrote to her and anxiously solicited her approval. "If you decree that I ought to publish my book," wrote one such correspondent to Hypatia, "I will dedicate it to orators and philosophers together." If, on the other hand, "it does not seem to you worthy," the letter continues, "a close and profound darkness will overshadow it, and mankind will never hear it mentioned."

Wrapped in the traditional philosopher's cloak, called a *tribon*, and moving about the city in a chariot, Hypatia was one of Alexandria's most visible public figures. Women in the ancient world often lived sequestered lives, but not she. "Such was her self-possession and ease of manner, arising from the refinement and cultivation of her mind," writes a contemporary, "that she not unfrequently appeared in public in presence of the magistrates." Her easy access to the ruling elite did not mean that she constantly meddled in politics. At the time of the earlier attacks on the cult images, she and her followers evidently held themselves aloof, telling themselves perhaps that the smashing of inanimate statues left intact what really mattered. But with the agitation against the Jews it must have become clear that the flames of fanaticism were not going to die down.

Hypatia's support for Orestes' refusal to expel the city's Jewish population may help to explain what happened next. Rumors began to circulate that her absorption in astronomy, mathematics, and philosophy—so strange, after all, in a woman—was sinister: she must be a witch, practicing black magic. In March 415 the crowd, whipped into a frenzy by one of Cyril's henchmen, erupted. Returning to her house, Hypatia was pulled from her chariot and taken to a church that was formerly a temple to the emperor. (The setting was no accident: it signified the transformation of paganism into the one true faith.) There, after she was stripped of her clothing, her skin was flayed off with broken bits of pottery. The mob then dragged her corpse outside the city walls and burned it. Their hero Cyril was eventually made a saint.

The murder of Hypatia signified more than the end of one remarkable person; it effectively marked the downfall of Alexandrian intellectual life and was the death knell for the whole intellectual tradition that underlay the text that Poggio recovered so many centuries later. The Museum, with its dream of assembling all texts, all schools, all ideas, was no longer at the protected center of civil society. In the years that followed the library virtually ceased to be mentioned, as if its great collections, virtually the sum of classical culture, had vanished without a trace. They had almost certainly not disappeared all at once—such a momentous act of destruction would have been recorded. But if one asks, Where did all the books go? the answer lies not only in the quick work of the soldiers' flames and the long, slow, secret labor of the bookworm. It lies, symbolically at least, in the fate of Hypatia.

The other libraries of the ancient world fared no better. A survey of Rome in the early fourth century listed twenty-eight public libraries, in addition to the unnumbered private collections in aristocratic mansions. Near the century's end, the historian Ammianus Marcellinus complained that Romans had virtually abandoned serious reading. Ammianus was not lamenting barbarian raids or Christian fanaticism. No doubt these were at work, somewhere in the background of the phenomena that struck him. But what he observed, as the empire slowly crumbled, was a loss of cultural moorings, a descent into febrile triviality. "In place of the philosopher the singer is called in, and in place of the orator the teacher of stagecraft, and while the libraries are shut up forever like tombs, w͏ ͏ manufactured and lyres as large as carriages. noted sourly, people were driving their chariots ᷓ through the crowded streets.

When, after a long, slow death agony, the Roman Empire in the West finally collapsed—the last emperor, Romulus Augustulus, quietly resigned in 476 CE—the Germanic tribes that seized one province after another had no tradition of literacy. The barbarians who broke into the public buildings and seized the villas may not have been actively hostile to learning, but they certainly had no interest in preserving its material traces. The former owners of the villas, dragged off to slavery on some remote farmstead, would have had more important household goods to salvage and take with them than books. And, since the conquerors were for the most part Christians, those among them who learned to read and write had no incentive to study the works of the classical pagan authors. Compared to the unleashed forces of warfare and of faith, Mount Vesuvius was kinder to the legacy of antiquity.

But a prestigious cultural tradition that has shaped the inner lives of the elite does not disappear easily, even in those who welcome its burial. In a letter written in 384 CE, Jerome—the scholarly saint to whom we owe the story of Lucretius' madness and suicide—described an inner struggle. Ten years earlier, he recalled, he was on his way from Rome to Jerusalem, where he planned to withdraw from all worldly entanglements, but still he took his prized classical library with him. He was committed to disciplining his body and saving his soul, but he could not forgo the addictive pleasures of his mind: "I would fast, only to read Cicero afterwards. I would spend many nights in vigil, I would shed bitter tears called from my inmost heart by the remembrance of my past sins; and then I would take up Plautus again." Cicero, Jerome understood, was a pagan who argued for a thoroughgoing skepticism toward all dogmatic claims, including the claims of religion, but the elegance of his prose seemed irresistible. Plautus was, if anything, worse: his comedies were populated by pimps, whores, and hangers-on, but their zany wit was delicious. Delicious but poisonous: whenever Jerome turned from these literary delights to the Scriptures, the holy texts seemed crude and uncultivated. His love for the beauty and elegance of Latin was such that when he determined to learn Hebrew, he initially found the experience almost physically repellent: "From the judicious precepts of Quintilian, the rich and fluent eloquence of Cicero, the graver style of Fronto, and the smoothness of Pliny," he wrote in 411, "I turned to this language of hissing and broken-winded words."

What saved him, Jerome wrote, was a nightmare. He had fallen gravely ill, and in his delirium, he dreamed that he had been dragged before God's judgment seat. Asked to state his condition, he replied that he was a Christian. But the Judge sternly replied, "You lie; you are a Ciceronian, not a Christian" (*Ciceronianus es, non Christianus*). These terrible words might have signaled his eternal damnation, but the Lord, in his mercy, instead ordered that Jerome merely be whipped. The sinner was pardoned, "on the understanding that the extreme of torture should be inflicted on me if ever I read again the works of Gentile authors." When he awoke, Jerome found that his shoulders were black and blue.

Jerome went on to settle in Bethlehem, where he established two monasteries, one for himself and his fellow monks, the other for the pious women who had accompanied him. There he lived for thirty-six years, studying, engaging in vehement theological controversies, and, most importantly, translating Hebrew Scriptures into Latin and revising the Latin translation of the New Testament. His achievement, the great Latin Bible translation known as the Vulgate, was in the sixteenth century declared by the Catholic Church to be "more authentic" than the original.

There is, as Jerome's nightmare suggests, a distinctly destructive element in his piety. Or rather, from the perspective of his piety, his intense pleasure in pagan literature was destroying him. It was not a matter merely of spending more of his time with Christian texts but of giving up the pagan texts altogether. He bound himself with a solemn oath: "O Lord, if ever again I possess worldly books or read them, I have denied thee." This renunciation of the authors he loved was a personal affair: he had in effect to cure himself of a dangerous addiction in order to save his soul. But the addiction—and hence the need for renunciation—was not his alone. What he found so alluring was what kept many others like him in thrall to pagan authors. He therefore had to persuade others to make the sacrifice he had made. "What has Horace to do with the Psalter," he wrote to one of his followers, "Virgil with the Gospels and Cicero with Paul?"

For many generations, learned Christians remained steeped, as Jerome was, in a culture whose values had been shaped by the pagan classics. Platonism contributed to Christianity its model of the soul; Aristotelianism its Prime Mover; Stoicism its model of Providence. All the more reason why those Christians repeated to themselves exemplary stories of renunciation. Through the telling of these stories, they acted out, as in a dream, the abandonment of the rich cultural soil in which they, their parents, and their grandparents were nurtured, until one day they awoke to find that they actually had abandoned it.

The knights of renunciation, as in a popular romance, were almost always glamorous figures who cast off the greatest symbol of their status—their intimate access to an elite education—for the sake of the religion they loved. The moment of renunciation came after rigorous training in grammar and rhetoric, engagement with the literary masterpieces, immersion in the myths. Only in the sixth century did Christians venture to celebrate as heroes those who dispensed entirely with education, and even then one can observe a certain hesitation or compromise. Here is Gregory the Great's celebration of St. Benedict:

> He was born in the district of Norcia of distinguished parents, who sent him to Rome for a liberal education. But when he saw many of his fellow students falling headlong into vice, he stepped back from the threshold of the world in which he had just set foot. For he was afraid that if he acquired any of its learning he, too, would later plunge, body and soul, into the dread abyss. In his desire to please God alone, he turned his back on further studies, gave up home and inheritance and resolved to embrace the religious life. He took this step, well aware of his ignorance, yet wise, uneducated though he was.

What flickers through such moments of abdication is a fear of being laughed at. The threat was not persecution—the official religion of the empire by this time was Christian—but ridicule. A fate no doubt preferable to being thrown to the lions, laughter in the ancient world nonetheless had very sharp teeth. What was ridiculous about Christianity, from the perspective of a cultivated pagan, was not only its language—the crude style of the Gospels' Greek resting on the barbarous otherness of Hebrew and Aramaic—but also its exaltation of divine humiliation and pain conjoined with an arrogant triumphalism.

When Christianity had completely secured its position, it managed to destroy most of the expressions of this hostile laughter. A few traces, however, survive in the quotations and summaries of Christian apologists. Some of the jibes were common to all of Christianity's polemical enemies—Jesus was born in adultery, his father was a nobody, and any claims to divine dignity are manifestly disproved by his poverty and his shameful end—but others bring us closer to the specific strain of mockery that surged up from Epicurean circles, when they encountered the messianic religion from Palestine. That mockery and the particular challenge it posed for early Christians set the stage for the subsequent disappearance of the whole Epicurean school of thought: Plato and Aristotle, pagans who believed in the immortality of the soul, could ultimately be accommodated by a triumphant Christianity; Epicureanism could not.

Epicurus did not deny the existence of gods. Rather, he thought that if the concept of divinity made any sense at all, the gods could not possibly be concerned with anything but their own pleasures. Neither creators of the universe nor its destroyers, utterly indifferent to the doings of any beings other than themselves, they were deaf to our prayers or our rituals. The Incarnation, Epicureans scoffed, was a particularly absurd idea. Why should the humans think of themselves as so superior to bees, elephants, ants, or any of the available species, now or in eons to come, that god should take their form and not another? And why then, among all the varieties of humans, should he have taken the form of a Jew? Why should anyone with any sense credit the idea of Providence, a childish idea contradicted by any rational adult's experience and observation? Christians are like a council of frogs in a pond, croaking at the top of their lungs, "For our sakes was the world created."

Christians could try, of course, to reverse the mockery. If such doctrines as the Incarnation and the resurrection of the body seemed absurd—"figments of diseased imagination," as one pagan put it, "and the futile fairy-tales invented by poets' fancy"—what about the tales that pagans profess to believe:

> Vulcan is lame and crippled; Apollo after years and years still beardless . . . Neptune has sea-green eyes; Minerva grey, like a cat's, Juno those of an ox . . . Janus has two faces, ready to walk backwards; Diana is sometimes short-kilted for the hunt, while at Ephesus she is figured with many breasts and paps.

But there is, of course, something uncomfortable about the "back-to-you" strategy, since the alleged ridiculousness of one set of beliefs hardly shores up the validity of another.

Christians knew, moreover, that many pagans did not believe in the literal truth of their own myths and that there were some—Epicureans prominent among them—who called into question virtually all religious systems and promises. Such enemies of faith found the doctrine of bodily resurrection particularly risible, since it was contradicted both by their scientific theory of atoms and by the evidence of their own senses: the rotting corpses that testified with nauseating eloquence to the dissolution of the flesh.

The early Church Father Tertullian vehemently insisted that, despite all appearances, everything would come back in the afterlife, down to the last details of the mortal body. He knew all too well the responses he would get from the doubters:

> What will be the use of the hands themselves and the feet and all the working parts of the body, when even trouble about food will cease? What will be the use of the kidneys . . . and of the other genital organs of both sexes and the dwelling places of the foetus and the streams from the nurse's breasts, when sexual inter-

course and conception and upbringing alike will cease
to be? Finally, what use will the whole body be, which
will of course have absolutely nothing to do?

"The crowd mocks," Tertullian wrote, "judging that nothing
is left over after death," but they will not have the last laugh: "I
will rather laugh at the crowd at the time when they are cruelly burning up themselves." On the Day of Judgment, each
man will be brought forth before the heavenly tribunal, not
a piece of him, not a shadow, not a symbolic token, but rather
the whole of him, as he lived on the earth. And that means
teeth and intestines and genitals, whether or not their mortal
functions have ceased forever. "Yes!" Tertullian addressed his
pagan listeners. "We too in our day laughed at this. We are
from among yourselves. Christians are made, not born!"

Some critics pointed out with a derisory smile that many
features of the Christian vision were stolen from much more
ancient pagan stories: a tribunal in which souls are judged,
fire used for punishment in an underground prison house, a
divinely beautiful paradise reserved for the spirits of the holy.
But Christians replied that these ancient beliefs were all distorted reflections of the true Christian mysteries. The eventual
success of this argumentative strategy is suggested by the very
word we have been using for those who clung to the old poly-
theistic faith. Believers in Jupiter, Minerva, and Mars did not
think of themselves as "pagans": the word, which appeared in
the late fourth century, is etymologically related to the word
"peasant." It is an insult, then, a sign that the laughter at rustic
ignorance had decisively reversed direction.

The charge of doctrinal plagiarism was easier for Christians
to deal with than the charge of absurdity. Pythagoreans who
believed in bodily resurrection had the right general idea; it was
simply an idea that needed correction. But Epicureans who said

that the whole idea of resurrection was a grotesque violation of everything that we know about the physical universe could not be so easily corrected. It made some sense to argue with the former, but the latter were best simply silenced.

Though early Christians, Tertullian among them, found certain features in Epicureanism admirable—the celebration of friendship, the emphasis on charity and forgiveness, a suspicion of worldly ambition—by the early fourth century, the task had become clear: the atomists had to disappear. The followers of Epicurus had already aroused considerable enmity outside the Christian community. When the emperor known as Julian the Apostate (c. 331–363), who attempted to revive paganism against the mounting Christian onslaught, drew up a list of works that it was important for pagan priests to read, he also noted some titles that he explicitly wished to exclude: "Let us not," he wrote, "admit discourses by Epicureans." Jews, likewise, termed anyone who departed from the rabbinic tradition *apikoros*, an Epicurean.

But Christians particularly found Epicureanism a noxious threat. If you grant Epicurus his claim that the soul is mortal, wrote Tertullian, the whole fabric of Christian morality unravels. For Epicurus, human suffering is always finite: "if it is slight, he [Epicurus] says, you may despise it, if it is great it will not be long." But to be Christian, Tertullian countered, is to believe that torture and pain last forever: "Epicurus utterly destroys religion," wrote another Church Father; take Providence away, and "confusion and disorder will overtake life."

Christian polemicists had to find a way to turn the current of mockery against Epicurus and his followers. Ridiculing the pagan pantheon did not work in this case, since Epicureanism eloquently dismantled the whole sacrificial worship of the gods and dismissed the ancient stories. What had to be done was to refashion the account of the founder Epicurus so that he appeared no longer as an apostle of moderation in the service of reasonable pleasure but instead as a Falstaffian figure of riotous excess. He was a fool, a pig, a madman. And his principal Roman disciple, Lucretius, had to be comparably made over.

But it was not enough to blacken the reputations of Epicurus and Lucretius, to repeat endlessly that they were stupid, swinishly self-indulgent, insane, and, finally, suicidal. It was not enough even, by this means, to suppress the reading of their works, to humiliate anyone who might express interest in them, to discourage copies from ever being made. Even more than the theory that the world consisted only of atoms and void, the main problem was the core ethical idea: that the highest good is the pursuit of pleasure and the diminution of pain. What had to be undertaken was the difficult project of making what appeared simply sane and natural—the ordinary impulses of all sentient creatures—seem like the enemy of the truth.

Centuries were required to accomplish this grand design, and it was never fully completed. But the grand outlines may be seen in the late third and early fourth century in the works of a North African convert from paganism to Christianity: Lactantius. Appointed tutor to the son of the emperor Constantine, who had established Christianity as the religion of the empire, Lactantius wrote a series of polemics against Epicureanism. That philosophy had, he acknowledges, a substantial following, "not because it brings forward any truth, but because the attractive name of pleasure invites many." Christians must refuse the invitation and understand that pleasure is a code name for vice.

The task, for Lactantius, was not only to draw believers away from their pursuit of human pleasures; it was also to persuade them that God was not, as Epicureans believed, entirely absorbed within the orbit of divine pleasures and hence indifferent to the fate of humans. Instead, as Lactantius wrote in a celebrated work written in 313 CE, God cared about humans, just as a father cared about his wayward child. And the sign of that care, he wrote, was anger. God was enraged at man—that was the characteristic manifestation of His love—and wanted to smite him over and over again, with spectacular, unrelenting violence.

A hatred of pleasure-seeking and a vision of God's providential rage: these were death knells of Epicureanism, henceforward branded by the faithful as "insane." Lucretius had urged the person who felt the prompting of sexual desire to satisfy it: "a dash of gentle pleasure sooths the sting." (4.177) Christianity, as a story rehearsed by Gregory demonstrates, pointed in a different direction. The pious Benedict found himself thinking of a woman he had once seen, and, before he knew what was happening, his desires were aroused:

> He then noticed a thick patch of nettles and briers next to him. Throwing his garment aside he flung himself into the sharp thorns and stinging nettles. There he rolled and tossed until his whole body was in pain and covered with blood. Yet, once he had conquered pleasure through suffering, his torn and bleeding skin served to drain the poison of temptation from his body. Before long, the pain that was burning his whole body had put out the fires of evil in his heart. It was by exchanging these two fires that he gained the victory over sin.

What worked for the saint in the early sixth century would, as monastic rules made clear, work for others. In one of the great cultural transformations in the history of the West, the pursuit of pain triumphed over the pursuit of pleasure.

The infliction of pain was hardly unknown in the world of Lucretius. The Romans were specialists in it, dedicating vast sums and huge arenas to public spectacles of violence. And it was not only in the Colosseum that Romans could glut themselves on injury, pain, and death. Plays and poems, based on the ancient myths, were often blood-drenched, as were paintings and sculptures. Violence was part of the fabric of everyday life. Schoolmasters and slaveholders were expected to flog their victims, and whipping was a frequent prelude to Roman executions. This is why in the gospel account, prior to his crucifixion, Jesus was tied to a column and scourged.

But for the pagans, in the great majority of these instances, pain was understood not as a positive value, a stepping stone to salvation, as it was by pious Christians intent on whipping themselves, but as an evil, something visited upon rulebreakers, criminals, captives, unfortunate wretches, and—the only category with dignity—soldiers. Romans honored a brave soldier's voluntary acceptance of pain, but that acceptance was far different from the ecstatic embrace celebrated in hundreds of convents and monasteries. The heroes of Roman stories willingly met what they could not, in good conscience, avoid or what they felt they had to endure in order to prove to their enemies their dauntless courage. Outside the orbit of that heroic obligation, there lay the special philosophical discipline that enabled the classical sage to regard inescapable pain—of kidney stones, for example—with equanimity. And for everyone, from the most exalted philosopher to the humblest artisan, there was the natural pursuit of pleasure.

In pagan Rome, the most extravagant version of this pursuit of pleasure came together in the gladiatorial arena with the most extravagant infliction and endurance of pain. If Lucretius offered a moralized and purified version of the Roman pleasure principle, Christianity offered a moralized and purified version of the Roman pain principle. Early Christians, brooding on the sufferings of the Saviour, the sinfulness of mankind, and the anger of a just Father, found the attempt to cultivate pleasure manifestly absurd and dangerous. At best a trivial distraction, pleasure was at worst a demonic trap, figured in medieval art by those alluring women beneath whose gowns one can glimpse reptilian claws. The only life truly worth imitating—the life of Jesus—bore ample witness to the inescapable presence in mortal existence of sadness and pain, but not of pleasure. The earliest pictorial depictions of Jesus were uniform in their melancholy sobriety. As every pious reader of Luke's Gospel knew, Jesus wept, but there were no verses that described him laughing or smiling, let alone pursuing pleasure.

It was not difficult for Christians of the fifth and sixth centuries to find reasons to weep: the cities were falling apart, the fields were soaked in the blood of dying soldiers, robbery and rape were rampant. There had to be some explanation for the catastrophic behavior of human beings over so many generations, as if they were incapable of learning anything from their historical experience. Theology provided an answer deeper and more fundamental than this or that flawed individual or institution: humans were by nature corrupt. Inheritors of the sin of Adam and Eve, they richly deserved every miserable catastrophe that befell them; they needed to be punished; they had coming to them an endless diet of pain. Indeed, it was only through this pain that a small number could find the narrow gate to salvation.

The most ardent early believers in this doctrine, those fired by an explosive mix of fear, hope, and fierce enthusiasm, were determined to make the pain to which all humankind was condemned their active choice. In doing so, they hoped to pay to an angry God the dues of suffering that He justly and implacably demanded. They possessed something of the martial hardness admired by traditional Roman culture, but, with a few exceptions, the goal was not the achievement of Stoical indifference to pain. On the contrary. Their whole project depended on experiencing an intense sensitivity to hunger, thirst, and loneliness. And when they whipped themselves with thorny branches or struck themselves with jagged stones, they made no effort to suppress their cries of anguish. Those cries were part of the payment, the atonement that would, if they were successful, enable them to recover in the afterlife the happiness that Adam and Eve had lost.

By the year 600 there were over three hundred monasteries and convents in Italy and Gaul. Many of these were still small— little more than fortified villas, with their outbuildings—but they possessed a spiritual rationale and an institutional coherence that conferred upon them stability in an unstable world. Their inhabitants were drawn from those who felt compelled to transform their lives, to atone for their own sins and for the sins of others, to secure eternal bliss by turning their backs on ordinary pleasures. Over time, their numbers were supplemented by many less fervent souls who had in effect been given to the Church by their parents or guardians.

In monasteries and convents driven by the belief that redemption would only come through abasement, it is not surprising that forms of corporal punishment—*virgarum verbera* (hitting with rods), *corporale supplicium* (bodily punishment), *ictus* (blows), *vapulatio* (cudgeling), *disciplina* (whipping), and *flagellatio*—were routinely inflicted on community members who broke the rules. Disciplinary practices that would, in pagan society, have been disgraces inflicted only on social inferiors were meted out with something like democratic indifference to rank. Typically, the guilty party had to carry the rod that was used for the beating, and then sitting on the ground and constantly repeating the words *Mea culpa*, submit to blows until the abbot or abbess was satisfied.

The insistence that punishment be actively embraced by the

victims—literalized in the kissing of the rod—marked a deliberate Christian trampling on the Epicurean credo of pursuing pleasure and avoiding pain. After all, the experience of pain was not only punishment; it was a form of pious emulation. Christian hermits, brooding on the sufferings of the Saviour, mortified their flesh, in order to experience in their own bodies the torments that Jesus had had to undergo. Though these acts of self-scourging began to be reported in late antiquity—they were novel and strange enough in the beginning to attract widespread attention—it was not until the eleventh century that a monastic reformer, the Italian Benedictine Peter Damian, established voluntary self-flagellation as a central ascetic practice acceptable to the Church.

It had taken a thousand years to win the struggle and secure the triumph of pain seeking. "Did our Redeemer not endure scourging?" Damian asked those critics who called into question the celebration of the whip. Weren't the apostles and many of the saints and martyrs flogged? What better way to follow in their footsteps, what surer method of imitating Christ, than to suffer the blows that they suffered? To be sure, Damian concedes, in the case of these glorious predecessors, someone else was doing the whipping. But in a world in which Christianity has triumphed, we have to do the whipping for ourselves. Otherwise the whole dream and doctrine of the imitation of Christ would have to be abandoned. "The body has to be shaped like a piece of wood," explained one of the many texts that followed in Damian's wake, "with beatings and whippings, with canes, scourges, and discipline. The body has to be tortured and starved, so that it submits to the spirit and takes perfect shape." In the pursuit of this spiritual goal, all boundaries, restraints, and inhibitions drop away. Shame at appearing naked before the eyes of others has no place, nor does the embarrassment of being seen trembling, howling, or sobbing.

Here is a description of the Dominican nuns of Colmar, penned at the turn of the fourteenth century by a sister named Catherine von Gebersweiler who had lived in the convent since childhood:

> At Advent and during the whole of Lent, the sisters would make their way after matins into the main hall or some other place devoted to their purpose. There they abused their bodies in the most acute fashion with all manner of scourging instruments until their blood flowed, so that the sound of the blows of the whip rang through the entire convent and rose more sweetly than any other melody to the ears of the Lord.

This is no mere sadomasochistic fantasy: a vast body of evidence confirms that such theaters of pain, the ritualized heirs to St. Benedict's spontaneous roll in the stinging nettles, were widespread in the late Middle Ages. They were noted again and again as a distinctive mark of holiness. St. Teresa, "although she was slowly wasting away, tormented herself with the most painful whips, frequently rubbed herself with fresh stinging nettles, and even rolled about naked in thorns." St. Clare of Assisi "tore apart the alabaster container of her body with a whip for forty-two years, and from her wounds there arose heavenly odors that filled the church." St. Dominic cut into his flesh every night with a whip affixed with three iron chains. St. Ignatius of Loyola recommended whips with relatively thin straps, "summoning pain into the flesh, but not into the bones." Henry Suso, who carved the name of Jesus on his chest, had an iron cross fixed with nails pressed into his back and whipped himself until the blood flowed. Suso's contemporary, Elsbeth of Oye, a nun from Zurich, whipped herself so energetically that the bystanders in the chapel were spattered with her blood.

The ordinary self-protective, pleasure-seeking impulses of

the lay public could not hold out against the passionate convictions and overwhelming prestige of their spiritual leaders. Beliefs and practices that had been the preserve of religious specialists, men and women set apart from the vulgar, everyday imperatives of the "world," found their way into the mainstream, where they thrived in societies of flagellants and periodic bursts of mass hysteria. What was once in effect a radical counterculture insisted with remarkable success that it represented the core values of all believing Christians.

Of course, people continued to pursue pleasure—the Old Adam could not be so easily eradicated. In peasants' huts and the halls of the great, along country lanes, in prelates' palaces, and behind the high walls of the monasteries, there was drinking, overeating, raucous laughter, merry dancing, and plenty of sex. But virtually no one in moral authority, no one with a public voice, dared speak up to justify any of it. The silence was not, or not only, the consequence of timidity or fear. Pleasure seeking had come to seem philosophically indefensible. Epicurus was dead and buried, almost all of his works destroyed. And after St. Jerome in the fourth century briefly noted that Lucretius had committed suicide, there were no attacks on Epicurus' great Roman disciple. He was forgotten.

The survival of the disciple's once celebrated poem was left to fortune. It was by chance that a copy of *On the Nature of Things* made it into the library of a handful of monasteries, places that had buried, seemingly forever, the Epicurean pursuit of pleasure. It was by chance that a monk laboring in a scriptorium somewhere or other in the ninth century copied the poem before it moldered away forever. And it was by chance that this copy escaped fire and flood and the teeth of time for some five hundred years until, one day in 1417, it came into the hands of the humanist who proudly called himself *Poggius Florentinus*, Poggio the Florentine.

CHAPTER FIVE

BIRTH AND REBIRTH

FLORENCE AT THE dawn of the fifteenth century had few of the architectural features with which it is now graced, features that deliberately evoke on a grand scale the dream of the ancient past. Brunelleschi's magnificent cupola on the Duomo, the city's vast cathedral—the first large dome constructed since Roman antiquity and to this day the principal feature of the city's skyline—did not yet exist, nor did his elegantly arched loggia of the Foundling Hospital or his other projects carefully constructed on principles derived from antiquity. The cathedral's baptistery lacked the famous classicizing doors designed by Ghiberti, and the Church of S. Maria Novella was without Leon Battista Alberti's harmonious, gracefully symmetrical facade. The architect Michelozzi had not designed the beautiful, austere buildings for the Convent of San Marco. The wealthiest families of the city—the Medici, the Pitti, the Rucelli—had not yet built their grand palaces, whose columns, arches, and carved capitals conspicuously emphasize classical order and proportion.

The walled city was distinctly medieval in appearance, closed in and dark. Its densely populated central zone was crowded with high towers and fortified stone buildings, with twisting narrow lanes and alleys made still darker by projecting upper stories and covered balconies. Even on the old bridge—the Ponte Vecchio—that crossed the Arno, shops crammed tightly next to each other made it impossible to glimpse an open landscape. From the air, it might have looked as though the city possessed many open spaces, but these were for the most part the walled interior courtyards of the huge monasteries built by the rival religious orders: the Dominicans' S. Maria Novella, the Franciscans' S. Croce, the Augustinian Hermits' S. Spirito, the Carmelites' S. Maria del Carmine, and others. Secular, open, public spaces were few and far between.

It was to this somber, constricted, congested city, subject to periodic outbreaks of bubonic plague, that Poggio Bracciolini came as a young man in the late 1390s. He had been born in 1380 in Terranuova, an undistinguished backwater within the territory that Florence controlled. Years later Tomaso Morroni, one of his polemical enemies, wrote that Poggio was the bastard son of peasants who eked out a living from the soil. The account cannot be taken seriously—it is one of many libels that Renaissance humanists, Poggio among them, hurled recklessly at one another, like punch-drunk pugilists. But, growing up where he did, he was undoubtedly familiar with Tuscan farms, whether he toiled on one or not. It was difficult for Poggio to claim a long line of illustrious ancestors, or rather, in order to do so with a straight face after he had established himself in the world, he had to purchase a fraudulent 350-year-old coat of arms.

A more plausible story, one Poggio himself seems to have allowed at certain points in his life, is that his father Guccio was a notary, though a tax record of the period describes him as a *spetiale*, that is, a druggist. Perhaps he was both. Notaries were not figures of great dignity, but in a contractual and intensely litigious culture, they were legion. The Florentine notary Lapo Mazzei describes six or seven hundred of them crowded into the town hall, carrying under their arms bundles of documents, "each folder thick as half a bible." Their knowledge of the law enabled them to draw up local regulations, arrange village elections, compose letters of complaint. Town officials who were meant to administer justice often had no clue how to proceed; the notaries would whisper in their ears what they were meant to say and would write the necessary documents. They were useful people to have around.

There was, in any case, an indubitable link in Poggio's family to a notary, his maternal grandfather Michaelle Frutti. The link is worth noting because in 1343, many years before Poggio's birth, Ser Michaelle signed a notarial register with a strikingly beautiful signature. Penmanship would turn out to play an oddly important role in the grandson's story. In the concatenation of accidents that led to the recovery of Lucretius' poem, Poggio's handwriting was crucial.

Other children were born to Guccio Bracciolini and his wife Jacoba—two daughters (one of whom died very young) and another son, about whom his older brother Poggio had angry complaints later in his life. To judge from his father's tax payments, Poggio's early years were reasonably comfortable; but around 1388, when he was eight years old, things took a very bad turn. Guccio had to sell his house and property, flee from his creditors, and move with his family to nearby Arezzo. According to Tomaso Morroni, young Poggio was sent out to the fields to labor for someone named Luccarus. When he was caught cheating Luccarus, Morroni reports, Poggio was condemned to be crucified and was pardoned only because of his tender years. Once again we should not take these slanders seriously, except as symptoms of the boundless loathing of squabbling scholars. In Arezzo, Poggio must have been attending a school, learning the elements of Latin, and mastering the art of handwriting, not ploughing someone's fields or dodging the executioner. But that he had few resources he himself attested later in his life, recalling that he arrived in Florence *cum quinque solidis*—with five pennies in his pocket.

It was at some point in the 1390s, well before he turned twenty, that the impoverished young man came to Florence. He probably had in hand a letter of recommendation from his schoolteacher in Arezzo, and he might have acquired as well a smattering of legal knowledge from brief studies in Bologna. After a time he was reunited with his improvident father and the rest of his family, all of whom eventually moved to Florence. But when he initially set foot in the Piazza della Signoria or looked up for the first time at Giotto's beautiful belltower next to the Duomo, Poggio was by himself, a nobody.

With a population hovering around 50,000, Florentine political, social, and commercial life was dominated by a small number of powerful mercantile and noble families: the Albizzi, Strozzi, Peruzzi, Capponi, Pitti, Buondelmonti, and a few others. The leading families signaled their presence and importance through conspicuous expenditure. "It is much sweeter to spend money than to earn it," wrote Giovanni Rucellai, whose family had grown rich in wool dyeing and banking; "spending gave me deeper satisfaction." The wealthy were attended by large numbers of clients, bailiffs, accountants, clerics, secretaries, messengers, tutors, musicians, artists, servants, and slaves. The labor shortage after the Black Death in 1348 had greatly increased the market for slaves, brought not only from Muslim Spain and Africa but also from the Balkans, Constantinople, and the shores of the Black Sea. The traffic was allowed, provided that the slaves were infidels, not Christians, and Poggio must have seen a fair number of them, North Africans, Cypriots, Tartars, Greeks, Russians, Georgians, and others.

Florence was an oligarchy, and the small coterie of the wealthy and wellborn were the people who counted. Wealth lay in banking and landowning, as it usually does, and it derived as well from the weaving and finishing of cloth, for which the city was famous. The cloth business required a cosmopolitan outlook, strong nerves, and extraordinary attention to detail. The surviving archive of a single great merchant of this period, Francesco di Marco Datini of nearby Prato—not, by any means, the greatest of these early capitalists—contains some 150,000 letters, along with 500 account books or ledgers, 300 deeds of partnership, 400 insurance policies, several thousand bills of lading, letters of advice, bills of exchange, and checks. On the first pages of Datini's ledgers were inscribed the words: "In the name of God and of profit."

In Florence, God was served in the astonishing number of churches that adjoined one another in the crowded streets. He was served as well in the long, passionate sermons that drew huge crowds, in the harangues of itinerant friars, in the prayers, vows, offerings, and expressions of religious fear that recur in almost all writings, formal and informal, and must have saturated everyday speech, and in periodic bursts of popular piety.

Profit was served in a vibrant international cloth industry that required large numbers of trained workmen. Some of the most skilled of these were organized in powerful guilds that looked out for their interests, but other workmen labored for a pittance. In 1378, two years before Poggio's birth, the seething resentment of these miserable day laborers, the *populo minuto*, had boiled over into a full-scale bloody revolt. Gangs of artisans ran through the streets, crying, "Long live the people and the crafts!" and the uprising briefly toppled the ruling families and installed a democratic government. But the old order was quickly restored, and with it a regime determined to maintain the power of the guilds and the leading families.

After the defeat of the *Ciompi*, as the working-class revolutionaries were called, the resurgent oligarchs held on to power tenaciously for more than forty years, shaping Poggio's whole knowledge and experience of the city where he determined to make his fortune. He had to find a way into a conservative, socially bounded world. Fortunately for him, by innate skill and training he possessed one of the few gifts that would enable someone of his modest origins and resources to do so. The key that opened the first door through which he slipped was something that has come to mean next to nothing in the modern world: beautiful handwriting.

Poggio's way of fashioning letters was a move away from the intricately interwoven and angular writing known as Gothic hand. The demand for more open, legible handwriting had already been voiced earlier in the century by Petrarch (1304–1374). Petrarch complained that the writing then in use in most manuscripts often made it extremely difficult to decipher the text, "as though it had been designed," he noted, "for something other than reading." To make texts more legible, the individual letters had somehow to be freed from their interlocking patterns, the spaces between the words opened up, the lines spaced further apart, the abbreviations filled out. It was like opening a window and letting air into a tightly closed room.

What Poggio accomplished, in collaboration with a few others, remains startling. They took Carolingian minuscule—a scribal innovation of the ninth-century court of Charlemagne—and transformed it into the script they used for copying manuscripts and writing letters. This script in turn served as the basis for the development both of italics and of the typeface we call "roman." They were then in effect the inventors of the script we still think of as at once the clearest, the simplest, and the most elegant written representation of our words. It is difficult to take in the full effect without seeing it for oneself, for example, in the manuscripts preserved in the Laurentian Library in Florence: the smooth bound volumes of vellum, still creamy white after more than five hundred years, contain page after page of perfectly beautiful script, almost magical in its regularity and fineness. There are tiny pinholes on the margins, where the blank sheets must have been fixed to hold them steady, and scarcely visible score marks to form straight lines, twenty-six per page. But these aids cannot begin to explain how the tasks could have been accomplished with such clean elegance.

To have invented a way to design letters immediately recognizable and admired after six centuries is no small achievement. But the way Poggio fashioned his letters showed more than just unusual skill in graphic design; it signaled a creative response to powerful cultural currents stirring in Florence and throughout Italy. Poggio seems to have grasped that the call for a new cursive writing was only a small piece of a much larger project, a project that linked the creation of something new with a search for something ancient. To speak of this search as a project runs the risk of making it sound routine and familiar. In fact it was a shared mania, one whose origin can be traced back to Petrarch, who, a generation before Poggio's birth, had made the recovery of the cultural heritage of classical Rome a collective obsession.

Modern scholarship has found dozens of ways to qualify and diminish this obsession. Petrarch's admirers wrote as if the ancient past had been utterly forgotten, until their hero heroically recalled it to life, but it can be demonstrated that Petrarch's vision was less novel than it seemed. In addition to the fifteenth-century Renaissance, there had been other moments of intense interest in antiquity, both throughout medieval Italy and in the kingdoms of the north, including the great Carolingian Renaissance of the ninth century. And it was not these moments alone that kept the intellectual heritage of antiquity alive. Medieval compendia provided much more continuity with classical thought than believed by those under Petrarch's spell. In the

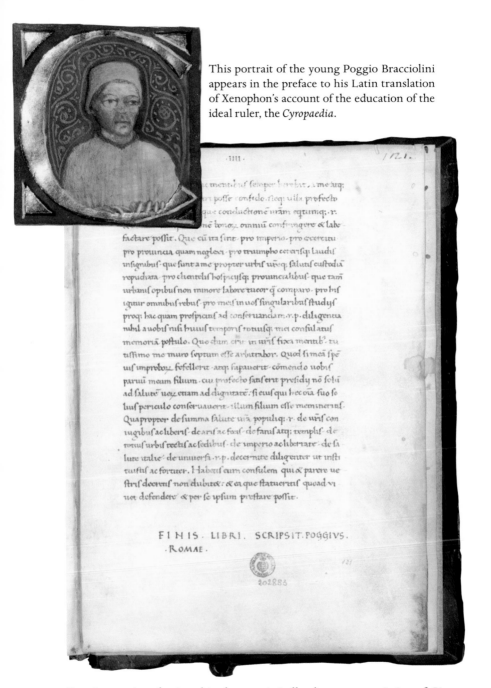

This portrait of the young Poggio Bracciolini appears in the preface to his Latin translation of Xenophon's account of the education of the ideal ruler, the *Cyropaedia*.

Poggio prominently signs his characteristically elegant transcription of Cicero, made in Rome in 1425. Poggio's handwriting was prized in his own lifetime and was one of the keys to his advancement.

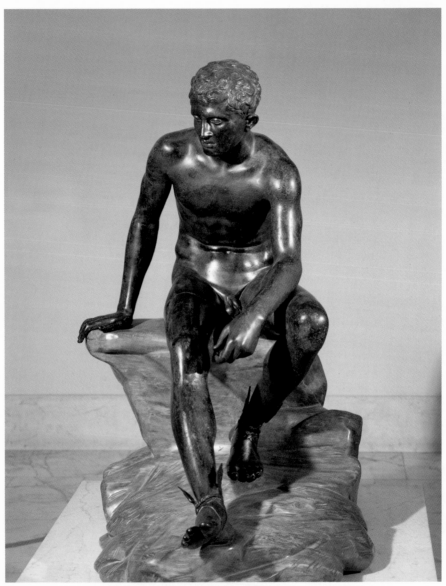

This bronze Seated Hermes was found in fragments in 1758 at the Villa of the Papyri in Herculaneum. A pair of winged sandals reveals his identity as the messenger god Hermes. To an Epicurean the figure's elegant repose might have suggested that the gods had no messages to deliver to mankind.

The enemies of Epicureanism associated it not with the thoughtful pose of the Seated Hermes but with the drunken abandonment of this Silenus, sprawled on a wineskin draped over a lion's pelt, found near the Hermes sculpture at the Villa of the Papyri.

The small bust of Epicurus, which retains its original base with the philosopher's name inscribed in Greek, was one of three such busts that adorned the Villa of the Papyri in Herculaneum. In his *Natural History* (chap. 35), the Roman author Pliny the Elder (23–79 CE) noted a vogue in his time for portrait busts of Epicurus.

"Then Pilate took Jesus and had him flogged" (John 19:1). The biblical text inspired images like this painting by the Austrian Michael Pacher and helped promote not only sympathy for the cruelly mistreated Messiah and rage at his tormentors but also a fervent desire to emulate his suffering.

The heretic Hus, forced to wear a mock paper crown declaring his misdeeds, is burned at the stake. Afterwards, to prevent any sympathetic bystander from collecting a relic of the martyr, his ashes are shoveled into the Rhine.

This portrait of Poggio appears in a manuscript of his work *De varietate fortunae*. The work, written when Poggio was sixty-eight years old, eloquently surveys the ruins of ancient Roman greatness.

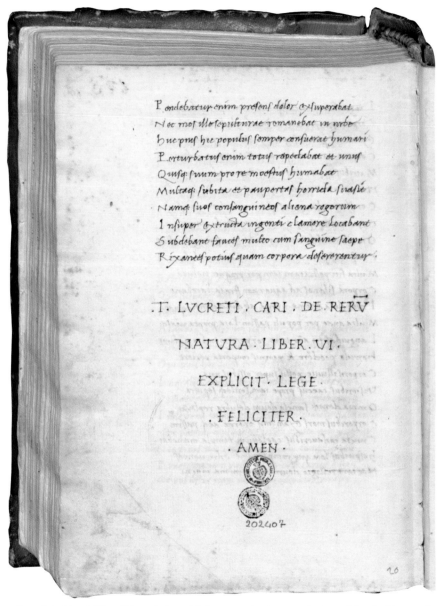

Pendebatur enim presens dolor exsuperabat
Nec mos ille sepulturae remanebat in urbe
Huc prius hic populus semper consuerat humari
Perturbatus enim totus raptabat et unus
Quisq; suum pro re moestus humabat
Multaq; subita et paupertas horrida suasit
Namq; suos consanguineos aliena rogorum
Insuper extructa ingenti clamore locabant
Subdebant faces multo cum sanguine saepe
Rixantes potius quam corpora desererentur

.T. LVCRETI . CARI . DE . RERV

NATVRA . LIBER . VI .

EXPLICIT . LEGE .

. FELICITER .

. AMEN .

202407

Poggio's friend Niccoli here brings his long-awaited transcription of *On the Nature of Things* to a close with the customary word "Explicit" (from the Latin for "unrolled"). He enjoins the reader to "read happily" ("Lege feliciter") and adds—in some tension with the spirit of Lucretius' poem—a pious "Amen."

At the center of Botticelli's painting stands Venus, surrounded by the ancient gods of the spring. The complex choreography derives from Lucretius' description of the great seasonal renewal of the earth: "Spring comes and Venus, preceded by Venus' winged harbinger, and mother Flora, following hard on the heels of Zephyr, prepares the way for them, strewing all their path with a profusion of exquisite hues and scents" (5:737–40).

Montaigne's signature on the title page of his heavily annotated Lucretius—the great edition published in 1563 and edited by Denis Lambin—was written over by a subsequent owner—"Despagnet"—and hence not identified for what it is until the twentieth century.

A bronze statue of Bruno, sculpted by Ettore Ferrari, was erected in 1889 in Rome's Campo de' Fiori on the spot where he was burned at the stake. In the monument, on the base of which are plaques devoted to other philosophers persecuted by the Catholic Church, the larger-than-life Bruno looks broodingly in the direction of the Vatican.

high Middle Ages, scholastic philosophers, reading Aristotle through the lens of the brilliant Arabic commentator Averroës, constructed a sophisticated, highly rational account of the universe. And even Petrarch's vaunted aesthetic commitment to classical Latinity—his dream of walking in the footsteps of the ancients—had been evident for at least seventy years before his birth. Much of what Petrarch and his followers claimed for the novelty of their approach was tendentious, self-congratulatory exaggeration.

But it is difficult entirely to demystify the movement to which Petrarch gave rise, if only because he and his contemporaries were so articulate about their experience. To them at least it did not seem obvious that the search on which they embarked was only a polite stroll onto well-trodden ground. They saw themselves as adventurous explorers both in the physical world—the mountains they crossed, the monastic libraries they investigated, the ruins they dug up—and in their inner world of desire. The urgency of the enterprise reflects their underlying recognition that there was nothing obvious or inevitable about the attempt to recover or imitate the language, material objects, and cultural achievements of the very distant past. It was a strange thing to do, far stranger than continuing to live the ordinary, familiar life that men and women had lived for centuries, making themselves more or less comfortable in the midst of the crumbling, mute remains of antiquity.

Those remains were everywhere visible in Italy and throughout Europe: bridges and roads still in use after more than a millennium, the broken walls and arches of ruined baths and markets, temple columns incorporated into churches, old inscribed stones used as building materials in new constructions, fractured statues and broken vases. But the great civilization that left these traces had been destroyed. The remnants could serve as walls to incorporate into new houses, as reminders that all things pass and are forgotten, as mute testimony to the triumph of Christianity over paganism, as literal quarries to be mined for precious stones and metals. Generations of men and women, in Italy and elsewhere in Europe, had developed effective techniques for the recycling of classical fragments, in their writing as well as their building. The techniques bypassed any anxiety about meddling with the leftovers of a pagan culture: as broken shards whether of stone or of language, these leftovers were at once useful and unthreatening. What more would anyone want with the rubble over which the living had clambered for more than a thousand years?

To insist on the original, independent meaning of this rubble would cause trouble and moral perplexity. A passion for antiquity could certainly not be justified on the basis of curiosity alone, for curiosity had long been rigorously condemned as a mortal sin. The religion of the pagans was widely regarded as the worship of demons, and, even setting aside that fear, the Christian faithful was urged to remember the cultural achievements of ancient Greece and Rome as the quintessential works of the world, the kingdom of man, set against the transcendent, timeless kingdom of God.

Petrarch was a devout Christian, and throughout his life he reflected with ardent seriousness on his spiritual condition. And yet he was, over the course of a complex career of restless journeying, diplomacy, soul-searching, and compulsive writing, a man held in the grip of a fascination with pagan antiquity that he himself could never completely fathom. Though he was for long periods of his life a relatively solitary figure, Petrarch did not keep this fascination to himself. He insisted with missionary zeal on the expressive power, the beauty, and the challenge of all that lay broken and buried beneath the crushing weight of neglect.

A gifted scholar, Petrarch began to search for ancient texts that had been forgotten. He was not the first to do so, but he managed to invest this search with a new, almost erotic urgency and pleasure, superior to all other treasure seeking:

> Gold, silver, jewels, purple garments, houses built of marble, groomed estates, pious paintings, caparisoned steeds, and other things of this kind offer a mutable and superficial pleasure; books give delight to the very marrow of one's bones. They speak to us, consult with us, and join with us in a living and intense intimacy.

Copying, comparing, and correcting the ancient Latin texts that he found, Petrarch returned them to circulation by sharing them with a vast network of correspondents to whom, often rising at midnight to sit at his desk, he wrote with manic energy. And he responded to the ancient writers as if they were somehow a living part of this network, intimate friends and family with whom he could share his thoughts. When he found a great cache of Cicero's private letters to his wealthy friend Atticus, candid letters filled with glimpses of egotism, ambition, and resentment, Petrarch did not hesitate to write a letter to Cicero, reproaching him for failing to live up to his own high principles.

For his own present, where he was forced to live, Petrarch professed limitless contempt. He lived in a sordid time, he complained, a time of coarseness, ignorance, and triviality that would quickly vanish from human memory. But his was the kind of contempt that seems only to intensify charisma and celebrity. His fame steadily grew, and with it the cultural significance of his obsession with the past. In succeeding generations that obsession was partly routinized and settled into an influential new educational curriculum, the humanities (*studia humanitatis*), with emphasis on a mastery of Greek and Latin language and literature and a particular focus on rhetoric. But the humanism that Petrarch himself helped to create and that he communicated to his closest friends and disciples— preeminently, to Giovanni Boccaccio (1313–1374) and Coluccio Salutati (1331–1406)—was not a strictly academic affair.

The early humanists felt themselves, with mingled pride, wonder, and fear, to be involved in an epochal movement. In part the movement involved recognizing that something that had seemed alive was really dead. For centuries, princes and prelates had claimed that they were continuing the living tradi- tions of the classical world and had appropriated, in some form or other, the symbols and the language of the past. But Petrarch and those he inspired insisted that this easy appropriation was a lie: the Roman Empire did not actually exist in Aachen, where the ruler who called himself the "Holy Roman Emperor" was crowned; the institutions and ideas that had defined the world of Cicero and Virgil had been torn to pieces, and the Latin written by the philosophers and theologians of the past six or seven hundred years was an ugly and distorted image, like that reflected in a badly made mirror, of what had once been so beau- tifully eloquent. It was better not to pretend any longer, but to acknowledge that there was no continuity. Instead, there was a corpse, long buried and by now disintegrated, under one's feet.

But this acknowledgment was only the necessary first step. Once one recognized what was gone, once one had mourned the tragic loss, it was possible to prepare the way for what lay on the other side of death: nothing less than resurrection. The pattern was, of course, familiar to every good Christian—and Petrarch, in holy orders, was a very good Christian indeed— but the resurrection in this case was in this world, not in the next. The object of recovery was fundamentally cultural and secular.

Poggio arrived in Rome a quarter of a century after Petrarch's death, at a time when the charismatic moment of the movement had already begun to fade. The sense of creative daring was gradually giving way to a spirit of antiquarianism and with it a desire to discipline, correct, and regulate all relations with the ancient past. Poggio and his generation became increasingly caught up in the desire to avoid mistakes in Latin grammar and to catch the blunders of others. But the lingering sense of the strangeness of the recovery of classical antiquity helps to explain the peculiar impact of his handwriting. The script that he fashioned was not a direct evocation of the handwriting used by the ancient Romans: all traces of that handwriting had long since vanished, leaving only the carved inscriptions in handsome capital letters on stone and occasional rough graffiti. But Poggio's script was a graphic expression of the deep longing for a different style of beauty, a cultural form that would signal the recovery of something precious that had been lost. The shape of his letters was based on the manuscript style of certain Carolingian scribes. But Poggio and his contemporaries did not identify this style with the court of Charlemagne; they called it *lettera antica*, and, in doing so, they dreamed not of Charlemagne's tutor Alcuin but of Cicero and Virgil.

In order to earn money the young Poggio copied books and documents, probably a very large number of them. His handwriting and his skill in copying—for which he became celebrated in his lifetime—must have been sufficiently remarkable from the beginning to enable him to pay for lessons. He improved his Latin, which was already quite advanced, by studying with a gifted scholar from Ravenna, Giovanni Malpaghino, a restless, quarrelsome man who had in his youth been Petrarch's secretary and amanuensis and who had made a living lecturing in Venice, Padua, Florence, and elsewhere on

Cicero and Roman poetry. Poggio's earnings paid too for his training as a notary, training that had the advantage of being cheaper and shorter than the long course of study required to become a lawyer.

At twenty-two years old, Poggio stood for his exam, not in the university but before a panel of lawyers and notaries. He had managed to survive the vagaries of his impoverished childhood and was poised to begin a career. The first notarial document in his hand is a letter of recommendation for his own father, who had fled from Florence to Rimini to escape an irate money-lender. We do not have a clue what Poggio thought when he penned this copy. Perhaps what already mattered more to him was the person in whose name the letter of recommendation was written: Coluccio Salutati, the great chancellor of the Florentine Republic.

The chancellor of the Florentine Republic was in effect the permanent secretary of state for foreign affairs. Florence was an independent state in control of a substantial swath of territory in central Italy and engaged in a constant, high-stakes chess game with the other powerful states of the Italian peninsula, especially Venice and Milan in the north, Naples in the south, and the papacy in Rome, weakened by internal divisions but still rich, dangerous, and meddlesome. Each of these rivals was prepared, if its position seemed threatened, to take the risky step of calling for aid, in money and troops, from the rulers of the Continent who welcomed the opportunity to intervene. All of the players in the game were ambitious, cunning, treacherous, ruthless, and armed, and the chancellor's conduct of diplomatic relations, including relations with the Church, was crucial not merely for the well-being of the city but for its very survival in the face of the threats from France, the Holy Roman Empire, and Spain.

When Poggio arrived on the scene in Florence, in the

late 1390s, Salutati—who had begun life as a lowly provincial notary—had filled this post for some twenty-five years, conducting intrigues, hiring and ridding himself of mercenaries, drafting precise instructions to ambassadors, negotiating treaties, seeing through the ruses of his enemies, forging alliances, issuing manifestos. Virtually everyone—the city's bitterest enemies as well as its most patriotic citizens—understood that in its chancellor Florence had someone truly exceptional, endowed not only with legal knowledge, political cunning, and diplomatic skill, but also with psychological penetration, a gift for public relations, and unusual literary skill.

Like Petrarch, with whom he had corresponded, Salutati felt the concentrated force of the buried past and had embarked on a scholarly search for the vestiges of classical culture. Like Petrarch, he was an intensely devout Christian who at the same time found almost nothing to cherish, at least stylistically, in anything written between Cassiodorus in the sixth century and Dante in the thirteenth. Like Petrarch, Salutati sought instead to imitate the style of Virgil and Cicero, and, though he recognized that he lacked Petrarch's literary genius—*Ego michi non placeo* ("I do not like myself"), he ruefully wrote—he astonished his contemporaries with the power of his prose.

Above all, Salutati shared with Petrarch the conviction that the recovery of the past had to be of more than antiquarian interest. The goal of reading was not to make oneself sound exactly like one of the ancients, even if that were possible. "I much prefer that my own style be my own," Petrarch wrote, "uncultivated and rude, but made to fit, as a garment, to the measure of my mind, rather than to someone else's, which may be more elegant, ambitious, and adorned, but one that, deriving from a greater genius, continually slips off, unfitted to the humble proportions of my intellect." Though there is clearly a large dose of false modesty here, there is also a genuine desire fashion a new and original voice not by disappearing into the old masters but by taking those masters into the self. The ancient authors, Petrarch wrote to Boccaccio, "have become absorbed into my being and implanted not only in my memory but in the marrow of my bones, and have become one with my mind so that even if I never read them again in my life, they would inhere in me with their roots sunk in the depths of my soul." "I have always believed," Salutati wrote in the same spirit, that "I must imitate antiquity not simply to reproduce it, but in order to produce something new. . . ."

To prove its worth, Petrarch and Salutati both insisted, the whole enterprise of humanism had not merely to generate passable imitations of the classical style but to serve a larger ethical end. And to do so it needed to live fully and vibrantly in the present. But here the disciple parted from his master, for while Petrarch, who was born in exile and never fully identified with a particular homeland, moved throughout his life from place to place—shuttling from royal palace to city to papal court to rural retreat, despairing of stable attachments and feeling the pull toward a contemplative withdrawal from the world—Salutati wanted to produce something new in the city-state he passionately loved.

At the center of Florence's cramped urban landscape of fortified towers and walled monasteries was the Palazzo della Signoria, the political heart of the republic. It was here for Salutati that the city's glory resided. The independence of Florence—the fact that it was not a client of another state, that it was not dependent on the papacy, and that it was not ruled by a king, a tyrant, or a prelate but governed by a body of its own citizens—was for Salutati what most mattered in the world. His letters, dispatches, protocols, and manifestos, written on behalf of the ruling priors of Florence, are stirring documents, and they were read and copied throughout Italy. They demonstrated that ancient rhetoric was alive, that it effectively stirred up political emotions and awakened old dreams. A supremely gifted diplomat and politician, Salutati had a range of voices, a range almost impossible to convey quickly, but something of his spirit may be gauged from a letter of February 13, 1376, to the town of Ancona. Ancona was, like Florence, an independent commune, and Salutati was urging its citizens to revolt against the papal government that had been imposed upon them: "Will you always stand in the darkness of slavery? Do you not consider, O best of men, how sweet liberty is? Our ancestors, indeed the whole Italian race, fought for five hundred years . . . so that liberty would not be lost." The revolt he was trying to incite was, of course, in Florence's strategic interest, but in attempting to arouse a spirit of liberty, Salutati was not being merely cynical. He seems genuinely to have believed that Florence was the heir to the republicanism on which ancient Roman greatness had been founded. That greatness, the proud claim of human freedom and dignity, had all but vanished from the broken, dirty streets of Rome, the debased staging ground of sordid clerical intrigues, but it lived, in Salutati's view, in Florence. And he was its principal voice.

He knew that he would not be its voice forever. As he reached his seventies, troubled by intensifying religious scruples and anxious about the many threats to the city he loved, Salutati looked to a group of gifted young men he had taken under his wing. Poggio was among these young men, though we do not know precisely how Salutati identified him or the others whom he trained, in the hope that one or another would continue his labor. The most promising student was Leonardo Bruni of Arezzo, a man about ten years older than Poggio, and like Poggio, from a very modest background. Bruni had set out to study law, but, along with other intellectually gifted men of his generation and particularly those in the orbit of Salutati, he had been seized by a passion for classical studies. In his case, the decisive factor was the study of ancient Greek, made possible when in 1397 Salutati invited the preeminent Byzantine scholar Manuel Chrysoloras to reside in Florence and give classes in a language that had been almost completely forgotten. "At the coming of Chrysoloras," Bruni later recalled, "I was made to halt in my choice of lives, seeing that I held it wrong to desert law, and yet I reckoned it a crime to omit so great an occasion of learning the Greek literature." The lure proved irresistible: "Conquered at last by these reasonings, I delivered myself over to Chrysoloras with such passion that what I had received from him by day in hours of waking, occupied my mind at night in hours of sleep."

In the circle jockeying for recognition by the great Salutati, one might have expected Poggio most to identify with the earnest, hardworking, ambitious Bruni, a penniless, provincial outsider endowed only with his own acute intelligence. But though he admired Bruni—who eventually served as a brilliant, deeply patriotic chancellor of Florence and was the author, among other works, of the first great history of the city—the young Poggio formed his deepest bond of friendship with another one of Salutati's students, the hypersensitive, argumentative aesthete Niccolò Niccoli.

Some sixteen years older than Poggio, Niccoli had been born to one of the city's wealthiest families. His father had made a fortune in the manufacture of wool cloth, along with money-lending, grain futures, and other enterprises. Tax records from the 1390s indicate that Niccolò Niccoli and his five brothers were wealthier than most of the residents in their quarter of the city, including such ruling families as the Brancacci and the Pitti. (Modern tourists to Florence can gauge the scale of this wealth by recalling the grandeur of the Pitti Palace, built some twenty years after Niccoli's death.)

By the time that Poggio came to know him, Niccoli's fortunes, and those of his brothers, were in decline. Though they
were still very rich men, the brothers were quarreling bitterly
among themselves, and the family as a whole seems to have
been unwilling or unable to play the political game that was
always necessary in Florence to protect and enhance accumulated wealth. Only those who actively exercised political power
in the city and kept a sharp eye out for their interests could avert
the crushing and often vindictive taxes that were levied on vulnerable fortunes. Taxes were used in Florence, as the historian
Guicciardini cannily remarked a century later, like a dagger.

Niccolò Niccoli spent all he had on a ruling passion that kept
him from the civic pursuits that might have helped him secure
some of the family wealth. The wool trade and commodity
speculation were not for him, any more than serving the republic in the Signoria, the executive body of government, or on
the important councils known as the Twelve Good Men and
the Sixteen Standard-bearers of the Militia. Even more than his
humanist mentor and friends, Niccoli was obsessed with the
vestiges of Roman antiquity and had no time for anything else.
He determined, probably at an early age, to have no career and
hold no civic offices, or rather, he determined to use his inherited wealth to live a beautiful and full life by conjuring up the
ghosts of the ancient past.

In the Florence of Niccoli's time, the family was the central institution, socially, economically, and psychologically,
and for anyone who did not choose to enter the special world
of the Church—and particularly for anyone with inherited
wealth—there was overwhelming pressure to marry, to have
children, and to augment the family fortunes. "Marriage gives
an abundance of all sorts of pleasure and delight," wrote Niccoli's younger contemporary, Leon Battista Alberti, summing
up widely held views,

If intimacy increases good will, no one has so close and continued a familiarity with anyone as with his wife; if close bonds and a united will arise through the revelation and communication of your feelings and desires, there is no one to whom you have more opportunity to communicate fully and reveal your mind than to your own wife, your constant companion; if, finally, an honorable alliance leads to friendship, no relationship more entirely commands your reverence than the sacred tie of marriage. Add to all this that every moment brings further ties of pleasure and utility, confirming the benevolence filling our hearts.

And if the picture painted here was exceedingly rosy, it was reinforced by dire warnings. Woe to the man, intoned San Bernardino, the greatest popular preacher of the time, who has no wife:

If he is rich and has somewhat, the sparrows eat it, and mice. . . . Know you what his bed is like? He lies in a ditch, and when he has put a sheet on his bed, he never takes it off again, until it is torn. And in the room in which he eats, the floor is covered with a melon rind and bones and salad leaves. . . . He wipes the trenchers off: the dog licks them, and so washes them. Know you how he lives? Like a brute beast.

Niccoli rejected both the inducements and the warnings. He chose to remain single, so that, it was said, no woman would distract him from his studies. "Studies" is a perfectly accurate term—he was a deeply scholarly and learned man—but it does not adequately convey the overarching vision of a mode of life immersed in the past that Niccoli arrived at early and that he pursued with a tenacious single-mindedness. As for the rest, all that ordinarily constitutes the pursuit of happiness, he seems to have been indifferent: "He had a housekeeper," his early biographer Vespasiano writes, "to provide for his wants."

Niccoli was one of the first Europeans to collect antiquities as works of art, prized possessions with which he surrounded himself in his Florentine apartments. Such collecting is by now such a familiar practice among the very rich that it is easy to lose sight of the fact that it was once a novel idea. Pilgrims to Rome in the Middle Ages had long been accustomed to gawking at the Colosseum and other "marvels" of paganism on their way to worshipping at the places that actually mattered, the revered Christian shrines of saints and martyrs. Niccoli's collection in Florence represented a very different impulse: not the accumulation of trophies but the loving appreciation of aesthetic objects.

As word got round that an eccentric man was willing to pay handsomely for ancient heads and torsos, farmers who might in the past have burned any marble fragments that they ploughed up for the lime they could extract from them or used the old carved stones for the foundations of a pigsty began instead to offer them for sale. On display in Niccoli's elegant rooms, along with antique Roman goblets, pieces of ancient glassware, medals, cameos, and other treasures, the sculptures inspired in others the impulse to collect.

Poggio could not possibly hope to be served his meals, as his friend was, on ancient Roman plates or disburse gold coins, as his friend did, for antique cameos that he happened to glimpse around the necks of street urchins. But he could share and deepen the desire that underlay Niccoli's acquisitions, the desire to understand and to reenter imaginatively the cultural world that had fashioned the beautiful objects with which he surrounded himself. The two friends studied together, traded historical anecdotes about the Roman Republic and Empire, pondered the religion and mythology represented by the statues of the gods and the heroes, measured the foundations of ruined villas, discussed the topography and the organization of ancient cities, and above all enriched their detailed understanding of the Latin language they both loved and which they routinely used in their personal letters and perhaps in private conversation as well.

From these letters it is clear that Niccolò Niccoli cared about one thing even more passionately than the ancient sculptures that were being exhumed from the earth: the classical and patristic texts that his fellow humanists were ferreting out of monastic libraries. Niccoli loved to possess these texts, to study them, and to copy them slowly, ever so slowly, in handwriting even more beautiful than Poggio's. Perhaps indeed their friendship coalesced at least as much around the forms of letters—Niccoli shares with Poggio the credit for the invention of humanist script—as around the forms of ancient thought.

Manuscripts of ancient texts were expensive to acquire, but to the avid collector no price seemed too great. Niccoli's library was famous among humanists in Italy and elsewhere, and, though he was often reclusive, crotchety, and fiercely opinionated, he generously welcomed into his house scholars who wished to consult his collections. When in 1437 he died at the age of seventy-three, he left eight hundred manuscripts, by far the largest and best collection in Florence.

Guided by Salutati's vision, Niccoli had formulated an idea of what to do with these texts. Petrarch and Boccaccio had both contemplated keeping together the manuscripts they had acquired, after they died, but their valuable collections were in fact sold off, dispersed, or simply neglected. (Many of the precious codices that Petrarch painstakingly gathered and that he brought to Venice, to serve as the core of what he dreamed would be a new Alexandrian Library, were shut away and forgotten in a damp palazzo where they crumbled into dust.) Niccoli did not want to see the work of his lifetime suffer a similar fate. He drew up a will in which he called for the manuscripts to be kept together, forbade their sale or dispersion, prescribed strict rules for loans and returns, appointed a committee of trustees, and left a sum of money to build a library. The building would be constructed and the collection housed in a monastery; but Niccoli emphatically did not want this to be a monastic library, closed off to the world and reserved for the monks. He specified that the books would be available not for the religious alone but for all learned citizens, *omnes cives studiosi*. Centuries after the last Roman library had been shut down and abandoned, Niccoli had brought back into the world the idea of the public library.

In the late 1390s, when Poggio first met Niccoli, the mania for collecting that led to this remarkable result must only have been in its early stages, but the friends bonded in their shared insistence on the superiority of all things ancient—setting aside matters of faith—over anything that followed. The astonishing literary ambition and creativity characteristic of Petrarch had largely shriveled up in them, as had the patriotic zeal and the passion for liberty that had fueled Salutati's humanism. What took their place was something far less expansive in spirit, something harder and more punishing: a cult of imitation and a craving for exactitude. Perhaps the younger generation simply lacked the overpowering talent of their elders, but it was as if these gifted disciples of Salutati had deliberately rejected the bold desire to bring something truly new into the world. Despising the new, they dreamed only of calling back to life something old. This dream, narrow and arid in spirit, was doomed to failure; but, all the same, it had surprising results.

To those outside the charmed circle of young humanists, the emerging attitude toward language and culture could seem repellent. "In order to appear well read to the mob," wrote one disgusted contemporary, "they shout about the piazza how many diphthongs the ancients had and why today only two are in use." Even Salutati was uneasy, and with good reason, for though the fervent classicism of Poggio and Niccoli was clearly indebted to him, it was also a parting of the ways, as he understood, and in some subtle sense a repudiation.

On the death of Petrarch on July 19, 1374, the grieving Salutati had declared that Petrarch was a greater prose writer than Cicero and a greater poet than Virgil. By the 1390s, this praise seemed to Poggio and Niccoli ridiculous, and they pressed Salutati to repudiate it. In all the intervening centuries, no one, they argued, had bettered the great classic writers in stylistic perfection. It was impossible. Since ancient times all there had been, in their view, was a long, tragic history of stylistic corruption and loss. Indifferent or ignorant, even supposedly well-educated medieval writers had forgotten how to form sentences correctly, in the proper manner of the masters of classical Latin, or to use words with the elegance, accuracy, and precision with which they had once been wielded. Moreover, the surviving samples of classical texts had been corrupted, so that they could no longer serve as correct models, even if anyone had the ambition to use them as such. The "ancients" cited by medieval scholastics, Niccoli argued, "would not have recognized as their own the writings attributed to them, preserved as they are in corrupt texts and translated without taste and sense."

Petrarch, who repeatedly insisted that the mastery of a classical style was by itself inadequate for the achievement of true literary or moral greatness, had once stood on the steps of the Capitol and had himself crowned poet laureate—as if the spirit of the ancient past had truly been reborn in him. But from the perspective of the radical, hard-core classicism of the younger generation, nothing truly worthwhile had been achieved by

Dante, Petrarch, or Boccaccio, let alone by lesser lights: "While the literary legacy of antiquity is in such a pitiful state, no real culture is possible, and any disputation is necessarily built on shaky ground."

These were unmistakably Niccoli's views, but they were not his precise words. Rather, they were the words attributed to him in a dialogue by Leonardo Bruni. For apart from letters to intimate friends, Niccoli wrote virtually nothing. How could he, given his hypercritical sourness and narrow, unrelenting classicism? Friends sent their Latin texts to him and anxiously awaited his corrections, which were almost invariably punishing, stern, and unforgiving. But Niccoli was at his most unforgiving in relation to himself.

Niccolò Niccoli was, Salutati observed, Poggio's "second self." But Poggio did not suffer from the crippling inhibitions that virtually silenced his friend. In the course of his long career, he wrote books on such subjects as hypocrisy, avarice, true nobility, whether an old man should marry, the vicissitudes of fortune, the miseries of the human condition, and the history of Florence. "He had a great gift of words," his younger contemporary Vespasiano da Bisticci wrote of him, adding, "He was given to strong invective, and all stood in dread of him." If Poggio, the master of invective, was not willing to grant to his old master that any writer of the past millennium could equal, let alone outstrip, the eloquence of the ancients, he was willing to concede that Petrarch had accomplished something: Petrarch was the first, Poggio granted, "who with his labor, industry, and watchful attention called back to light the studies almost brought to destruction, and opened the path to those others who were eager to follow."

That was the path on which Niccoli had decisively embarked, casting aside everything else in his life. Poggio, for his part, was happy to join him, but he had somehow to make a living. He had fantastic skill as a scribe, but that would hardly have supported him in the manner he hoped to live. His command of classical Latin would have enabled him to embark on a career as a teacher, but this was a life with very few of the amenities he sought. Universities generally lacked buildings, libraries, endowments; they consisted of scholars and masters, and humanists were usually paid much less than professors of law and medicine. Most teachers of the humanities lived itinerant lives, traveling from city to city, giving lectures on a few favorite authors, and then restlessly moving on, in the hope of finding new patrons. Poggio had had the opportunity to witness such lives, and they did not appeal to him. He wanted something much more stable and settled.

At the same time Poggio lacked the patriotic zeal—the passion for the city and for republican liberty—that inspired Salutati and had been stirred in Bruni. And he lacked as well the calling that might have led him to take religious orders and embark on the life of a priest or a monk. His spirit was emphatically secular and his desires were in and of the world. Still, he had to do something. In the fall of 1403, armed with a letter of recommendation from Salutati, the twenty-three-year-old Poggio set off for Rome.

CHAPTER SIX

IN THE LIE FACTORY

OR AN AMBITIOUS provincial upstart like Poggio, the swirling, swollen orbit of the pope was the principal magnet, but Rome held out other opportunities. The powerful Roman noble families—most prominently, the Colonna or the Orsini—could always find some way to make use of someone endowed with excellent Latin and exquisite handwriting. Still more, the bishops and cardinals residing in Rome had their own smaller courts, in which a notary's ability to draft and pen legal documents was a sought-after skill. Upon his arrival, Poggio found a place in one of these courts, that of the cardinal of Bari. But this was only a brief halt on the way to the higher goal of papal service—whether in the palace (the *palatium*) or the court (the *curia*). Before the year was out, the staunchly republican Salutati had pulled enough strings at the court of the reigning pope, Boniface IX, to help his prized pupil get what he most wanted, the coveted position of scribe—apostolic scriptor.

Most of the papal bureaucrats were from Rome and its surroundings; many of them, like Poggio, had some training in the law. Though scriptors were expected to attend mass every day before work, their post was a secular one—they busied themselves principally with the business side of the papacy, the side that entailed rationality, calculation, administrative skill, and legal acumen. The pope was (or at least claimed to be) the absolute ruler of a large swath of central Italy, extending north into the Romagna and to the territories controlled by the Venetian Republic. Many of the cities over which he ruled were perennially restive, the policies of the surrounding states were as aggressive, treacherous, and grasping as his own, foreign powers were always poised to make their own armed incursions into the peninsula. To hold his own, he needed all of the diplomatic cunning, money, and martial ferocity he could muster, and hence he needed and maintained a large governmental apparatus.

The pope was, of course, the absolute ruler of a much larger spiritual kingdom, one that extended, in principle at least, to the entire human race and affected to shape its destiny both in this world and in the next. Some of those he claimed as his subjects professed surprise at his presumption—as did the New World peoples whom the pope in the late fifteenth century grandly signed over en masse to be vassals of the kings of Spain and Portugal—and others, such as the Jews or the Eastern Orthodox Christians, stubbornly resisted. But the great majority of Christians in the West, even if they lived in distant regions, or were ignorant of the Latin in which he conducted his affairs, or knew something of the spectacular moral failings that stained his office, believed that they stood in a special relationship to the pope's unique authority. They looked to the papacy to determine points of doctrine in a dogmatic religion that claimed these points were crucial for the fate of the soul and enforced this claim with fire and sword. They sought papal dispensations—that is, exemptions from the rules of canon law—in such matters as marriages and annulments and a thousand other delicate social relations. They jockeyed for appointment to various offices and confirmation of valuable benefices. They looked for everything that people hope an immensely wealthy and powerful lawmaker, landowner, and spiritual leader will confer upon them or deny to their rivals. In the early fifteenth century, when Poggio got his bearings in Rome, cases came into the papal court for settlement at the rate of two thousand a week.

All of this activity—far exceeding any other chancery court in Europe—required skilled personnel: theologians, lawyers, notaries, clerks, secretaries. Petitions had to be drawn up in the proper form and filed. Minutes had to be carefully kept. Decisions had to be recorded. Orders were transcribed and copied. Papal bulls—that is, decrees, letters patent, and charters—were copied and sealed. Abbreviated versions of these bulls were prepared and disseminated. The bishop of Rome had a large household staff, as befitted his princely rank; he had a huge entourage of courtiers, advisers, clerks, and servants, as befitted his political office and his ceremonial significance; he had an enormous chancery, as befitted his juridical power; and he had a massive religious bureaucracy, as befitted his spiritual authority.

This was the world Poggio entered and in which he hoped to thrive. A position in the curia could serve as a step toward highly remunerative advancement in the Church hierarchy, but those who aspired to such advancement became churchmen. Poggio certainly understood that ordination was the route to wealth and power, and, unmarried as he was, there was no obstacle to his taking it. (He may already have had a mistress and illegitimate children, but that certainly was no obstacle). And yet he held back.

He knew himself well enough to understand that he lacked a religious vocation. That, of course, did not stop many of his contemporaries, but he did not like what he observed in those who had made this choice anyway. "I am determined not to assume the sacerdotal office," he wrote to his friend Niccoli, "for I have seen many men whom I have regarded as persons of good character and liberal dispositions, degenerate into avarice, sloth, and dissipation, in consequence of their introduction into the priesthood." This degeneration would, he thought, almost certainly be his own fate, one he was determined to avoid: "Fearing lest this should be the case with myself, I have resolved to spend the remaining term of my pilgrimage as a layman." He was, to be sure, turning his back on a particularly comfortable and secure existence in a very insecure world, but for Poggio the cost of this security was too high: "I do not think of the priesthood as liberty, as many do," he confided to Niccoli, "but as the most severe and oppressive form of service." The life course he opted for instead may seem to us a peculiarly constrained one—a lay bureaucrat in the service of the pope—but to Poggio the refusal of orders evidently felt liberating, as if he were guarding an inner core of independence.

He needed every bit of independence that he could muster. The Roman curia was, from a moral perspective, a notoriously perilous place, a peril deftly summed up by a Latin proverb of the time: *Curialis bonus, homo sceleratissimus* ("Good curialist, wickedest of men"). The atmosphere he breathed is most brilliantly conveyed by a strange work of the 1430s, written when Poggio was still very much at the center of the curia. The work, entitled *On the Excellence and Dignity of the Roman Court,* is by a younger humanist contemporary, the Florentine Lapo da Castiglionchio. It is a dialogue, in the style of Cicero, a form much favored at the time by writers who wished to air controversial and even dangerous views without taking full responsibility for them. Hence, at the start of Lapo's imaginary conversation, a character called Angelo—not Lapo himself, of course, heaven forbid—violently assails the moral bankruptcy of the curia, a place "in which crime, moral outrage, fraud, and deceit take the name of virtue and are held in high esteem." The thought that this sink of hypocrisy makes a claim to religious faith is grotesque: "What can be more alien to religion than the curia?"

Lapo, professing to speak in his own voice, rises to the defense of the papal court. The place attracts crowds of petitioners, to be sure, but we know that God wants to be worshipped by multitudes. Therefore he must be particularly gratified by the magnificent spectacles of worship staged in His honor by the richly dressed priests. And for ordinary mortals, the curia is the best place to acquire the virtue known as prudence, since there are so many types of people in attendance from all over the world. Just to observe the wide array of outlandish costumes and accents and ways of wearing one's beard is in itself a valuable lesson in the range of human customs. And the court is also the best place to study the humanities. After all, Lapo writes, as "the pope's domestic secretary" (and hence a very influential figure), "there is Poggio of Florence, in whom there is not only the highest erudition and eloquence, but also a unique gravity, seasoned with plenty of great wit and urbanity."

True, he concedes, it is disturbing that bribery and corruption lie at the heart of the curia, but these problems are the work of a small group of miserable thieves and perverts who have brought the place into disrepute. Perhaps the pope will notice the scandal one day and undertake to clean his house, but in any case one should in life always keep in mind what was intended, not what is actually done.

Angelo, evidently persuaded by these arguments, begins to wax enthusiastic over the cunning of the lawyers in the curia, with their subtle grasp of the weaknesses and intimate secrets of everyone and their ability to exploit all opportunities to make money. And, given the huge sums that are paid for bits of paper with papal seals, what fantastic profits are reaped! The place is a gold mine. There is no need any longer to affect the poverty of Christ: that was necessary only at the beginning in order to avoid the imputation of bribing people to believe. Times have changed, and now riches, so essential for any important enterprise, are in order for whoever can acquire them. Priests are allowed to amass all the wealth they want; they only have to be poor in spirit. To want high priests actually to be poor, rather than the immensely rich men that they are, displays a kind of "mindlessness."

So the dialogue runs on, with deadpan seriousness and wide-eyed enthusiasm. The curia, the friends agree, is a great place not only for serious study but also for lighter amusements such as gaming, horsemanship, and hunting. Just think of the dinner parties at the papal court—witty gossip, along with fantastic food and drink served by beautiful, young, hairless boys. And for those whose tastes do not run in the direction of Ganymede, there are the abundant pleasures of Venus. Mistresses, adulterous matrons, courtesans of all descriptions occupy a central place in the curia, and appropriately so, since the delights they offer have such a central place in human happiness. Lewd songs, naked breasts, kissing, fondling, with small white lapdogs trained to lick around your groin to excite desire—and all for remarkably low prices.

This expansive enthusiasm for outrageously corrupt behavior and the frantic pursuit of wealth must be a sly satirical game. Yet *On the Excellence and Dignity of the Roman Court* is a very peculiar satire, and not merely because its gushing praise for what the reader is presumably meant to despise evidently took in some contemporaries. The problem is that when he wrote the work, Lapo was busily seeking appointment in the curia for himself. It is possible, of course, that he felt ambivalent about his attempt: people often despise the very institutions they are frantically trying to enter. But perhaps compiling this inventory of the vices of the curia was something more than an expression of ambivalence.

There is a moment in the work in which Lapo praises the gossip, obscene stories, jokes, and lies that characterize the conversation of the apostolic scribes and secretaries. No matter, he says, whether the things that are reported are true or false. They are all amusing and, in their way, instructive:

> No one is spared, whether he is absent or present, and everyone is equally attacked, to the great guffawing and laughter of all. Dinner parties, tavern life, pandering, bribes, thefts, adultery, sexual degradation, and shameful acts are publicly revealed. From this one acquires not only pleasure but also the greatest utility, since the life and character of all is thus placed before your eyes.

Lapo is no doubt being ironic, but he is also, in the very manner of his irony, showing that he gets the cynical joke and thereby demonstrating his suitability to participate in the conversations he pillories. This was in effect a way of presenting himself to the members of the curia, and above all to "Poggio of Florence."

By the time Lapo came on the scene, in the 1430s, Poggio had risen from scriptor to the much more powerful and remunerative position of papal secretary. At any one time there were about a hundred scriptors in the papal court, but only six apostolic secretaries. The latter had direct access to the pope himself and hence far greater influence. A careful suggestion here, a well-timed word there, could make all the difference in the outcome of an important case or the disposition of a wealthy benefice.

Among the secretaries, there was one in particular who was known as the *secretarius domesticus* or *secretus*, that is, the pope's private or intimate secretary. This coveted position was the golden apple, and, after years of maneuvering, Poggio—whose father had once fled from Arezzo a step ahead of his creditors—finally plucked it. When ambitious Lapo or any other office seeker surveyed the court, it was easy enough to see that Poggio was foremost among "the pope's men."

But why then should Lapo have thought to ingratiate himself with Poggio by painting a slyly ironic picture of the corrupt institution to which he hoped to be appointed? Because already in the 1430s, and probably for a long time before this, Poggio had established himself at the very center of what he called "the Bugiale," the Lie Factory. There, in a room at the court, the papal secretaries would regularly gather to exchange stories and jokes. "Nobody was spared," Poggio wrote, in a phrase echoed by Lapo, "and whatever met with our disapprobation was freely censured; oftentimes the Pope himself was the first subject-matter of our criticism." The chatter, trivial, mendacious, sly, slanderous, often obscene, was the kind of speech that is almost forgotten before its sound fades away, but Poggio seems not to have forgotten any of it. He went back to his desk and, in his best Latin, fashioned the conversations he had had in the Lie Factory into something he entitled the *Facetiae.*

It is almost impossible for jokes that are centuries old to retain any life. The fact that a few of the jokes of Shakespeare or Rabelais or Cervantes continue to make us smile is something of a miracle. Almost six hundred years old, Poggio's *Facetiae* is by now largely interesting only as a symptom. These relics, like the remains of long-dead insects, tell us what once buzzed about in the air of the Vatican. Some of the jokes are professional complaints, of the sort secretaries must always have had: the boss routinely claims to detect mistakes and demands rewriting, but, if you bring him the identical document, which you pretend to have corrected, he will take it into his hand, as if to peruse it, give it a glance, and then say, "Now it is all right: go, seal it up. . . ." Some are stories, half-skeptical, half-credulous, about popular miracles and prodigies of nature. A few reflect wryly on Church politics, as when Poggio compares the pope who conveniently forgot his promise to end the schism to a quack from Bologna who announced that he was going to fly: "At the end of the day, when the crowd had watched and waited, he had to do something, so he exposed himself and showed his ass."

Most of the stories in the *Facetiae* are about sex, and they convey, in their clubroom smuttiness, misogyny mingled with both an insider's contempt for yokels and, on occasion, a distinct anticlerical streak. There is the woman who tells her husband that she has two cunts (*duos cunnos*), one in front that she will share with him, the other behind that she wants to give, pious soul that she is, to the Church. The arrangement works because the parish priest is only interested in the share that belongs to the Church. There is the clueless priest who in a sermon against lewdness (*luxuria*) describes practices that couples are using to heighten sexual pleasure; many in the congregation take note of the suggestions and go home to try them out for themselves. There are dumb priests who, baffled by the fact that in confession almost all the women say that they have been faithful in matrimony and almost all the men confess to extramarital affairs, cannot for the life of them figure out who the women are with whom the men have sinned. There are many tales about seductive friars and lusty hermits, about Florentine merchants nosing out profits, about female medical woes magically cured by lovemaking, about cunning tricksters, bawling preachers, unfaithful wives, and foolish husbands. There is the fellow humanist—identified by name as Francesco Filelfo— who dreams that he puts his finger into a magic ring that will keep his wife from ever being unfaithful to him and wakes to find that he has his finger in his wife's vagina. There is the quack doctor who claims that he can produce children of different types—merchants, soldiers, generals—depending on how far he pushes his cock in. A foolish rustic, bargaining for a soldier, hands his wife over to the scoundrel, but then, thinking himself sly, comes out of hiding and hits the quack's ass to push his cock further in: "Per Sancta Dei Evangelia," the rustic shouts triumphantly, "hic erit Papa!" "This one is going to be pope!"

The *Facetiae* was a huge success.

If Poggio's work—the best known jokebook of its age— captures anything of the atmosphere of the papal court, it is less surprising that Lapo tried to call attention to himself by signaling openly a strange blend of moral outrage and cynicism. (As it turned out, a few months after he penned his *Dialogue in Praise of the Papal Court*, poor Lapo died of plague at the age of thirty-three.) By the sixteenth century, the Catholic hierarchy, deeply alarmed by the Protestant Reformation, would attempt to stamp out within its own ranks this current of subversive humor. Poggio's *Facetiae* was on a list, alongside books by Boccaccio, Erasmus, and Machiavelli, that the Church wished to burn. But in the world Poggio inhabited, it was still permissible, even fashionable, to reveal what was, in any case, widely understood. Poggio could write of the institution where he spent most of his working life that "there is seldom room for talent or honesty; every thing is obtained through intrigue or luck, not to mention money, which seems to hold supreme sway over the world."

Ambitious young intellectuals, living by their wits, the papal scribes and secretaries looked about and felt that they were cleverer, more complex, more worthy of advancement than the overstuffed prelates they served. Theirs was, predictably, a world of resentment: we complained, Poggio writes, "of the inadequate men who hold the highest dignities of the Church, discreet and learned men being left out in the cold, whilst ignorant and worthless persons are exalted."

Theirs was also, equally predictably, a world of intense sniping, competitiveness, and backbiting. We have, in the snide remarks about Poggio's parentage, already had a taste of what they dished out to one another, and Poggio's own "jokes" about his enemy, the rival humanist Filelfo, are cut from the same cloth:

> At a meeting of the Pope's Secretaries, in the Pontifical palace, attended, as usual, by a number of men of great learning, conversation had turned upon the filthy and disgusting life led by that villain, Francesco Filelfo, who was, on all sides, charged with numerous outrages, and someone inquired if he was of noble extraction,—"To be sure," said one of his fellow-countrymen, assuming a most earnest look, "to be sure he is, and his nobility is even most illustrious; for his father constantly wore silk in the morning."

And then, eager to make sure that his readers get the point of the wisecrack, Poggio adds an explanatory note (always a sign of a damp squib): "meaning by that that Filelfo was the bastard of a priest. When officiating, priests are generally clothed with silk."

At this distance, much of this squabbling seems childish. But these were adults intent on drawing blood, and on occasion the blows were not only rhetorical. In 1452, Poggio had been having a running quarrel with another papal secretary, the notoriously morose humanist George of Trebizond, over the burning question of who deserved more credit for several translations of ancient texts. When Poggio screamed at his rival that he was a liar, George struck Poggio with his fist. The two sulked back momentarily to their desks, but then the fight resumed, the seventy-two-year-old Poggio grabbling the fifty-seven-year-old George's cheek and mouth with one hand while attempting to gouge out his eye with the other. After it was over, in an angry note to Poggio about the fracas, George represented himself as having acted with exemplary restraint: "Rightly I could have bitten off the fingers you stuck in my mouth; I did not. Since I was seated and you were standing, I thought of squeezing your testicles with both hands and thus lay you out; I did not do it." The whole thing seems a grotesque farce, akin to one of the stories in Poggio's jokebook, except for its real-world consequences: with his better contacts and more genial manner, Poggio had George expelled from the curia. Poggio ended his life covered with honors; George died obscure, resentful, and poor.

In a celebrated nineteenth-century book on "the revival of learning," John Addington Symonds, recounting these gladiatorial struggles among humanist scholars, suggests that "they may be taken as proof of their enthusiasm for their studies." Perhaps. However wild their insults, the arguments swirled around fine points of Latin grammar, accusations of mistakes in diction, subtle questions of translation. But the extravagance and bitterness of the charges—in the course of a quarrel over Latin style, Poggio accused the younger humanist Lorenzo Valla of heresy, theft, lying, forgery, cowardice, drunkenness, sexual perversion, and insane vanity—discloses something rotten in the inner lives of these impressively learned individuals.

Though he was knocking at the door trying to gain admission, Lapo seems to have understood and analyzed the sickness of the whole environment. The problem was not only a matter of this or that difficult personality; it was structural. The papal court had, to serve its own needs, brought into being a class of rootless, ironic intellectuals. These intellectuals were committed to pleasing their masters, on whose patronage they utterly depended, but they were cynical and unhappy. How could the rampant cynicism, greed, and hypocrisy, the need to curry favor with perverse satraps who professed to preach morality to the rest of mankind, the endless jockeying for position in the court of an absolute monarch, not eat away at whatever was hopeful and decent in anyone who breathed that air for very long? What—apart from attempts at character assassination and outright assassination—could be done with the seething feeling of rage?

One way that Poggio dealt with the sickness—to which he himself had quickly succumbed and from which he was never entirely cured—was through laughter, the abrasive, obscene laughter of the *Facetiae*. The laughter must have given him some relief, though evidently not enough. For he also wrote a succession of dialogues—*On Avarice, Against the Hypocrites, On Nobility, On the Vicissitudes of Fortune, On the Misery of Human Life*, and so forth—in which he adopted the stance of a serious moralist. There are clear links between the jokes and the moral essays, but the moral essays allowed Poggio to explore the issues only hinted at in the comical anecdotes.

The essay *Against the Hypocrites*, for example, has its share of stories of clerical seducers, but the stories are part of a larger, much more serious analysis of an institutional dilemma: why churchmen, and especially monks, are particularly prone to hypocrisy. Is there a relation, Poggio asks, between religious vocation and fraud? A full answer would certainly involve sexual motives, but those motives alone cannot adequately account for the swarms of hypocrites in a place such as the curia, including monks notable for their ostentatious piety and their ascetic pallor who are feverishly seeking benefices, immunities, favors, privileges, positions of power. Nor can sexual intrigues adequately explain the still larger swarms of robed hypocrites in the world outside the curia, charismatic preachers who mint money with their sonorous voices and their terrible threats of hellfire and damnation, observant friars who claim to adhere strictly to the Order of St. Francis but have the morals of bandits, mendicant friars with their little sacks, their long hair and longer beards, and their fraudulent pretense of living in holy poverty, confessors who pry into the secrets of every man and woman. Why don't all these models of extravagant religiosity simply shut themselves up in their cells and commit themselves to lives of fasting and prayer? Because their conspicuous professions of piety, humility, and contempt for the world are actually masks for avarice, laziness, and ambition. To be sure, someone in the conversation concedes, there are some good and sincere monks, but very, very few of them, and one may observe even those slowly drawn toward the fatal corruption that is virtually built into their vocation.

"Poggio," who represents himself as a character in the dialogue, argues that hypocrisy is better at least than open violence, but his friend Aliotti, an abbot, responds that it is worse, since everyone can perceive the horror of a confessed rapist or murderer, but it is more difficult to defend oneself against a sly deceiver. How is it possible then to identify hypocrites? After all, if they are good at their simulations, it is very difficult to distinguish the frauds from genuinely holy figures. The dialogue lists the warning signs. You should be suspicious of anyone who

> displays an excessive purity of life;
> walks barefoot through the streets, with a dirty face and shabby robes;
> shows in public a disdain for money;
> always has the name of Jesus Christ on his lips;
> wants to be called good, without actually doing anything particularly good;
> attracts women to him to satisfy his wishes;
> runs here and there outside his monastery, seeking fame and honors;

makes a show of fasting and other ascetic practices;
induces others to get things for himself;
refuses to acknowledge or return what is given to him in
trust.

Virtually any priest or monk who is at the curia is a hypocrite,
writes Poggio, for it is impossible to fulfill the highest purposes
of religion there. And if you happen at the curia to see someone who is particularly abject in his humility, beware: he is
not merely a hypocrite but the worst hypocrite of all. In general, you should be wary of people who seem too perfect, and
remember that it is actually quite difficult to be good: "Difficile
est bonum esse."

Against the Hypocrites is a work written not in the wake of
Martin Luther by a Reformation polemicist but a century earlier, by a papal bureaucrat living and working at the center of
the Roman Catholic hierarchy. It indicates that the Church,
though it could and did respond violently to what it perceived
as doctrinal or institutional challenges, was willing to tolerate
extremely sharp critiques from within, including critiques from
secular figures like Poggio. And it indicates too that Poggio and
his fellow humanists in the curia struggled to channel their
anger and disgust into more than obscene laughter and violent
quarrels with one another.

The greatest and most consequential work in this critical
spirit was written by Poggio's bitter enemy, Lorenzo Valla.
Valla famously used his brilliant command of Latin philology
to demonstrate that the "Donation of Constantine," the document in which the Roman emperor purportedly gave possession of the Western Empire to the pope, was a forgery. After the
publication of this piece of detective work, Valla was in considerable danger. But the Church's tolerance for internal critique
extended, at least for a brief period in the fifteenth century,

even to this extreme edge: the humanist pope Nicholas V eventually appointed Valla to the post of apostolic secretary, and thus this most independent and critical of spirits was, like Poggio, employed by the curia he had so relentlessly exposed and ridiculed.

Poggio lacked Valla's radicalism and originality. One of the speakers in *Against the Hypocrites* briefly floats an argument that might have led in a perilous direction, moving from the theatrical pretense of holiness in the Catholic Church to the fraudulent use of oracles in pagan religion as a means to overawe and manipulate the vulgar. But the subversive link—which Machiavelli would exploit to shocking effect in the next century in constructing a disenchanted analysis of the political uses of all religious faith— is never quite made, and Poggio's work merely ends with a fantasy of stripping the hypocrites of their protective cloaks. In the afterlife, we are told, the dead, in order to enter the infernal kingdom, have to pass through gates of different diameters. Those who are known by the custodian to be clearly bad or good pass through the wide gates; through the narrow ones go those about whom it is not clear whether they are honest or hypocritical. The honest souls pass through, with only minimal scratching; the hypocrites have their skin entirely lacerated.

This fantasy of laceration manages to combine Poggio's aggression and his pessimism: the hypocrites will all be exposed and definitively punished, but it is not until the afterlife that it is possible even to reveal who they are. If anger always hovers within him just beneath the surface of his laughter, so too despair—at the impossibility of reforming abuses, at the steady loss of everything worth treasuring, at the wretchedness of the human condition—hovers just beneath his anger.

Like many of his colleagues, Poggio was an indefatigable letter writer, and through these letters we glimpse him grappling with the cynicism, disgust, and worldweariness that seems to have afflicted everyone in the papal entourage. Monasteries, he writes to a friend, are "not congregations of the faithful or places of religious men but the workshops of criminals"; the curia is "a sink of men's vices." (158) Everywhere he looks around Rome, people are tearing down ancient temples to get the lime from the stones, and within a generation or two most of the glorious remains of the past, so much more precious than our own miserable present, will be gone. He is wasting his life and must find an escape route: "I must try everything, so that I may achieve something, and so stop being a servant to men and have time for literature."

Yet though he indulged at moments in fantasies of changing his life—"to abandon all these worldly concerns, all the empty cares, annoyances, and daily plans, and to flee into the haven of poverty, which is freedom and true quiet and safety"—Poggio recognized sadly that such a route was not open to him. "I do not know what I can do outside the Curia," he wrote to Niccoli, "except teach boys or work for some master or rather tyrant. If I had to take up either one of these, I should think it utter misery. For not only is all servitude a dismal thing, as you know, but especially so is serving the lusts of a wicked man. As for school teaching, may I be spared that! For it would be better to be subject to one man than to many." He would stay at the curia, then, in the hope that he would make enough money to enable him to retire early: "My one ambition: by the hard work of a few years to achieve leisure for the rest of my life." As it turned out, the "few years" would prove to be fifty.

The pattern of dreaming and deferral and compromise is an altogether familiar one: it is the epitome of a failed life. But Poggio did not succumb to it, though he had every reason to do so. He lived in a world not only pervaded by corruption and greed but also repeatedly battered by conspiracies, riots, wars, and outbreaks of plague. He worked in the Roman curia, but the curia was not even stable in its location in Rome, since the pope and his entire court repeatedly were forced to flee the city. He grappled, as everyone in his world had to grapple, with the constant presence of pain—from which there was no medical relief—and with the constant threat of death. He could easily have contracted into brittle, defensive cynicism, relieved only by unfulfilled fantasies of escape.

What saved him was an obsessive craving, his book mania.

In 1406, when he learned that his great mentor Salutati had died, Poggio was grief-stricken. The great old man had seized upon anyone in whom he had seen "some gleam of intellect" and had helped those whom he had so identified with instruction, guidance, letters of recommendation, money, and, above all, the use of his own books. "We have lost a father," he wrote; "we have lost the haven and refuge of all scholars, the light of our nation." Poggio claimed that he was weeping as he wrote his letter, and there is no reason to doubt the genuineness of his words: "Express my sympathy to his sons," he wrote to Niccoli in Florence, "and tell them that I am plunged in grief. This too I want to find out from you: what you think will happen to his books."

"I was upset and terrified," Poggio wrote Niccoli in July 1449, "by the death of Bartolomeo de Montepulciano," the close friend with whom he had explored the monastic libraries of Switzerland. But a moment later his mind shifts to what he had just discovered at Monte Cassino: "I found a book containing Julius Frontinus' *De aquaeductu urbis.*" And in a letter written a week later, the same pattern recurs. He begins by mentioning two ancient manuscripts that he has copied and that he wishes, he notes, "to be ruled in red and bound."

> I could not write you this from the City on account of my grief over the death of my dearest friend and on account of my confusion of spirit, deriving partly from

fear and partly from the sudden departure of the Pope. I had to leave my house and settle all my things; a great deal had to be done at once so that there was no opportunity for writing or even for drawing breath. There was besides the greatest grief, which made everything else much harder. But to go back to the books.

"But to go back to the books . . ." This is the way out, the escape from the pervasive fear and bafflement and pain. "My country has not yet recovered from the plague which troubled it five years ago," he writes in September, 1430; "Now again it seems that it will succumb to a massacre equally violent." And then a moment later: "But let us get back to our own affairs. I see what you write about the library." If it is not plague that threatens, it is war: "Every man waits his destined hour; even the cities are doomed to their fate." And then the same note: "Let us spend our leisure with our books, which will take our minds off these troubles, and will teach us to despise what many people desire." In the north the powerful Visconti of Milan are raising an army; Florentine mercenaries are besieging Lucca; Alfonso in Naples is stirring up trouble, and the emperor Sigismond is applying intolerable pressure on the pope. "I have already decided what I shall do even if things turn out as many people fear; namely, that I shall devote myself to Greek literature. . . ."

Poggio was highly self-conscious about these letters, and expected them to circulate, but his book mania, expressed again and again, seems unguarded, candid, and authentic. It was the key to a feeling he characterized with a word that otherwise seems singularly inappropriate to a papal bureaucrat: freedom. "Your Poggio," he wrote, "is content with very little and you shall see this for yourself; sometimes I am free for reading, free from all care about public affairs which I leave to my superiors. I live free as much as I can." Freedom here has nothing to do with political liberty or a notion of rights or the license to say whatever he wished or the ability to go wherever he chose. It is rather the experience of withdrawing inwardly from the press of the world—in which he himself was so ambitiously engaged—and ensphering himself in a space apart. For Poggio, that experience was what it meant to immerse himself in an ancient book: "I am free for reading."

Poggio savored the feeling of freedom at those times when the usual Italian political disorder became particularly acute or when the papal court was in an uproar or when his own personal ambitions were thwarted or, perhaps equally threatening, when those ambitions were realized. Hence it was a feeling to which he must have clung with particular intensity when sometime after 1410, having amply displayed his gifts as a humanist scribe, a learned writer, and a court insider, he accepted the most prestigious and most dangerous appointment of his career: the post of apostolic secretary to the sinister, sly, and ruthless Baldassare Cossa, who had been elected pope.

CHAPTER SEVEN

A PIT TO
CATCH FOXES

To SERVE AS the pope's apostolic secretary was the pinnacle of curial ambition: though he was only in his early thirties, Poggio's skills had taken him from nothing to the top of the heap. And the heap at this moment was swarming with diplomatic maneuvers, complex business transactions, rumors of invasion, heresy hunts, threats, feints, and double-dealing, for Baldassare Cossa—Pope John XXIII, as he called himself—was a master of intrigue. Poggio would have been involved in controlling access to the pontiff, digesting and passing along key information, taking notes, articulating policies that had only been roughly sketched, crafting the Latin missives sent to princes and potentates. He was necessarily privy to secrets and to strategies, for the apostolic secretary had to be initiated into his master's plans for dealing with the two rival claimants to the papal throne, with a Holy Roman Emperor determined to end the schism, with heretics in Bohemia, with neighboring powers poised to seize territories controlled by the Church. The sheer quantity of work on Poggio's desk must have been enormous.

Yet during this period Poggio found the time to copy in his beautiful handwriting the three long books of Cicero's *On the Laws* (*De legibus*), along with his oration on Lucullus. (The man-

uscript is in the Vatican Library: Cod. Vatican. lat. 3245.) Somehow then he managed to hold on at least to moments of what he
called his freedom. But that freedom—the plunging back into
the ancient past—appears always to have heightened his alien-
ation from the present. To be sure, his love for classical Latin
did not lead him to idealize, as some of his contemporaries did,
ancient Roman history: Poggio understood that history to have
had its full measure of human folly and wickedness. But he was
aware that the city in which he lived was a pathetic shadow of
its past glory.

The population of Rome, a small fragment of what it had
once been, lived in detached settlements, one at the Capitol
where the massive ancient Temple of Jupiter had once stood,
another near the Lateran whose old imperial palace had been
given by Constantine to the bishop of Rome, yet another around
the crumbling fourth-century Basilica of St. Peter's. Between
these settlements spread a wasteland of ruins, hovels, rubble-
strewn fields, and the shrines of martyrs. Sheep grazed in the
Forum. Armed thugs, some in the pay of powerful families, others operating on their own, swaggered through dirty streets,
and bandits lurked outside the walls. There was virtually no
industry, very little trade, no thriving class of skilled artisans or
burghers, no civic pride, and no prospect of civic freedom. One
of the only spheres of serious enterprise was the trade in digging out the metal clasps that had knitted the ancient buildings
together and in peeling off the thin sheets of marble veneer so
that they could be reused in churches and palaces.

Though most of Poggio's writings come from later in his
career, there is no indication that he ever felt anything other
than a kind of soul-sickness at the contemporary world in which
he was immersed. His career triumph in the pontificate of John
XXIII must have given him some pleasure, but it only intensified this immersion and hence intensified both the soul-sickness

and the fantasy of an escape. Like Petrarch before him, Poggio cultivated an archaeologist's sense of what had once existed, so that vacant spaces and the jumble of contemporary Rome were haunted by the past. "The hill of the Capitol, on which we sit," he wrote, "was formerly the head of the Roman empire, the citadel of the earth, the terror of kings; illustrated by the footsteps of so many triumphs, enriched with the spoils and tributes of so many nations." Now just look at it:

> This spectacle of the world, how is it fallen! How changed! How defaced! The path of victory is obliterated by vines, and the benches of the senators are concealed by a dunghill. . . . The forum of the Roman people, where they assembled to enact their laws and elect magistrates, is now inclosed for the cultivation of pot-herbs or thrown open for the reception of swine and buffaloes.

The relics of the fallen greatness only made the experience of the present more melancholy. In the company of his humanist friends, Poggio could try to conjure up what it all must once have looked like: "Cast your eyes on the Palatine hill, and seek, among the shapeless and enormous fragments, the marble theatre, the obelisks, the colossal statues, the porticoes of Nero's palace." But it was to the shattered present that, after his brief imaginary excursions into antiquity, the papal bureaucrat always had to return.

That present, in the turbulent years that Rome was ruled by John XXIII, must have threatened not only to extinguish the occasional "freedom" Poggio prized but also to drag him into cynicism so deep that there could be no escape. For the question with which Poggio and others in Rome grappled was how they could retain even the shreds of a moral sensibility while living and working in the court of this particular pope. A decade older than his apostolic secretary Poggio, Baldassare Cossa had been born on the small volcanic island of Procida, near Naples. His noble family held the island as its personal possession, the hidden coves and well-defended fortress evidently well suited to the principal family occupation, piracy. The occupation was a dangerous one: two of his brothers were eventually captured and condemned to death. Their sentence was commuted, after much pulling of strings, to imprisonment. It was said by his enemies that the young Cossa participated in the family business, owed to it his lifelong habit of wakefulness at night, and learned from it his basic assumptions about the world.

Procida was far too small a stage for Baldassare's talents. Energetic and astute, he early displayed an interest in what we might call higher forms of piracy. He studied jurisprudence at the University of Bologna—in Italy it was legal studies rather than theology that best prepared one for a career in the Church—where he obtained doctorates in both civil and canon law. At his graduation ceremony, a colorful affair in which the successful candidate was conducted in triumph through the town, Cossa was asked what he was going to do now. He answered, "To be Pope."

Cossa began his career, as Poggio did, in the court of his fellow Neapolitan Boniface IX, whom he served as private chamberlain. In this capacity he helped to oversee the open sale of Church offices and the feverish market in indulgences. He also helped to organize the hugely profitable jubilee when pilgrims to Rome's principal churches were granted a plenary indulgence, that is, a remission of the horrible pain of purgatorial fires in the afterlife. The massive crowds filled the city's inns, patronized the taverns and brothels, filed across the narrow bridges, prayed at the sacred shrines, lit candles, gawked at wonder-working pictures and statues, and returned home with talismanic souvenirs.

The original idea was that there would be a jubilee once every hundred years, but the demand was so great and the consequent profits so enormous that the interval was shortened first to fifty years, then thirty-three, and then twenty-five. In 1400, shortly before Poggio arrived on the scene, the huge numbers of pilgrims drawn to Rome by the dawning of a new century led the pope to issue a plenary indulgence, though only a decade had passed since the last jubilee. To enhance its profits, the Church came up with a variety of offers that may reflect Cossa's practical intelligence. Hence, for example, people who desired the spiritual benefits conferred by the pilgrimage to Rome—exemption from thousands of years of postmortem torments in Purgatory—but who wanted to avoid the difficult journey over the Alps could obtain the same indulgences by visiting certain shrines in Germany, provided that they paid what the longer trip would have cost.

Cossa's gifts were not limited to clever marketing schemes. Appointed governor of Bologna, he proved himself to be a highly successful civil and military commander, as well as a vigorous orator. He was in many ways the embodiment of those qualities—astute intelligence, eloquence, boldness in action, ambition, sensuality, limitless energy—that together form the ideal of the Renaissance man. But even for an age accustomed to a gap between religious professions and lived realities, the cardinal deacon of Bologna, as Cossa was called, seemed an unusual figure to be wearing clerical vestments. Though he was, as Poggio's friend Bruni remarked, a hugely gifted man of the world, it was obvious that he did not have a trace of a spiritual vocation.

This widespread perception of his character helps account for the peculiar blend of admiration, fear, and suspicion that he aroused and that led people to believe that he was capable of anything. When on May 4, 1410, Pope Alexander V died immediately after a visit to Bologna for a dinner with his friend the cardinal deacon, it was widely rumored that he had been poisoned. The suspicions did not prevent Cossa's faction of fellow cardinals from electing him to succeed Alexander as pope. Perhaps they were simply frightened. Or perhaps it seemed to them that Cossa, only forty years old, had the skills needed to end the disgraceful schism in the Church and to defeat the rival claims by the doggedly inflexible Spaniard Pedro de Luna, who styled himself Pope Benedict XIII, and the intransigent Venetian Angelo Correr, who styled himself Pope Gregory XII.

If this was the cardinals' hope, they were soon disappointed, but they could not have been altogether surprised. The schism had already lasted more than thirty years and had eluded all attempts at resolution. Each of the claimants had excommunicated the followers of the others and had called down divine vengeance upon them. Each combined attempts to seize the moral high ground with thuggish tactics. Each had powerful allies but also strategic weaknesses that made achieving unity through military conquest impossible. Everyone understood that the situation was intolerable. The competing national factions—the Spanish, French, and Italians each backing a different candidate—undermined the claim to the existence of a catholic, that is, universal, church. The spectacle of multiple squabbling popes called the whole institution into question. The situation was embarrassing, distasteful, dangerous. But who could solve it?

Fifteen years earlier, the theologians at the University of Paris had placed a large chest in the cloister of the Mathurins and asked anyone who had any idea how to end the schism to write it down and drop it in the slot that had been cut in the lid. More than ten thousand notes were deposited. Fifty-five professors, assigned to read through the notes, reported that three principal methods had been proposed. The first, the so-called "Way of Cession," required the simultaneous abdication of those who claimed to be pope, followed by the proper election of a single candidate; the second, the "Way of Compromise," envisaged arbitration at the end of which one of the existing claimants would emerge as the sole pope; the third, the "Way of Council," called for the convening of the bishops of all of the Catholic world who would, by formal vote in an ecumenical assembly, have the final authority to resolve the dispute.

The first two methods had the advantage of being relatively simple, cost-effective, and straightforward; however, they had, like military conquest, the disadvantage of being impossible. Calls for simultaneous abdication met with the predictable results, and attempts to set the preconditions for arbitration inevitably broke down into hopeless squabbling. That left the option of the "Way of Council," strongly supported by the Holy Roman Emperor-elect, King Sigismund of Hungary, who was at least nominally allied to Cossa's faction in Rome.

Surrounded by his cardinals and secretaries, in the massive pagan mausoleum that had been converted into the fortified Castel St. Angelo, the wily pope could see no reason to accede to pressure to convene an ecumenical assembly. Such an assembly, which would inevitably unleash long-standing hostility to Rome, could only threaten his position. So he temporized and delayed, busying himself with making and unmaking alliances, with maneuvering against his ambitious enemy to the south, Ladislas, king of Naples, and with filling the papal coffers. After all, there were innumerable petitions to be considered, bulls to be issued, the papal states to defend, administer, and tax, Church offices and indulgences to be sold. Poggio and the other secretaries, scriptors, abbreviators, and minor court bureaucrats were kept very busy.

The stalemate might have continued indefinitely—that, in any case, is what the pope must have hoped for—had it not been for an unexpected turn of events. In June 1413, Ladislas's army suddenly broke through Rome's defenses and sacked the city, robbing houses, pillaging shrines, breaking into palaces and carting off treasures. The pope and his court escaped to Florence, where they could count on some limited protection: the Florentines and the Neapolitans were enemies. But to survive as pope, Cossa now absolutely needed the support of Sigismund—then residing in Como—and urgent negotiations made clear that this support would only come if the pope agreed to convoke a general council.

His back to the wall, Cossa proposed that the council be held in Italy, where he could marshal his principal allies, but the emperor objected that the long journey across the Alps would be too difficult for the more elderly bishops. The council, he declared, should be in Constance, a city in his territory, nestled in the mountains between Switzerland and Germany on the shores of the Bodensee. Though the location was hardly to the pope's liking, by the fall of 1413 his agents—*exploratores*—were in Constance, inquiring about lodging and provisions, and by the following summer the pope and his court were on the move, as were powerful churchmen and their servants from everywhere in Europe, all converging on the one small South German town.

A citizen of Constance, Ulrich Richental, was fascinated enough by what was going on around him to write a circumstantial chronicle of the events. From Richental we learn that the pope traveled over the Alps with an enormous retinue, some six hundred men. From other sources, we know that among this group (or shortly to join them) were the greatest humanists of the time: Poggio Bracciolini, Leonardo Bruni, Pier Paolo Vergerio, Cencio Rustici, Bartolomeo Aragazzi da Montepulciano, Zomino (Sozomeno) da Pistoia, Benedetto da Piglio, Biagio Guasconi, Cardinals Francesco Zabarella, Alamano Adimari, Branda da Castiglione, the archbishop of Milan

Bartolomeo della Capra, and his future successor Francesco Pizzolpasso. The pope was a thug, but he was a learned thug, who appreciated the company of fine scholars and expected court business to be conducted in high humanist style.

The trip across the mountains was never easy, even in late summer. At one point the pope's carriage tipped over, dumping him in the snow. When, in October 1414, he looked down at Constance and its lake ringed by mountains, he turned to his train—among whom, of course, was Poggio—and said, "This is the pit where they catch foxes."

If he had only the competing factions within the Italian church to deal with, Cossa would probably have been confident that he could evade the fox trap; after all, he had for several years prevailed, or at least managed to maintain his hold upon the papal throne in Rome. The problem was that others, many from beyond the reach of his patronage or his poisons, were streaming into Constance from all over Christendom: some thirty cardinals, three patriarchs, thirty-three archbishops, one hundred abbots, fifty provosts (ecclesiastical officials), three hundred doctors of theology, five thousand monks and friars, and about eighteen thousand priests. In addition to the emperor and his large retinue, there were also, by invitation, many other secular rulers and their representatives: the electors Ludwig von der Pfalz and Rudolph of Saxony, the dukes of Bavaria, Austria, Saxony, Schleswig, Mecklenburg, Lorraine, and Teck, the margrave of Brandenburg, the ambassadors of the kings of France, England, Scotland, Denmark, Poland, Naples, and the Spanish realms, along with a vast array of lesser nobles, barons, knights, lawyers, professors, and public officials. Each of these in turn had small armies of retainers, guards, servants, cooks, and the like, and the whole assembly attracted hordes of sight-seers, merchants, mountebanks, jewelers, tailors, shoemakers, apothecaries, furriers, grocers, barbers, scribes, jugglers, acro-bats, street singers, and hangers-on of all types. The chronicler Richental estimates that over seven hundred whores came to town and hired their own houses, plus "some who lay in stables and wherever they could, beside the private ones whom I could not count."

The arrival of somewhere between 50,000 and 150,000 visitors put a huge strain on Constance and invited every kind of abuse. Officials tried to combat crime in the usual way—staging public executions—and set rules for the range and quality of services that visitors should expect: so, for example, "Every fourteen days the tablecloths and sheets and whatever needed washing should be changed for clean." Food for the visitors (and their 30,000 horses) was a constant concern, but the area was well stocked, and the rivers made it possible to renew supplies. Bakers with movable carts went through the streets with little ovens in which they baked rolls, pretzels, and pastries stuffed with spiced chicken and other meats. In inns and makeshift food stalls set up in booths and tents, cooks prepared the usual range of meats and fowl, along with thrush, blackbirds, wild boar, roe venison, badger, otter, beaver, and hare. For those who preferred fish, there were eels, pike, sturgeon, garfish, bream, whitefish, gudgeons, catfish, bullheads, dace, salt cod, and herring. "There were also frogs and snails for sale," Richental adds with distaste, "which the Italians bought."

Once he and his own court had been provided for in suitable style, the practical arrangements were the least of Cossa's concerns. Against his wishes, the council determined to organize itself and conduct its votes by blocs or "nations"—Italians, French, Germans, Spanish, and English—an arrangement that diminished his own special position and the influence of his core supporters. With his power rapidly melting away he took care to insist on his prestige. If he could hardly claim any moral high ground, he could at least establish his ceremonial significance. He needed to show the whole enormous assembly that he was no mere Neapolitan fox; he was the Vicar of Christ, the embodiment of spiritual radiance and worldly grandeur.

Clad in white vestments and a white miter, on October 28, 1414, Baldassare Cossa made his entry into Constance on a white horse. Four burghers of the town carried a golden canopy over his head. Two counts, one Roman and the other German, walked by his side, holding his bridle. Behind them rode a man on a great horse from whose saddle rose a long staff bearing a huge umbrella—Richental mistook it for a hat—made of red and gold cloth. The umbrella, broad enough to spread over three horses, was topped by a golden knob on which stood a golden angel holding a cross. Behind the umbrella came nine cardinals on horseback, all in long, red mantles, with red hoods, and all wearing wide red hats. Other clerics and the staff of the curia, including Poggio, followed, along with attendants and servants. And at the front of the procession stretched a line of nine white horses, covered with red saddlecloths. Eight of these were laden with garments—the pope's wardrobe was evidence of his hold upon his sacred identity—and the ninth, a little bell jingling on its head, bore on its back a casket of silvergilt covered with a red cloth to which were attached two silver candlesticks with burning candles. Within the casket, at once jewel box and tomb, was the Holy Sacrament, the blood and body of Christ. John XXIII had arrived.

Ending the schism was the council's most important item of business, but it was not the only one. Two other major issues were the reform of ecclesiastical government—that was also not happy news for John XXIII—and the repression of heresy. The latter held out some promise for the cornered fox, almost the only tactical weapon he could find. The correspondence that the secretaries copied out for their pope attempted to turn the focus away from the schism and from papal corruption and toward someone whose name Poggio must have begun to write in official documents again and again.

Forty-four-year-old Jan Hus, a Czech priest and religious reformer, had been for some years a thorn in the side of the Church. From his pulpit and in his writings, he vehemently attacked the abuses of clerics, condemning their widespread greed, hypocrisy, and sexual immorality. He denounced the selling of indulgences as a racket, a shameless attempt to profit from the fears of the faithful. He urged his congregants not to put their faith in the Virgin, the cult of the saints, the Church, or the pope, but in God alone. In all matters of doctrine he preached that Holy Scripture was the ultimate authority.

Hus boldly meddled not with doctrine alone but with the politics of the Church at a moment of growing national restiveness. He argued that the state had the right and the duty to supervise the Church. Laymen could and should judge their spiritual leaders. (It is better, he said, to be a good Christian than a wicked pope or prelate.) An immoral pope could not possibly claim infallibility. After all, he said, the papacy was a human institution—the word "pope" was nowhere in the Bible. Moral probity was the test of a true priest: "If he is manifestly sinful, then it should be supposed, from his works, that he is not just, but the enemy of Christ." And such an enemy should be stripped of his office.

It is easy to see why Hus had been excommunicated for his teachings in 1410 and why the Church dignitaries who gathered in Constance were exercised about his refusal to submit. Protected by powerful Bohemian noblemen, he continued to disseminate dangerous views, views that threatened to spread. And one can see as well why Cossa, his back to the wall, thought that it might be advantageous to shift the council's focus to Hus, and not only as a convenient distraction. For the Bohemian, feared and hated by the Church establishment, was articulating as a principle precisely what Cossa's enemies in that same establishment were proposing to do: to disobey and depose a pope accused of corruption. Perhaps this uneasy mirroring helps to explain a strange charge that was circulated in Constance about Hus: that he was an extraordinary magician who could read the thoughts of all who approached him within a certain distance.

Hus, who had repeatedly asked for the opportunity to explain himself before a Church council, had been formally invited to present his views in person before the prelates, theologians, and rulers at Constance. The Czech reformer had the visionary's luminous confidence that his truths, should he only be allowed to articulate them clearly, would sweep away the cobwebs of ignorance and bad faith.

As someone who had been charged with heresy, he was also understandably wary. Hus had recently seen three young men, two of whom were his students, beheaded by the authorities. Before he left the relative safety of his protectors in Bohemia, he applied for and received a certificate of orthodoxy from the grand inquisitor of the diocese of Prague, and he received as well a guarantee of free passage from the emperor Sigismund. The safe-conduct, bearing the large imperial seal, promised "protection and safeguard" and requested that Hus be allowed "freely and securely" to "pass, sojourn, stop, and return." The Bohemian nobles who accompanied him rode ahead to meet with the pope and ask whether Hus would be allowed to remain in Constance free from the risk of violence. "Had he killed my own brother," John replied, "not a hair of his head should be touched while he remained in the city." With these assurances, not long after the grand arrival of the beleaguered pope, the reformer reached Constance.

Hus's arrival on November 3 must have seemed a godsend, as it were, to John XXIII. The heretic was hated by the upright in the Church as well as by the crooked. He and his principal associate, Jerome of Prague, were known followers of the English heretic John Wycliffe, whose advocacy of vernacular translations of the Bible, insistence on the primacy of Scripture-based faith over works, and attacks on clerical wealth and the selling of indulgences had led to his condemnation in the previous century. Wycliffe had died in his bed, much to the disappointment of his ecclesiastical enemies, but the council now ordered that his remains be dug up and cast out of consecrated ground. It was not an auspicious sign for their reception of Jan Hus.

Notwithstanding the assurances that the pope, the council, and the emperor had given him, Hus was almost immediately vilified and denied the opportunity to speak in public. On November 28, barely three weeks after he arrived, he was arrested on order of the cardinals and taken to the prison of a Dominican monastery on the banks of the Rhine. There he was thrown into an underground cell through which all the filth of the monastery was discharged. When he fell seriously ill, he asked that an advocate be appointed to defend his cause, but he was told that, according to canon law, no one could plead the cause of a man charged with heresy. In the face of protests from Hus and his Bohemian supporters about the apparent violation of his safe-conduct, the emperor chose not to intervene. He was, it was said, uncomfortable about what seemed a violation of his word, but an English cardinal had reportedly reassured him that "no faith need be kept with heretics."

If Cossa thought that the persecution of Hus would distract the council from its determination to end the schism or silence his own enemies, he was sorely mistaken. As the mood in the papal court turned grim, the pope continued to stage extravagant public displays. Richental describes the spectacles:

> When the Pope was to give his blessing, a bishop in a
> mitre came first into the balcony, carrying a cross, and

behind the cross came two bishops in white mitres, carrying two tall burning candles in their hands and set the candles burning in the window. Then came four cardinals, also in white mitres, or sometimes six, or at other times less. Sometimes also our lord King came into the balcony. The cardinals and the King stood in the windows. After them came Our Holy Father the Pope, wearing the most costly priest's robes and a white mitre on his head. Under the vestments as for Mass he wore one more robe than a priest and had gloves on his hands and a large ring, set with a rare great stone, on the middle finger of his right hand. He stood in the central window, so that everyone saw him. Then came his singers, all with burning candles so that the balcony shone as if it were on fire, and they took their places behind him. And a bishop went up to him and took off his mitre. Thereupon the Pope began to chant. . . .

But what was going on away from the gawking public was more and more disquieting. Though he continued to preside over the council meetings, the pope had lost control of the agenda, and it was clear that the emperor Sigismund, who had arrived in Constance on December 25, was not inclined to save him.

Cossa still had allies. At a session of the council on March 11, 1415, discussing how they might obtain a single pope for the whole Church, the archbishop of Mainz stood up and said that he would never obey anyone but John XXIII. But there was no chorus of support, of the kind he must have hoped to trigger. Instead, the patriarch of Constantinople exclaimed, *"Quis est iste ipse? Dignus est comburendus!*—Who is that fellow? He deserves to be burned!"* The archbishop walked out, and the session broke up.

The fox saw that the trap was about to be sprung. Constance, he said, was not safe. He no longer felt secure. He wanted to move the council to some place more suitable. The king demurred, and the town council of Constance hastened to offer reassurance: "If His Holiness had not sufficient security," the burghers declared, "they would give him more and guard him against all the world, even though a disastrous fate should compel them to eat their own children." Cossa, who had made comparably extravagant promises to Jan Hus, was evidently not appeased. On March 20, 1415, at approximately 1 p.m., he fled. Wearing a gray cape with a gray cowl wrapped around him so that no one could see his face, he rode quietly through the town gates. Next to him rode a crossbowman, along with two other men, both muffled up. In the evening and all through the night, the pope's adherents—his servants and attendants and secretaries—left town as stealthily as they could. But the word quickly spread. John XXIII was gone.

In the following weeks Cossa's enemies, who tracked the fugitive to Schaffhausen where he had fled to an ally's castle, drew up a bill of indictment against him. As menacing rumors circulated and his remaining allies started to crumble, he fled again, this time too in disguise, and his court—among whom, presumably, was his apostolic secretary, Poggio—was thrown into further confusion: "The members of the Curia all followed him in haste and wild disorder," one of the contemporary chroniclers puts it; "for the Pope was in flight and the rest in flight too, by night, though with no pursuers." Finally, under great pressure from the emperor, Cossa's principal protector gave over his unwelcome guest, and the world had the edifying spectacle of a pope put under guard as a criminal.

Seventy charges were formally read out against him. Fearing their effect on public opinion, the council decided to suppress the sixteen most scandalous charges—never subsequently revealed—and accused the pontiff only of simony, sodomy, rape, incest, torture, and murder. He was charged with poisoning his predecessor, along with his physician and others. Worst of all—at least among the charges that were made public—was one that his accusers dredged up from the ancient struggle against Epicureanism: the pope was said to have maintained stubbornly, before reputable persons, that there was no future life or resurrection, and that the souls of men perish with their bodies, like brutes.

On May 29, 1415, he was formally deposed. Stricken from the roster of official popes, the name John XXIII was once again available, though it took more than five hundred years for another pope—the remarkable Angelo Roncalli—to be courageous enough in 1958 to adopt the name for himself.

Shortly after the deposition, Cossa was briefly imprisoned in Gottlieben Castle on the Rhine, where Hus, near starvation, had been chained in irons for more than two months. It is not known whether the pope and the heretic, so implausibly united in abject misery, were brought together by their captors. At this point, if Poggio was still with his master—and the record does not make that clear—he would have parted from him for the last time. All of the former pope's attendants were dismissed, and the prisoner, soon transferred to another place of confinement, was henceforward surrounded by German-speaking guards with whom he could only communicate in sign language. Effectively cut off from the world, he occupied himself by writing verses on the transitory nature of all earthly things.

The pope's men were suddenly masterless. Some scrambled quickly to find employment with one or another of the prelates and princes in Constance. But Poggio remained unemployed, a bystander to events in which he was no longer a party. He stayed on in Constance, but we do not know if he was present when Hus was finally brought before the council—the moment the reformer had longed for and upon which he had staked his life—only to be mocked and shouted down when he attempted to speak. On July 6, 1415, at a solemn ceremony in the cathedral of Constance, the convicted heretic was formally unfrocked. A round paper crown, almost eighteen inches high and depicting three devils seizing a soul and tearing it apart, was placed upon his head. He was led out of the cathedral past a pyre on which his books were in flames, shackled in chains, and burned at the stake. In order to ensure that there would be no material remains, the executioners broke his charred bones into pieces and threw them all into the Rhine.

There is no direct record of what Poggio personally thought of these events in which he had played his small part, the part of a bureaucrat who helps the ongoing functioning of a system that he understands is vicious and hopelessly corrupt. It would have been dangerous for him to speak out, even had he been inclined to do so, and he was, after all, in the service of the papacy whose power Hus was challenging. (A century later, Luther, mounting a more successful challenge, remarked: "We are all Hussites without knowing it.") But when, some months later, Hus's associate, Jerome of Prague, was also put on trial for heresy, Poggio was not able to remain silent.

A committed religious reformer with degrees from the universities of Paris, Oxford, and Heidelberg, Jerome was a famous orator whose testimony on May 26, 1416, made a powerful impression on Poggio. "I must confess," he wrote to his friend Leonardo Bruni, "that I never saw any one who in pleading a cause, especially a cause on the issue of which his own life depended, approached nearer to that standard of ancient eloquence, which we so much admire." Poggio was clearly aware that he was treading on dangerous ground, but the papal bureaucrat could not entirely restrain the humanist's passionate admiration:

> It was astonishing to witness with what choice of words,
> with what closeness of argument, with what confidence

of countenance he replied to his adversaries. So impressive was his peroration, that it is a subject of great concern, that a man of so noble and excellent a genius should have deviated into heresy. On this latter point, however, I cannot help entertaining some doubts. But far be it from me to take upon myself to decide in so important a matter. I shall acquiesce in the opinion of those who are wiser than myself.

This prudent acquiescence did not altogether reassure Bruni. "I must advise you henceforth," he told Poggio in reply, "to write upon such subjects in a more guarded manner."

What had happened to lead Poggio, ordinarily careful not to court real danger, to write so unguardedly to his friend? In part, the rashness might have been provoked by the trauma of what he had just seen: his letter is dated May 30, 1416, which is the day that Jerome was executed. Poggio was writing in the wake of witnessing something particularly horrible, as we know from the chronicler Richental who also recorded what happened. As the thirty-seven-year-old Jerome was led out of the city, to the spot where Hus was burned and where he too would meet his end, he repeated the creed and sang the litany. As had happened with Hus, no one would hear his confession; that sacrament was not granted to a heretic. When the fire was lit, Hus cried out and died quickly, but the same fate, according to Richental, was not granted to Jerome: "He lived much longer in the fire than Hus and shrieked terribly, for he was a stouter, stronger man, with a broad, thick, black beard." Perhaps these terrible shrieks explain why Poggio could not any longer remain discreetly silent, why he felt compelled to testify to Jerome's eloquence.

Shortly before he was so unnerved by Jerome's trial and execution, hoping to cure the rheumatism in his hands (a serious concern for a scribe), Poggio decided to visit the celebrated medicinal baths at Baden. It was not an altogether easy trip from Constance: first twenty-four miles on the Rhine by boat to Schaffhausen, where the pope had fled; then, because the river descended steeply at that point over cliffs and rocks, ten miles on foot to a castle called Kaiserstuhl. From this spot, Poggio saw the Rhine cascading in a waterfall, and the loud sound made him think of classical descriptions of the fall of the Nile.

At the bathhouse in Baden, Poggio was amazed by what he saw: "Old women as well as younger ones," he wrote to a friend in Florence, "going naked into the water before the eyes of men and displaying their private parts and their buttocks to the onlookers." There was a sort of lattice between the men's and women's baths, but the separation was minimal: there were, he observed, "many low windows, through which the bathers can drink together and talk and see both ways and touch each other as is their usual custom."

Poggio refused to enter the baths himself, not, he insisted, from any undue modesty but because "it seemed to me ridiculous that a man from Italy, ignorant of their language, should sit in the water with a lot of women, completely speechless." But he watched from the gallery that ran above the baths and described what he saw with the amazement that someone from Saudi Arabia might bring to an account of the beach scene at Nice.

There were, he observed, bathing suits of some sort, but they concealed very little: "The men wear nothing but a leather apron, and the women put on linen shifts down to their knees, so cut on either side that they leave uncovered neck, bosom, arms, and shoulders." What would cause a crisis in Poggio's Italy and perhaps trigger violence seemed simply to be taken for granted in Baden: "Men watched their wives being handled by strangers and were not disturbed by it; they paid no attention and took it all in the best possible spirit." They would have been at home in Plato's Republic, he laughed, "where all property was held in common."

The rituals of social life at Baden seemed dreamlike to Poggio, as if they were conjuring up the vanished world of Jove and Danae. In some of the pools, there was singing and dancing, and some of the girls—"good looking and well-born and in manner and form like a goddess"—floated on the water while the music was playing: "They draw their clothes slightly behind them, floating along the top of the water, until you might think they were winged Venuses." When men gaze down at them, Poggio explains, the girls have a custom to ask playfully for something. The men throw down pennies, especially to the prettiest, along with wreaths of flowers, and the girls catch them sometimes in their hands, sometimes in their clothes, which they spread wider. "I often threw pennies and garlands," Poggio confessed.

Confident, easy in themselves, and contented, these are people "for whom life is based on fun, who come together here so that they may enjoy the things for which they hunger." There are almost a thousand of them at the baths, many drinking heavily, Poggio wrote, and yet there is no quarreling, bickering, or cursing. In the simple, playfully unselfconscious behavior before him, Poggio felt he was witnessing forms of pleasures and contentment that his culture had lost:

> We are terrified of future catastrophes and are thrown into a continuous state of misery and anxiety, and for fear of becoming miserable, we never cease to be so, always panting for riches and never giving our souls or

our bodies a moment's peace. But those who are content with little live day by day and treat any day like a
feast day.

He is describing the scenes at the baths, he tells his friend, "so
that you may understand from a few examples what a great
center of the Epicurean way of thinking this is."

With his contrasting vision of anxious, work-obsessed,
overly disciplined Italians and happy-go-lucky, carefree Germans, Poggio believed he glimpsed for a moment the Epicurean pursuit of pleasure as the highest good. He knew perfectly
well that this pursuit ran counter to Christian orthodoxy. But
in Baden it was as if he found himself on the threshold of a mental world in which Christian rules no longer applied.

In his reading, Poggio had frequently stood on that threshold. He never ceased to occupy himself with the pursuit of lost
classical texts. Judging from a remark by Niccoli, he spent some
of his time in Constance looking through library collections—
there in the monastery of St. Mark he evidently found a copy
of an ancient commentary on Virgil. In the early summer of
1415, probably just after his master had been formally deposed
and he found himself definitively out of work, he made his way
to Cluny, in France, where he found a codex with seven orations by Cicero, two of which had been unknown. He sent this
precious manuscript to his friends in Florence and also made a
copy in his own hand, inscribed with a remark deeply revealing
of his mood:

> These seven orations by Marcus Tullius had through
> the fault of the times been lost to Italy. By repeated
> searches through the libraries of France and Germany,
> with the greatest diligence and care, Poggio the Floren-
> tine all alone brought them out of the sordid squalor in

which they were hidden and back into the light, returning them to their pristine dignity and order and restor-
ing them to the Latin muses.

When he wrote these words, the world around Poggio was falling to pieces, but his response to chaos and fear was always to
redouble his immersion in books. In the charmed circle of his
bibliomania, he could rescue the imperiled legacy of the glorious past from the barbarians and return it to the rightful heirs.

A year later, in the summer of 1416, in the wake of the execution of Jerome of Prague and shortly after the interlude at
Baden, Poggio was once again out book-hunting, this time
accompanied by two other Italian friends on a visit to the
monastery of St. Gall, about twenty miles from Constance. It
was not the architectural features of the great medieval abbey
that drew the visitors; it was a library of which Poggio and his
friends had heard extravagant rumors. They were not disappointed: a few months later Poggio wrote a triumphant letter
to another friend back in Italy, announcing that he had located
an astonishing cache of ancient books. The capstone of these
was the complete text of Quintilian's *Institutes*, the most important ancient Roman handbook on oratory and rhetoric. This
work had been known to Poggio and his circle only in fragmen-
tary form. To recover the whole of it seemed to them wildly
exciting—"Oh wondrous treasure! Oh unexpected joy!" one
of them exclaimed—because it gave them back a whole lost
world, a world of public persuasion.

It was the dream of persuading an audience through the eloquence and conviction of public words that had drawn Hus and
Jerome of Prague to Constance. If Hus had been shouted down,
Jerome, dragged from the miserable dungeon where he had
been chained for 350 days, managed at least to make himself
heard. For a modern reader, there is something almost absurd

about Poggio's admiration for Jerome's "choice of words" and the effectiveness of his "peroration"—as if the quality of the prisoner's Latin were the issue; but it was precisely the quality of the prisoner's Latin that unsettled Poggio and made him doubt the validity of the charges against the heretic. For he could not, at least at this strange moment of limbo, disguise from himself the tension between the bureaucrat who worked for the sinister John XXIII and the humanist who longed for the freer, clearer air, as he imagined it, of the ancient Roman Republic. Poggio could find no real way to resolve this tension; instead, he plunged into the monastic library with its neglected treasures.

"There is no question," Poggio wrote, "that this glorious man, so elegant, so pure, so full of morals and wit, could not much longer have endured the filth of that prison, the squalor of the place, and the savage cruelty of his keepers." These words were not a further lapse into the kind of imprudent admiration of the eloquent, doomed Jerome that alarmed Leonardo Bruni; they are Poggio's description of the manuscript of Quintilian that he found at St. Gall:

> He was sad and dressed in mourning, as people are when doomed to death; his beard was dirty and his hair caked with mud, so that by his expression and appearance it was clear that he had been summoned to an undeserved punishment. He seemed to stretch out his hands and beg for the loyalty of the Roman people, to demand that he be saved from an unjust sentence.

The scene he had witnessed in May appears still vivid in the humanist's imagination as he searched through the monastery's books. Jerome had protested that he had been kept "in filth and fetters, deprived of every comfort"; Quintilian was found "filthy with mold and dust." Jerome had been confined, Poggio wrote to Leonardo Aretino, "in a dark dungeon, where it was impossible for him to read"; Quintilian, he indignantly wrote of the manuscript in the monastic library, was "in a sort of foul and gloomy dungeon . . . where not even men convicted of a capital offense would have been stuck away." "A man worthy of eternal remembrance!" So Poggio rashly exclaimed about the heretic Jerome whom he could not lift a finger to save. A few months later in the monastery of St. Gall, he rescued another man worthy of eternal remembrance from the barbarians' prison house.

It is not clear how conscious the link was in Poggio's mind between the imprisoned heretic and the imprisoned text. At once morally alert and deeply compromised in his professional life, he responded to books as if they were living, suffering human beings. "By Heaven," he wrote of the Quintilian manuscript, "if we had not brought help, he would surely have perished the very next day." Taking no chances, Poggio sat down and began copying the whole lengthy work in his beautiful hand. It took him fifty-four days to complete the task. "The one and only light of the Roman name, except for whom there was no one but Cicero and he likewise cut into pieces and scattered," he wrote to Guarino of Verona, "has through our efforts been called back not only from exile but from almost complete destruction."

The expedition to the monastery was expensive, and Poggio was perennially short of money: such was the consequence of his decision not to take the profitable route of priesthood. Back in Constance his money worries deepened, as he found himself dangling, without work and without clear prospects. His deposed master, Baldassare Cossa, was desperately negotiating a quiet retirement for himself. After spending three years in prison, he eventually bought his release and was made a cardinal in Florence, where he died in 1419, his elegant tomb by Donatello erected in the baptistery of the Duomo. Another pope Poggio had earlier worked for, the deposed Gregory XII, died during this same period. The last thing he said was "I have not understood the world, and the world has not understood me."

It was high time for a prudent, highly trained bureaucrat, almost forty years old, to look out for himself and find some stable means of support. But Poggio did nothing of the kind. Instead, a few months after his return from St. Gall, he left Constance again, this time apparently without companions. His craving to discover and to liberate whatever noble beings were hidden in the prison house had evidently only intensified. He had no idea what he would find; he only knew that if it was something ancient and written in elegant Latin, then it was worth rescuing at all costs. The ignorant, indolent monks, he was convinced, were locking away traces of a civilization far greater than anything the world had known for more than a thousand years.

Of course, all Poggio could hope to find were pieces of parchment, and not even very ancient ones. But for him these were not manuscripts but human voices. What emerged from the obscurity of the library was not a link in a long chain of texts, one copied from the other, but rather the thing itself, wearing borrowed garments, or even the author himself, wrapped in gravecloths and stumbling into the light.

"We accept Aesculapius as belonging among the gods because he called back Hippolytus, as well as others from the underworld," Francesco Barbaro wrote to Poggio after hearing of his discoveries;

> If people, nations, and provinces have dedicated shrines
> to him, what might I think ought to be done for you, if
> that custom had not already been forgotten? You have

revived so many illustrious men and such wise men,
who were dead for eternity, through whose minds and
teachings not only we but our descendants will be able
to live well and honourably.

Books that had fallen out of circulation and were sitting in
German libraries were thus transformed into wise men who
had died and whose souls had been imprisoned in the underworld; Poggio, the cynical papal secretary in the service of the
famously corrupt pope, was viewed by his friends as a culture
hero, a magical healer who reassembled and reanimated the
torn and mangled body of antiquity.

Thus it was that in January 1417, Poggio found himself once
again in a monastic library, probably Fulda. There he took from
the shelf a long poem whose author he may have recalled seeing mentioned in Quintilian or in the chronicle compiled by St.
Jerome: *T. LUCRETI CARI DE RERUM NATURA.*

CHAPTER EIGHT

THE WAY
THINGS ARE

On the Nature of Things is not an easy read. Totaling 7,400 lines, it is written in hexameters, the standard unrhymed six-beat lines in which Latin poets like Virgil and Ovid, imitating Homer's Greek, cast their epic poetry. Divided into six untitled books, the poem yokes together moments of intense lyrical beauty, philosophical meditations on religion, pleasure, and death, and complex theories of the physical world, the evolution of human societies, the perils and joys of sex, and the nature of disease. The language is often knotty and difficult, the syntax complex, and the overall intellectual ambition astoundingly high.

The difficulty would not in the least have fazed Poggio and his learned friends. They possessed wonderful Latin, rose eagerly to the challenge of solving textual riddles, and had often wandered with pleasure and interest through the still more impenetrable thickets of patristic theology. A quick glance at the first few pages of the manuscript would have sufficed to convince Poggio that he had discovered something remarkable.

What he could not have grasped, without carefully reading through the work and absorbing its arguments, was that he was unleashing something that threatened his whole mental universe. Had he understood this threat, he might still have returned the poem to circulation: recovering the lost traces of the ancient world was his highest purpose in life, virtually the only principle uncontaminated by disillusionment and cynical laughter. But, as he did so, he might have uttered the words that Freud reputedly spoke to Jung, as they sailed into New York Harbor to receive the accolades of their American admirers: "Don't they know we are bringing them the plague?"

One simple name for the plague that Lucretius brought—a charge frequently leveled against him, when his poem began once again to be read—is atheism. But Lucretius was not in fact an atheist. He believed that the gods existed. But he also believed that, by virtue of being gods, they could not possibly be concerned with human beings or with anything that we do. Divinity by its very nature, he thought, must enjoy eternal life and peace entirely untouched by any suffering or disturbance and indifferent to human actions.

If it gives you pleasure to call the sea Neptune or to refer to grain and wine as Ceres and Bacchus, Lucretius wrote, you should feel free to do so, just as you can dub the round world the Mother of the Gods. And if, drawn by their solemn beauty, you choose to visit religious shrines, you will be doing yourself no harm, provided that you contemplate the images of the gods "in peace and tranquillity." (6:78) But you should not think for a minute that you can either anger or propitiate any of these deities. The processions, the animal sacrifices, the frenzied dances, the drums and cymbals and pipes, the showers of snowy rose petals, the eunuch priests, the carved images of the infant god: all of these cultic practices, though compelling and impressive in their way, are fundamentally meaningless, since the gods they are meant to reach are entirely removed and separated from our world.

It is possible to argue that, despite his profession of religious belief, Lucretius was some sort of atheist, a particularly sly one perhaps, since to almost all believers of almost all religious faiths in almost all times it has seemed pointless to worship a god without the hope of appeasing divine wrath or acquiring divine protection and favor. What is the use of a god who is uninterested in punishing or rewarding? Lucretius insisted that such hopes and anxieties are precisely a toxic form of superstition, combining in equal measure absurd arrogance and absurd fear. Imagining that the gods actually care about the fate of humans or about their ritual practices is, he observed, a particularly vulgar insult—as if divine beings depended for their happiness on our mumbled words or good behavior. But that insult is the least of the problems, since the gods quite literally could not care less. Nothing that we can do (or not do) could possibly interest *them*. The serious issue is that false beliefs and observances inevitably lead to human mischief.

These views were certainly contrary to Poggio's own Christian faith and would have led any contemporary who espoused them into the most serious trouble. But by themselves, encountered in a pagan text, they were not likely to trigger great alarm. Poggio could have told himself, as did some later sympathetic readers of *On the Nature of Things*, that the brilliant ancient poet simply intuited the emptiness of pagan beliefs and hence the absurdity of sacrifices to gods who did not in fact exist. Lucretius, after all, had the misfortune of living shortly before the coming of the Messiah. Had he been born a century later, he would have had the opportunity of learning the truth. As it was, he at least grasped that the practices of his own contemporaries were worthless. Hence even many modern translations of Lucretius' poem into English reassuringly have it denounce as "superstition" what the Latin text calls simply *religio*.

But atheism—or, more accurately, the indifference of the gods—was not the only problem posed by Lucretius' poem. Its main concerns lay elsewhere, in the material world we all inhabit, and it is here that the most disturbing arguments arose, arguments that lured those who were most struck by their formidable power—Machiavelli, Bruno, Galileo, and others—into strange trains of thought. Those trains of thought had once been eagerly explored in the very land to which they now returned, as a result of Poggio's discovery. But a thousand years of virtual silence had rendered them highly dangerous.

By now much of what *On the Nature of Things* claims about the universe seems deeply familiar, at least among the circle of people who are likely to be reading these words. After all, many of the work's core arguments are among the foundations on which modern life has been constructed. But it is worth remembering that some of the arguments remain alien and that others are hotly contested, often by those who gladly avail themselves of the scientific advances they helped to spawn. And to all but a few of Poggio's contemporaries, most of what Lucretius claimed, albeit in a poem of startling, seductive beauty, seemed incomprehensible, unbelievable, or impious.

Here is a brief list, by no means exhaustive, of the elements that constituted the Lucretian challenge:

- **Everything is made of invisible particles.** Lucretius, who disliked technical language, chose not to use the standard Greek philosophical term for these foundational particles, "atoms," i.e., things that cannot be divided. He deployed instead a variety of ordinary Latin words: "first things," "first beginnings," "the bodies of matter," "the seeds of things." Everything is formed of these seeds and, on dissolution, returns to them in the end. Immutable, indivisible, invisible, and infinite in number, they are constantly in motion, clashing with one another, coming together to form new shapes, coming apart, recombining again, enduring.

• The elementary particles of matter—"the seeds of the things"—are eternal. Time is not limited—a discrete substance with a beginning and an end—but infinite. The invisible particles from which the entire universe is made, from the stars to the lowliest insect, are indestructible and immortal, though any particular object in the universe is transitory. That is, all the forms that we observe, even those that seem the most durable, are temporary: the building blocks from which they are composed will sooner or later be redistributed. But those building blocks themselves are permanent, as is the ceaseless process of formation, dissolution, and redistribution.

Neither creation nor destruction ever has the upper hand; the sum total of matter remains the same, and the balance between the living and the dead is always restored:

> And so the destructive motions cannot hold sway eternally and bury existence forever; nor again can the motions that cause life and growth preserve created things eternally. Thus, in this war that has been waged from time everlasting, the contest between the elements is an equal one: now here, now there, the vital forces conquer and, in turn, are conquered; with the funeral dirge mingles the wail that babies raise when they reach the shores of light; no night has followed day, and no dawn has followed night, which has not heard mingled with those woeful wails the lamentations that accompany death and the black funeral. (2.569–80)

The Spanish-born Harvard philosopher George Santayana called this idea—the ceaseless mutation of forms composed of indestructible substances—"the greatest thought that mankind has ever hit upon."

- The elementary particles are infinite in number but limited in shape and size. They are like the letters in an alphabet, a discrete set capable of being combined in an infinite number of sentences. (2.688ff.) And, with the seeds of things as with language, the combinations are made according to a code. As not all letters or all words can be coherently combined, so too not all particles can combine with all other particles in every possible manner. Some of the seeds of things routinely and easily hook onto others; some repel and resist one another. Lucretius did not claim to know the hidden code of matter. But, he argued, it is important to grasp that there is a code and that, in principle, it could be investigated and understood by human science.

- All particles are in motion in an infinite void. Space, like time, is unbounded. There are no fixed points, no beginnings, middles, or ends, and no limits. Matter is not packed together in a solid mass. There is a void in things, allowing the constitutive particles to move, collide, combine, and move apart. Evidence for the void includes not only the restless motion that we observe all around us, but also such phenomena as water oozing through the walls of caves, food dispersed through bodies, sound passing through walls of closed rooms, cold permeating to the bones.

    The universe consists then of matter—the primary particles and all that those particles come together to form—and space, intangible and empty. Nothing else exists.

- The universe has no creator or designer. The particles themselves have not been made and cannot be destroyed. The patterns of order and disorder in the world are not the product of any divine scheme. Providence is a fantasy.

    What exists is not the manifestation of any overarching plan or any intelligent design inherent in matter itself. No supreme choreographer planned their movements, and the seeds of things did not have a meeting in which they decided what would go where.

> But because throughout the universe from time everlasting countless numbers of them, buffeted and impelled by blows, have shifted in countless ways, experimentation with every kind of movement and combination has at last resulted in arrangements such as those that created and compose our world. (1.1024–28)

There is no end or purpose to existence, only ceaseless creation and destruction, governed entirely by chance.

- **Everything comes into being as a result of a swerve.** If all the individual particles, in their infinite numbers, fell through the void in straight lines, pulled down by their own weight like raindrops, nothing would ever exist. But the particles do not move lockstep in a preordained single direction. Instead, "at absolutely unpredictable times and places they deflect slightly from their straight course, to a degree that could be described as no more than a shift of movement." (2.218–20) The position of the elementary particles is thus indeterminate.

The swerve—which Lucretius called variously *declinatio, inclinatio,* or *clinamen*—is only the most minimal of motions, *nec plus quam minimum.* (2.244) But it is enough to set off a ceaseless chain of collisions. Whatever exists in the universe exists because of these random collisions of minute particles. The endless combinations and recombinations, resulting from the collisions over a limitless span of time, bring it about that "the rivers replenish the insatiable sea with plentiful streams of water, that the earth, warmed by the sun's fostering heat, renews her produce, that the family of animals springs up and thrives, and that the gliding ethereal fires have life." (1.1031–34)

- **The swerve is the source of free will.** In the lives of all sentient creatures, human and animal alike, the random swerve of elementary particles is responsible for the existence of free will. For if all of motion were one long predetermined chain, there would be no possibility of freedom. Cause would follow cause from eternity, as the fates decreed. Instead, we wrest free will from the fates.

  But what is the evidence that the will exists? Why should we not simply think that the matter in living creatures moves because of the same blows that propel dust motes? Lucretius' image is the split second on the race track after the starting gate is opened, before the straining horses, frantically eager to move, can actually propel their bodies forward. That split second is the thrilling spectacle of a mental act bidding a mass of matter into motion. And because this image did not quite answer to his whole purpose—because, after all, race horses are precisely creatures driven to move by the blows of their riders—Lucretius went on to observe that though an outside force may strike against a man, that man may deliberately hold himself back.

- **Nature ceaselessly experiments.** There is no single moment of origin, no mythic scene of creation. All living beings, from plants and insects to the higher mammals and man, have evolved through a long, complex process of trial and error. The process involves many false starts and dead ends, monsters, prodigies, mistakes, creatures that were not endowed with all the features that they needed to compete for resources and to create offspring. Creatures whose combination of organs enables them to adapt and to reproduce will succeed in establishing themselves, until changing circumstances make it impossible for them any longer to survive.

The successful adaptations, like the failures, are the result of a fantastic number of combinations that are constantly being generated (and reproduced or discarded) over an unlimited expanse of time. It is difficult to grasp this point, Lucretius acknowledged, but "what has been created gives rise to its own function." (4.835) That is, he explained, "Sight did not exist before the birth of the eyes, nor speech before the creation of the tongue." (4.836–37) These organs were not created in order to fulfill a purposed end; their usefulness gradually enabled the creatures in whom they emerged to survive and to reproduce their kind.

- **The universe was not created for or about humans.** The earth—with its seas and deserts, harsh climate, wild beasts, diseases—was obviously not purpose-built to make our species feel at home. Unlike many other animals, who are endowed at birth with what they need to survive, human infants are almost completely vulnerable: Consider, Lucretius wrote in a celebrated passage, how a baby, like a shipwrecked sailor flung ashore by fierce waves,

  > lies on the ground naked, speechless, and utterly helpless as soon as nature has cast it forth with pangs of labor from its mother's womb into the shores of light. (5.223–25)

  The fate of the entire species (let alone that of any individual) is not the pole around which everything revolves. Indeed, there is no reason to believe that human beings as a species will last forever. On the contrary, it is clear that, over the infinite expanses of time, some species grow, others disappear, generated and destroyed in the ceaseless process of change. There were other forms of life before us, which no longer exist; there will be other forms of life after us, when our kind has vanished.

- **Humans are not unique.** They are part of a much larger material process that links them not only to all other life forms but to inorganic matter as well. The invisible particles out of which living things, including humans, are composed are not sentient nor do they come from some mysterious source. We are made of the same stuff that everything else is made of.

  Humans do not occupy the privileged place in existence they imagine for themselves: though they often fail to recognize the fact, they share many of their most cherished qualities with other animals. To be sure, each individual is unique, but, thanks to the abundance of matter, the same is true of virtually all creatures: how else do we imagine that a calf recognizes its dam or the cow her calf? We have only to look attentively at the world around us to grasp that many of the most intense and poignant experiences of our lives are not exclusive to our species.

- **Human society began not in a Golden Age of tranquility and plenty, but in a primitive battle for survival.** There was no original paradisal time of plenty, as some have dreamed, in which happy, peaceful men and women, living in security and leisure, enjoyed the fruits of nature's abundance. Early humans, lacking fire, agriculture, and other means to soften a brutally hard existence, struggled to eat and to avoid being eaten.

  There may always have been some rudimentary capacity for social cooperation in the interest of survival, but the ability to form bonds and to live in communities governed by settled customs developed slowly. At first there was only random mating—either from mutual desire or from barter or rape—and the hunting and gathering of food. Mortality rates were extremely high, though not, Lucretius noted wryly, as high as they currently are, inflated by warfare, shipwreck, and overeating.

The idea that language was somehow given to humans, as a miraculous invention, is absurd. Instead, Lucretius wrote, humans, who like other animals used inarticulate cries and gestures in various situations, slowly arrived at shared sounds to designate the same things. So too, long before they were able to join together to sing melodious songs, humans imitated the warbling of birds and the sweet sound of a gentle breeze in the reeds and so gradually developed a capacity to make music.

The arts of civilization—not given to man by some divine lawmaker but painstakingly fashioned by the shared talents and mental power of the species—are accomplishments worth celebrating, but they are not unmixed blessings. They arose in tandem with the fear of the gods, the desire for wealth, the pursuit of fame and power. All of these originated in a craving for security, a craving that reaches back to the earliest experiences of the human species struggling to master its natural enemies. That violent struggle—against the wild beasts that threatened human survival—was largely successful, but the anxious, acquisitive, aggressive impulses have metastasized. In consequence, human beings characteristically develop weapons that turn against themselves.

· **The soul dies.** The human soul is made of the same material as the human body. The fact that we cannot physically locate the soul in a particular organ only means that it is made of exceedingly minute particles interlaced through the veins, flesh, and sinews. Our instruments are not fine enough to weigh the soul: at the moment of death, it dissolves "like the case of a wine whose bouquet has evaporated, or of a perfume whose exquisite scent has dispersed into the air." (3.221–2) We do not imagine that the wine or perfume contains a mysterious soul; only that the scent consists of very subtle material elements, too small to measure. So too of the human spirit: it consists of tiny elements hidden in body's most secret recesses. When the body dies—that is, when its matter is dispersed—the soul, which is part of the body, dies as well.

- **There is no afterlife.** Humans have both consoled and tormented themselves with the thought that something awaits them after they have died. Either they will gather flowers for eternity in a paradisal garden where no chill wind ever blows or they will be frog-marched before a harsh judge who will condemn them, for their sins, to unending misery (misery that somewhat mysteriously requires them after dying to have heat-sensitive skin, an aversion to cold, bodily appetite and thirst, and the like). But once you grasp that your soul dies along with your body, you also grasp that there can be no posthumous punishments or rewards. Life on this earth is all that human beings have.

- **Death is nothing to us.** When you are dead—when the particles that have been linked together, to create and sustain you, have come apart—there will be neither pleasure nor pain, longing nor fear. Mourners, Lucretius wrote, always wring their hands in anguish and say, "Never again will your dear children race for the prize of your first kisses and touch your heart with pleasure too profound for words." (3.895–98) But they do not go on to add, "You will not care, because you will not exist."

- **All organized religions are superstitious delusions.** The delusions are based on deeply rooted longings, fears, and ignorance. Humans project images of the power and beauty and perfect security that they would like to possess.

Fashioning their gods accordingly, they become enslaved to their own dreams.

Everyone is subject to the feelings that generate such dreams: they wash over you when you look up at the stars and start imagining beings of immeasurable power; or when you wonder if the universe has any limits; or when you marvel at the exquisite order of things; or, less agreeably, when you experience an uncanny string of misfortunes and wonder if you are being punished; or when nature shows its destructive side. There are entirely natural explanations for such phenomena as lightning and earthquakes—Lucretius spells them out—but terrified humans instinctively respond with religious fear and start praying.

· **Religions are invariably cruel.** Religions always promise hope and love, but their deep, underlying structure is cruelty. This is why they are drawn to fantasies of retribution and why they inevitably stir up anxiety among their adherents. The quintessential emblem of religion—and the clearest manifestation of the perversity that lies at its core—is the sacrifice of a child by a parent.

Almost all religious faiths incorporate the myth of such a sacrifice, and some have actually made it real. Lucretius had in mind the sacrifice of Iphegenia by her father Agamemnon, but he may also have been aware of the Jewish story of Abraham and Isaac and other comparable Near Eastern stories for which the Romans of his times had a growing taste. Writing around 50 BCE he could not, of course, have anticipated the great sacrifice myth that would come to dominate the Western world, but he would not have been surprised by it or by the endlessly reiterated, prominently displayed images of the bloody, murdered son.

· **There are no angels, demons, or ghosts.** Immaterial spirits of any kind do not exist. The creatures with which the Greek and Roman imagination populated the world— the Fates, harpies, daemons, genii, nymphs, satyrs, dryads, celestial messengers, and the spirits of the dead—are entirely unreal. Forget them.

· **The highest goal of human life is the enhancement of pleasure and the reduction of pain.** Life should be organized to serve the pursuit of happiness. There is no ethical purpose higher than facilitating this pursuit for oneself and one's fellow creatures. All the other claims—the service of the state, the glorification of the gods or the ruler, the arduous pursuit of virtue through self-sacrifice—are secondary, misguided, or fraudulent. The militarism and the taste for violent sports that characterized his own culture seemed to Lucretius in the deepest sense perverse and unnatural. Man's natural needs are simple. A failure to recognize the boundaries of these needs leads human beings to a vain and fruitless struggle for more and more.

Most people grasp rationally that the luxuries they crave are, for the most part, pointless and do little or nothing to enhance their well-being: "Fiery fevers quit your body no quicker, if you toss in embroidered attire of blushing crimson, than if you must lie sick in a common garment." (2.34–36) But, as it is difficult to resist fears of the gods and the afterlife, so too it is difficult to resist the compulsive sense that security, for oneself and one's community, can somehow be enhanced through exploits of passionate acquisitiveness and conquest. These exploits, however, only decrease the possibility of happiness and put everyone engaged in them at the risk of shipwreck.

The goal, Lucretius wrote in a celebrated and famously disturbing passage, must be to escape from the whole mad enterprise and observe it from a position of safety:

It is comforting, when winds are whipping up the waters of the vast sea, to watch from land the severe trials of another person: not that anyone's distress is a cause of agreeable pleasure; but it is comforting to see from what troubles you yourself are exempt. It is comforting also to witness mighty clashes of warriors embattled on the plains, when you have no share in the danger. But nothing is more blissful than to occupy the heights effectively fortified by the teaching of the wise, tranquil sanctuaries from which you can look down upon others and see them wandering everywhere in their random search for the way of life, competing for intellectual eminence, disputing about rank, and striving night and day with prodigious effort to scale the summit of wealth and to secure power. (2:1–13)

· **The greatest obstacle to pleasure is not pain; it is delusion.** The principal enemies of human happiness are inordinate desire—the fantasy of attaining something that exceeds what the finite mortal world allows—and gnawing fear. Even the dreaded plague, in Lucretius' account—and his work ends with a graphic account of a catastrophic plague epidemic in Athens—is most horrible not only for the suffering and death that it brings but also and still more for the "perturbation and panic" that it triggers.

It is perfectly reasonable to seek to avoid pain: such avoidance is one of the pillars of his whole ethical system. But how is it possible to keep this natural aversion from turning into panic, panic that only leads to the triumph of suffering? And, more generally, why are humans so unhappy?

The answer, Lucretius thought, had to do with the power of the imagination. Though they are finite and mortal, humans are gripped by illusions of the infinite—infinite pleasure and infinite pain. The fantasy of infinite pain helps to account for their proneness to religion: in the misguided belief that their souls are immortal and hence potentially subject to an eternity of suffering, humans imagine that they can somehow negotiate with the gods for a better outcome, an eternity of pleasure in paradise. The fantasy of infinite pleasure helps to account for their proneness to romantic love: in the misguided belief that their happiness depends upon the absolute possession of some single object of limitless desire, humans are seized by a feverish, unappeasable hunger and thirst that can only bring anguish instead of happiness.

Once again it is perfectly reasonable to seek sexual pleasure: that is, after all, one of the body's natural joys. The mistake, Lucretius thought, was to confound this joy with a delusion, the frenzied craving to possess—at once to penetrate and to consume—what is in reality a dream. Of course, the absent lover is always only a mental image and in this sense akin to a dream. But Lucretius observed in passages of remarkable frankness that in the very act of sexual consummation lovers remain in the grip of confused longings that they cannot fulfill:

> Even in the hour of possession the passion of the lovers fluctuates and wanders in uncertainty: they cannot decide what to enjoy first with their eyes and hands. They tightly squeeze the object of their desire and cause bodily pain, often driving their teeth into one another's lips and crushing mouth against mouth. (4.1076–81)

The point of this passage—part of what W. B. Yeats called "the finest description of sexual intercourse ever written"—is not to urge a more decorous, tepid form of lovemaking.

It is to take note of the element of unsated appetite that haunts even the fulfillment of desire. The insatiability of sexual appetite is, in Lucretius' view, one of Venus' cunning strategies; it helps to account for the fact that, after brief interludes, the same acts of love are performed again and again. And he understood too that these repeated acts are deeply pleasurable. But he remained troubled by the ruse, by the emotional suffering that comes in its wake, by the arousal of aggressive impulses, and, above all, by the sense that even the moment of ecstasy leaves something to be desired. In 1685, the great poet John Dryden brilliantly captured Lucretius' remarkable vision:

> . . . when the youthful pair more closely join,
>   When hands in hands they lock, and thighs in thighs
>   they twine;
> Just in the raging foam of full desire,
>   When both press on, both murmur, both expire,
>   They grip, they squeeze, their humid tongues they
>   dart,
>   As each would force their way to th'others heart.
>   In vain; they only cruise about the coast.
>   For bodies cannot pierce, nor be in bodies lost,
>   As sure they strive to be, when both engage
>   In that tumultuous momentary rage.
>   So tangled in the nets of love they lie,
>   Till man dissolves in that excess of joy.
>
> (4.1105–14)

- **Understanding the nature of things generates deep wonder.** The realization that the universe consists of atoms and void and nothing else, that the world was not made for us by a providential creator, that we are not the center of the universe, that our emotional lives are no more distinct than our physical lives from those of all other creatures, that our souls are as material and as mortal as our bodies—all these things are not the cause for despair. On the contrary, grasping the way things really are is the crucial step toward the possibility of happiness. Human insignificance—the fact that it is not all about us and our fate—is, Lucretius insisted, the good news.

It is possible for human beings to live happy lives, but not because they think that they are the center of the universe or because they fear the gods or because they nobly sacrifice themselves for values that purport to transcend their mortal existence. Unappeasable desire and the fear of death are the principal obstacles to human happiness, but the obstacles can be surmounted through the exercise of reason.

The exercise of reason is not available only to specialists; it is accessible to everyone. What is needed is to refuse the lies proffered by priests and other fantasymongers and to look squarely and calmly at the true nature of things. All speculation—all science, all morality, all attempts to fashion a life worth living—must start and end with a comprehension of the invisible seeds of things: atoms and the void and nothing else.

It might seem at first that this comprehension would inevitably bring with it a sense of cold emptiness, as if the universe had been robbed of its magic. But being liberated from harmful illusions is not the same as disillusionment. The origin of philosophy, it was often said in the ancient world, was wonder: surprise and bafflement led to a desire to know, and knowledge in turn laid the wonder to rest. But in Lucretius' account the process is something like the reverse: it is knowing the way things are that awakens the deepest wonder.

On the Nature of Things is that rarest of accomplishments: a great work of philosophy that is also a great poem. Inevitably, compiling a list of propositions, as I have done, obscures Lucretius' astonishing poetic power, a power he himself downplayed when he compared his verses to honey smeared around the lip of a cup containing medicine that a sick child might otherwise refuse to drink. The downplaying is not altogether surprising: his philosophical master and guide, Epicurus, was suspicious of eloquence and thought that the truth should be uttered in plain, unadorned prose.

But the poetic greatness of Lucretius' work is not incidental to his visionary project, his attempt to wrest the truth away from illusion-mongers. Why should the tellers of fables, he thought, possess a monopoly on the means that humans have invented to express the pleasure and beauty of the world? Without those means, the world we inhabit runs the risk of seeming inhospitable, and for their comfort people will prefer to embrace fantasies, even if those fantasies are destructive. With the aid of poetry, however, the actual nature of things—an infinite number of indestructible particles swerving into one another, hooking together, coming to life, coming apart, reproducing, dying, recreating themselves, forming an astonishing, constantly changing universe—can be depicted in its true splendor.

Human beings, Lucretius thought, must not drink in the poisonous belief that their souls are only part of the world temporarily and that they are heading somewhere else. That belief will only spawn in them a destructive relation to the environment in which they live the only lives that they have. These lives, like all other existing forms in the universe, are contingent and vulnerable; all things, including the earth itself, will eventually disintegrate and return to the constituent atoms from which they were composed and out of which other things will form in the perpetual dance of matter. But while we are alive, we should be filled with the deepest pleasure, for we are a small part of a vast process of world-making that Lucretius celebrated as essentially erotic.

Hence it is that, as a poet, a maker of metaphors, Lucretius could do something very strange, something that appears to violate his conviction that the gods are deaf to human petitions. *On the Nature of Things* opens with a prayer to Venus. Once again Dryden probably best renders in English the spirit of Lucretius' ardor:

> Delight of humankind and gods above,
> Parent of Rome, propitious Queen of Love,
> Whose vital power, air, earth, and sea supplies,
> And breeds whate'er is born beneath the rolling skies;
> For every kind, by thy prolific might,
> Springs and beholds the regions of the light:
> Thee, Goddess, thee, the clouds and tempests fear,
> And at thy pleasing presence disappear;
> For thee the land in fragrant flowers is dressed,
> For thee the ocean smiles and smooths her wavy
>   breast,
> And heaven itself with more serene and purer light is
>   blessed.
>
> (1.1–9)

The hymn pours forth, full of wonder and gratitude, glowing with light. It is as if the ecstatic poet actually beheld the goddess of love, the sky clearing at her radiant presence, the awakening earth showering her with flowers. She is the embodiment of desire, and her return, on the fresh gusts of the west wind, fills all living things with pleasure and passionate sexual longing:

For when the rising spring adorns the mead,
And a new scene of nature stands displayed,
When teeming buds and cheerful greens appear,
And western gales unlock the lazy year,
The joyous birds thy welcome first express
Whose native songs thy genial fire confess.
Then savage beasts bound o'er their slighted food,
Struck with thy darts, and tempt the raging flood.
All nature is thy gift: earth, air, and sea;
Of all that breathes, the various progeny,
Stung with delight, is goaded on by thee.
O'er barren mountains, o'er the flowery plain,
The leafy forest, and the liquid main
Extends thy uncontrolled and boundless reign.
Through all the living regions dost thou move
And scatterest, where thou goest, the kindly seeds of
   Love.

(1.9–20)

We do not know how the German monks who copied the Latin verses and kept them from destruction responded, nor do we know what Poggio Bracciolini, who must at least have glanced at them as he salvaged the poem from oblivion, thought they meant. Certainly almost every one of the poem's key principles was an abomination to right-thinking Christian orthodoxy. But the poetry was compellingly, seductively beautiful. And we can see with hallucinatory vividness what at least one Italian, later in the fifteenth century, made of them: we have only to look at Botticelli's great painting of Venus, ravishingly beautiful, emerging from the restless matter of the sea.

CHAPTER NINE

THE RETURN

"LUCRETIUS HAS NOT yet come back to me," Poggio wrote to his Venetian friend, the patrician humanist Francesco Barbaro, "although he has been copied." Evidently, then, Poggio had not been allowed to borrow the ancient manuscript (which he characteristically referred to as if it were the poet himself) and take it back to Constance with him. The monks must have been too wary for that and forced him instead to find someone to make a copy. He did not expect this scribe to deliver the result, important as it was, in person: "The place is rather far away and not many people come from there," Poggio wrote, "and so I shall wait until some people turn up who will bring him." How long would he be willing to wait? "If no one comes," he assured his friend, "I shall not put public duties ahead of private needs." A very strange remark, for what is public here and what is private? Poggio was, perhaps, telling Barbaro not to worry: official duties in Constance (whatever they might be) would not stand in the way of getting his hands on Lucretius.

When the manuscript of *On the Nature of Things* finally did reach him, Poggio evidently sent it off at once to Niccolò Niccoli, in Florence. Either because the scribe's copy was crudely made or simply because he wanted a version for himself, Poggio's friend undertook to transcribe it. This transcription in Niccoli's elegant hand, together with the copy made by the German scribe, spawned dozens of further manuscript copies—more than fifty are known to survive—and were the sources of all fifteenth-century and early sixteenth-century printed editions of Lucretius. Poggio's discovery thus served as the crucial conduit through which the ancient poem, dormant for a thousand years, reentered circulation in the world. In the cool gray and white Laurentian library that Michelangelo designed for the Medici, Niccoli's copy of the scribe's copy of the ninth-century copy of Lucretius' poem—Codex Laurentianus 35.30—is preserved. One of the key sources of modernity, it is a modest book, bound in fading, tattered red leather inlaid with metal, a chain attached to the bottom of the back cover. There is little to distinguish it physically from many other manuscripts in the collection, apart from the fact that a reader is given latex gloves to wear when it is delivered to the desk.

The copy that the scribe made and that Poggio sent from Constance to Florence is lost. Presumably, after completing his transcription, Niccoli sent it back to Poggio, who does not seem to have copied it in his own exquisite hand. Perhaps, confident in Niccoli's skills, Poggio or his heirs deemed the scribe's copy not worth preserving and in the end simply threw it away. Lost too is the manuscript that the scribe had copied and that presumably remained in the monastic library. Did it burn up in a fire? Was the ink carefully scraped off in order to make room for some other text? Did it finally molder away from neglect, the victim of damp and rot? Or did a pious reader actually take in its subversive implications and choose to destroy it? No remnants of it have been discovered. Two ninth-century manuscripts of *On the Nature of Things*, unknown to Poggio or any of his humanist contemporaries, did manage to make it through the almost impenetrable barrier of time. These manuscripts, named after their formats the Oblongus and the Quadratus, were cataloged in the collection of a great seventeenth-century Dutch scholar and collector, Isaac Voss, and have been in the Leiden University Library since 1689. Fragments of a third ninth-century manuscript, containing about 45 percent of Lucretius' poem, also turned out to survive and are now housed in collections in Copenhagen and Vienna. But by the time these manuscripts surfaced, Lucretius' poem, thanks to Poggio's discovery, had already long been helping to unsettle and transform the world.

It is possible that Poggio sent his copy of the poem to Niccoli without having done more than look at it briefly. He had much to occupy his mind. Baldassare Cossa had been stripped of the papacy and was languishing in prison. The second claimant to the throne of St. Peter, Angelo Correr, who had been forced to resign his title of Gregory XII, died in October 1417. The third claimant, Pedro de Luna, barricaded first in the fortress of Perpignan and then on the inaccessible rock of Peñiscola on the sea coast near Valencia, still tenaciously called himself Benedict XIII, but it was clear to Poggio and almost everyone else that Papa Luna's claim could not be taken seriously. The papal throne was vacant, and the council—which, like the current European Community, was riven with tensions among the English, French, German, Italian, and Spanish delegations—squabbled over the conditions that would have to be met before proceeding to elect a new pope.

In the long interval before an agreement was finally reached, many members of the curia had found paths to new employment; some, like Poggio's friend Bruni, had already returned to Italy. Poggio's own attempts were unsuccessful. The apostolic secretary to the disgraced pope had enemies, and he refused to appease them by distancing himself from his former master. Other bureaucrats in the papal court testified against the imprisoned Cossa, but Poggio's name does not appear on the list of witnesses for the prosecution. His best hope was that one of Cossa's principal allies, Cardinal Zabarella, would be named pope, but Zabarella died in 1417. When the electors finally met in secret conclave in the fall of 1418, they chose someone with no interest in surrounding himself with humanist intellectuals, the Roman aristocrat Oddo Colonna, who took the name Martin V. Poggio was not offered the post of apostolic secretary, though he could have stayed on at court in the lower rank of scriptor. Instead, he decided to make a very surprising and risky career move.

In 1419, Poggio accepted the post of secretary to Henry Beaufort, bishop of Winchester. The uncle of Henry V (Shakespeare's heroic warrior of Agincourt fame), Beaufort was the leader of the English delegation to the Council of Constance, where he evidently met and was impressed by the Italian humanist. For the wealthy and powerful English bishop, Poggio represented the most advanced and sophisticated type of secretary, someone deeply versed both in the Roman curial bureaucracy and in prestigious humanist studies. For the Italian secretary, Beaufort represented the salvaging of dignity. Poggio had the satisfaction of refusing what would have been in effect a demotion, had he returned to the Roman Curia. But he knew no English, and, if that did not greatly matter in the service of an aristocratic cleric whose mother tongue was French and who was comfortable in Latin and Italian, it did mean that Poggio could never hope to feel entirely at home in England.

The decision to move, as he approached his fortieth birthday, to a land where he had no family, allies, or friends was motivated by something other than pique. The prospect of a sojourn in a distant realm—much more remote and exotic than Tasmania would now seem to a contemporary Roman—excited the book hunter in Poggio. He had had spectacular successes in Switzerland and Germany, successes that had made his name famous in humanist circles. Other great discoveries might await him now in English monastic libraries. Those libraries had not yet been thoroughly searched by humanists endowed, as Poggio was, with a careful reading of known classical texts, an encyclopedic grasp of the clues to missing manuscripts, and remarkable philological acumen. If he had already been hailed as a demigod for his ability to resurrect the ancient dead, how would he be praised for what he might now bring to light?

In the event, Poggio remained in England for almost four years, but the stay was deeply disappointing. Bishop Beaufort was not the gold mine that Poggio, perennially short of money, had dreamed he would be. He was away much of the time—"as nomadic as a Scythian"—leaving his secretary with little or nothing to do. Except for Niccoli, his Italian friends seem all to have forgotten him: "I have been relegated to oblivion as though I were dead." The English people he met were almost uniformly disagreeable: "plenty of men given over to gluttony and lust but very few lovers of literature and those few barbarians, trained rather in trifling debates and in quibbling than in real learning."

His letters back to Italy were a litany of complaints. There was plague; the weather was miserable; his mother and brother wrote to him only to pester him for money that he did not have; he suffered from hemorrhoids. And the truly terrible news was that the libraries—at least the ones he visited—were from Poggio's point of view almost completely uninteresting. "I saw many monasteries, all crammed with new doctors," he wrote to Niccoli in Florence,

> none of whom you would even have found worth listening to. There were a few volumes of ancient writings, which we have in better versions at home. Nearly all the monasteries of this island have been built within the last four hundred years and that has not been an age which produced either learned men or the books which we seek; these books were already sunk without trace.

There might, Poggio conceded, be something or other at Oxford, but his master Beaufort was not planning a visit there, and his own resources were severely strained. It was time for his humanist friends to abandon their dreams of stupendous discoveries: "you had better give up hope of books from England, for they care very little for them here."

Poggio professed to find some consolation in embarking on a serious study of the Church Fathers—there was no shortage of theological tomes in England—but he felt painfully the absence of the classical texts he loved: "During my four years here I have paid no attention to the study of the Humanities," he complained, "and I have not read a single book that had anything to do with style. You can guess this from my letters, for they are not what they used to be."

In 1422, after ceaseless complaining, conniving, and cajoling, he finally secured for himself a new secretarial post at the Vatican. Obtaining the money for the voyage back was not easy—"I am hunting everywhere to find some means of leaving here at someone else's expense," he wrote frankly—but eventually he cobbled enough together. He returned to Italy, having uncovered no lost bibliographic treasures and having had no appreciable impact on the English intellectual scene.

On May 12, 1425, he wrote to remind Niccoli that he wished to see the text he had sent him some eight years earlier: "I wanted the Lucretius for two weeks and no more but you want to copy that and Silius Italicus, Nonius Marcellus, and Cicero's *Orations* all in one breath," he wrote; "because you talk of everything you will accomplish nothing." After a month had gone by, he tried again on June 14, suggesting that he was not alone in his eagerness to read the poem: "If you send me the Lucretius you will be doing a favor to many people. I promise you not to keep the book more than one month and then it will come back to you." But another year passed without any results; the wealthy collector seemed to feel that the best place for *On the Nature of Things* was on his own shelf, near the ancient cameos, the fragments of statues, and the precious glassware. There it sat, perhaps unread, a trophy. It was as if the poem had been reburied, now not in a monastery but in the humanist's gilded rooms.

In a letter sent on September 12, 1426, Poggio was still trying to recover it: "Send me the Lucretius too, which I should like to see for a little while. I shall send it back to you." Three years later, Poggio's patience was understandably wearing thin: "You have now kept the Lucretius for twelve years," he wrote on December 13, 1429; "it seems to me that your tomb will be finished sooner than your books will be copied." When he wrote again, two weeks later, impatience showed signs of giving way to anger, and, in a revealing slip of the pen, he exaggerated the number of years he had been waiting: "You have now kept the Lucretius for fourteen years and the Asconius Pedianus too. . . . Does it seem just to you that, if I sometimes want to read one of these authors, I cannot on account of your carelessness? . . . I want to read Lucretius but I am deprived of his presence; do you intend to keep him another ten years?" Then he added, in a more cajoling note, "I urge you to send me either the Lucretius or the Asconius, which I shall have copied as soon as possible and then I shall send them back to you to keep as long as you like."

But finally—the actual date is unknown—it was done. Released from the confinement of Niccoli's rooms, *On the Nature of Things* slowly made its way once again into the hands of readers, about a thousand years after it had dropped out of sight. There is no trace of Poggio's own response to the poem he had relaunched, nor is anything known of Niccoli's reactions, but there are signs—manuscript copies, brief mentions, allusions, subtle marks of influence—that it began quietly to circulate, at first in Florence, and then beyond.

Back in Rome, Poggio had meanwhile picked up the familiar pieces of his existence in the papal court: conducting often lucrative business, exchanging cynical jokes with his fellow secretaries at the "Lie Factory," writing to humanist friends about the manuscripts they coveted, quarrelling bitterly with rivals. In a busy life—the court rarely stayed in place for very long—he managed to find time to translate ancient texts from Greek to Latin, to make copies of old manuscripts, and to write moral essays, philosophical reflections, rhetorical treatises, diatribes, and funeral orations on the friends—Niccolò Niccoli, Lorenzo de' Medici, Cardinal Niccolò Albergati, Leonardo Bruni, Cardinal Giuliano Cesarini—who were passing away.

He also managed to father children, many children, with his mistress Lucia Pannelli: they had, if contemporary accounts are accurate, twelve sons and two daughters. To take the scandalmongering of the times at face value would be rash, but Poggio himself acknowledged the existence of illegitimate children. When a cardinal with whom he was on good terms reproached him for the irregularity of his life, Poggio conceded his fault but added acerbically, "Do we not every day, and in all countries, meet with priests, monks, abbots, bishops, and dignitaries of a still higher order, who have families of children by married women, widows, and even by virgins consecrated to the service of God?"

As Poggio accumulated more money—and his tax records suggest that he did so with increasing success after his return from England—his life slowly began to change. He remained passionately interested in the recovery of ancient texts, but his own voyages of discovery were behind him. In their place, he began to emulate his wealthy friend Niccoli by collecting antiquities: "I have a room full of marble heads," he boasted in 1427. In that same year Poggio purchased a house in Terranuova, the small town in Tuscany where he was born and where he would over the next years gradually increase his property holdings. He raised the money for the purchase, it was said, chiefly by copying a manuscript of Livy and selling it for the princely sum of 120 gold florins.

Poggio's debt-ridden father had once been forced to flee from the town; now Poggio contemplated creating there what he called his "Academy," to which he dreamed of someday retiring and living in style. "I fished out a marble bust of a woman, wholly undamaged, which I like very much," he wrote a few years later. "It was found one day when the foundations of some house were being dug. I took care to have it brought to me here and then to my little garden at Terra Nova, which I shall decorate with antiquities." About another cache of statues he purchased, he wrote that "when they arrive, I shall place them in my little gymnasium." Academy, garden, gymnasium: Poggio was recreating, at least in his fantasy, the world of the ancient Greek philosophers. And he was eager to confer upon it a high aesthetic polish. The sculptor Donatello, he remarks, saw one of the statues "and praised it highly."

All the same, Poggio's life was not perfectly settled and secure. At one point in 1433, when he was serving as apostolic secretary to Pope Eugenius IV (who had succeeded Martin V), there was a violent popular insurrection in Rome against the papacy. Disguised as a monk and leaving his followers to fend for themselves, the pope set out in a small boat on the Tiber to reach the port at Ostia, where a ship belonging to his Florentine allies awaited him. A mutinous crowd along the banks of the river recognized him and showered the boat with rocks, but the pope managed to escape. Poggio was not quite as fortunate: fleeing the city, he was captured by one of the bands of the pope's enemies. Negotiations for his release broke down, and he was eventually forced to ransom himself for a substantial sum of his own money.

But somehow each of these violent disruptions of his world was righted, sooner or later, and Poggio returned to his books and statues, his scholarly translations and quarrels, and the steady accumulation of wealth. The gradual changes in his life culminated in a momentous decision: on January 19, 1436, he married Vaggia di Gino Buondelmonti. Poggio was fifty-six years old; his bride eighteen. The marriage was not contracted for money but for a different form of cultural capital. The Buondelmonti were one of the ancient feudal families in Florence, a fact that Poggio—who wrote eloquently against taking pride in aristocratic bloodlines—manifestly loved. Against those who ridiculed his decision, he wrote a dialogue, "Should an Old Man Marry?" (*An seni sit uxor ducenda*). The predictable arguments, most of them charged with misogyny, are rehearsed and are met with the predictable replies, many of them equally dubious. Hence—according to the anti-marriage interlocutor, who is none other than Niccolò Niccoli—it is folly for any older man, let alone a scholar, to change his well-tried style of life for one that is inescapably alien and risky. His bride may prove to be peevish, morose, intemperate, sluttish, lazy. If she is a widow, she will inevitably dwell on the happy times she had with her late husband; if she is a young maiden, she will almost certainly prove to be temperamentally unsuited to the gravity of her aging spouse. And if there are children, the old man will experience the bitter pain of knowing that he will leave them before they reach maturity.

But no—according to the pro-marriage interlocutor—a man of mature years will compensate for the inexperience and igno-

rance of a young wife whom he will be able to mold like wax
to his will. He will temper her impetuous sensuality with his
wise restraint, and if they are blessed with children, he will
enjoy the reverence due to his advanced age. Why should he
assume that his life must inevitably be cut short? And, for however many years he is granted, he will experience the unspeakable pleasure of sharing his life with someone he loves, a second
self. Perhaps the most convincing moment comes when Poggio
speaks in his own voice to say, with unusual simplicity, that he
is very happy. Niccoli concedes that there may be exceptions to
the pessimistic rule.

As it turned out, in an age of what by our standards was
exceedingly low life expectancy, Poggio flourished, and he and
Vaggia had what seems to have been a happy marriage, one
that lasted almost a quarter of a century. They had five sons—
Pietro Paolo, Giovanni Battista, Jacopo, Giovanni Francesco,
and Filippo—and a daughter, Lucretia, all of whom survived
into adulthood. Four of the five sons embarked on ecclesiastical
careers; the exception, Jacopo, became a distinguished scholar.
(Jacopo made the mistake of being caught up in the Pazzi con-
spiracy to assassinate Lorenzo and Giuliano de' Medici and was
hanged in Florence in 1478.)

The fate of Poggio's mistress and their fourteen children is
not known. His friends congratulated the newly married Poggio
on his good fortune and his moral rectitude; his enemies circulated stories of his indifference to those he had thrown off.
According to Valla, Poggio cruelly rescinded the procedure by
which he had petitioned that four of the sons his mistress bore
him be declared legitimate. The charge may be a malicious
slander, of the kind rival humanists took vindictive pleasure
in, but there is no indication that Poggio went out of his way
to treat those he had abandoned with particular generosity or
kindness.

As a layman, Poggio was not obliged to leave the papal court after his marriage. He continued to serve the pope, Eugenius IV, through long years of bitter conflict between the papacy and the Church councils, feverish diplomatic maneuvering, denunciations of heretics, military adventures, precipitous flights, and outright war. On Eugenius's death in 1447, Poggio continued on as apostolic secretary to his successor, Nicholas V.

This was the eighth pope whom he had served in this capacity, and Poggio, now in his later sixties, may have been growing weary. He was, in any case, pulled in different directions. His writing occupied an increasing amount of his time, and he had a growing family to attend to. Moreover, his wife's deep family ties to Florence intensified the links that he had always carefully maintained to what he claimed as his native city, a city to which he returned at least once a year. But in many ways his service to the new pope must have been deeply satisfying, for prior to his election, Nicholas V—whose secular name was Tommaso da Sarzana—had distinguished himself as a learned humanist. He was the embodiment of that project of education in classical learning and taste to which Petrarch, Salutati, and other humanists had devoted themselves.

Poggio, who had met the future pope in Bologna and had come to know him well, had in 1440 dedicated to him one of his works, *On the Unhappiness of Princes*. Now, in the congratulatory epistle he hastened to send after the election, he assured the new pope that not all princes needed to be completely unhappy. To be sure, in his elevated position, he would not be able any longer to indulge himself in the joys of friendship and literature, but at least he would be able to "become the protector of men of genius and cause the liberal arts to raise their drooping heads." "Let me now entreat you, most holy father," Poggio added, "not to forget your ancient friends, of which number I profess myself to be one."

In the event, though the reign of Nicholas V was highly gratifying, it was not perhaps as perfectly idyllic as the apostolic secretary might have dreamed. During this period Poggio had his grotesque scuffle with George of Trebizond, complete with screams and blows. He must have been vexed as well that the pope, as if taking seriously the injunction to be the patron of men of genius, chose as another of the apostolic secretaries his bitter enemy Lorenzo Valla. Poggio and Valla promptly embarked on a vitriolic public quarrel, mingling snide comments about each other's mistakes in Latin with still nastier remarks about hygiene, sex, and family.

The ugliness of these quarrels must have intensified the dream of retirement that Poggio had been toying with since he had purchased the house in Terranuova and begun to collect ancient fragments. And the retirement project was not only his private fantasy; he was at this point in his life famous enough as a book hunter, scholar, writer, and papal official to command the attention of a broader public. He had carefully cultivated friends in Florence, marrying into an important family and allying himself with the interests of the Medici. Though he had lived and worked in Rome for most of his adult life, the Florentines were happy to claim him as one of their own. The Tuscan government passed a public revenue bill in his favor, noting that he had declared his intention eventually to retire to his native land and to dedicate the remainder of his time on earth to study. Whereas his literary pursuits would not permit him to acquire the wealth that came to those engaged in commerce, the bill declared, he and his children should thenceforth be exempted from the payment of all public taxes.

In April 1453, Carlo Marsuppini, the chancellor of Florence, died. Marsuppini was an accomplished humanist; at the time of his death, he was translating the *Iliad* into Latin. The office was no longer the actual locus of state power: the consolidation of Medici power had reduced the political significance of the chancellorship. Many years had passed since Salutati's command of classical rhetoric had seemed critical to the survival of the republic. But the pattern had been set for the Florentine post to be held by a distinguished scholar, including two terms by Poggio's old friend, the immensely gifted historian Leonardo Bruni.

The remuneration was generous and the prestige high. Florence conferred upon its humanist chancellors all the marks of respect and honor that the buoyant, self-loving city felt were its own due. Chancellors who died in office were honored with elaborate state funerals, surpassing those of any other citizen of the republic. When Poggio, seventy-three years old, was offered the vacant position, he accepted. For more than fifty years, he had worked at the court of an absolute monarch; now he would return as the titular leader of a city that prided itself on its history of civic freedom.

Poggio served as chancellor of Florence for five years. The chancellorship evidently did not function entirely smoothly under his leadership; he seems to have neglected the lesser duties of the office. But he attended to his symbolic role, and he made time to work on the literary projects he had pledged himself to pursue. In the first of these projects, a somber two-volume dialogue on *The Wretchedness of the Human Condition*, the conversation moves from a specific disaster—the fall of Constantinople to the Turks—to a general review of the catastrophes that befall virtually all men and women of every class and profession and in all times. One of the interlocutors, Cosimo de' Medici, suggests that an exception might be made for popes and princes of the Church who certainly seem to live lives of extraordinary luxury and ease. Speaking in his own voice, Poggio replies: "I am a witness (and I lived with them for fifty years) that I have found no one who seemed in any way happy to himself, who did not bemoan that life as harmful, disquieting, anxious, oppressed with many cares."

The unremitting gloominess of the dialogue could make it seem that Poggio had entirely succumbed to late-life melancholy, but the second of the works of this period, presented to the same Cosimo de' Medici, suggests otherwise. Drawing on the Greek he had first learned more than a half century earlier, Poggio translated (into Latin) Lucian of Samosta's richly comic novel *The Ass*, a magical tale of witchcraft and metamorphosis. And for his third enterprise, moving in still a different direction, he undertook to write an ambitious, highly partisan *History of Florence* from the mid-fourteenth century to his own time. The remarkable range of the three projects—the first seemingly suitable for a medieval ascetic, the second for a Renaissance humanist, the third for a patriotic civic historian—suggests the complexity both of Poggio's own character and of the city he represented. To the Florentine citizens of the fifteenth century the distinct strains seemed closely bound together, parts of a single, complex cultural whole.

In April 1458, shortly after his seventy-eighth birthday, Poggio resigned, declaring that he wished to pursue his studies and writing as a private citizen. His death followed eighteen months later, on October 30, 1459. Since he had resigned his office, the Florentine government could not give him a grand state funeral, but they buried him with appropriate ceremony in the Church of Santa Croce and hung his portrait, by Antonio Pollaiuolo, in one of the city's public halls. The city also commissioned a statue of him, which was erected in front of Florence's cathedral, Santa Maria del Fiore. When in 1560, a century later, the Duomo's facade was refashioned, the statue was moved to a different part of the building and now serves as one of a sculpted group of the twelve apostles. It is, I suppose, an honor for the likeness of any pious Christian to function in this way, but I do not imagine that Poggio would have been entirely pleased. He was always determined to receive appropriate public recognition.

Much of the recognition by now has vanished. His tomb in Santa Croce has disappeared, displaced by those of other celebrities. To be sure, the town where he was born has been renamed Terranuova Bracciolini, in honor of its native son, and in 1959, on the five hundredth anniversary of his death, his statue was erected in the leafy town square. But few of those who pass through, on their way to the nearby fashion factory outlets, can have any idea who is being commemorated.

Nonetheless, in his book-hunting exploits in the early fifteenth century, Poggio had done something amazing. The texts he returned to circulation gave him a claim to a place of honor amidst his more famous Florentine contemporaries: Filippo Brunelleschi, Lorenzo Ghiberti, Donatello, Fra Angelico, Paolo Uccello, Luca della Robbia, Masaccio, Leon Battista Alberti, Filippo Lippi, Piero della Francesca. Unlike Brunelleschi's massive cupola, the greatest dome constructed since classical antiquity, Lucretius' great poem does not stand out against the sky. But its recovery permanently changed the landscape of the world.

CHAPTER TEN

SWERVES

MORE THAN FIFTY manuscripts of *De rerum natura* from the fifteenth century survive today—a startlingly large number, though there must have been many more. Once Gutenberg's clever technology was commercially established, printed editions quickly followed. The editions were routinely prefaced with warnings and disavowals.

As the fifteenth century neared its end, the Dominican friar Girolamo Savonarola ruled Florence for several years as a strict "Christian republic." Savonarola's passionate, charismatic preaching had provoked large numbers of Florentines, the elite as well as the masses, into a short-lived but feverishly intense mood of repentance. Sodomy was prosecuted as a capital crime; bankers and merchant princes were attacked for their extravagant luxuries and their indifference to the poor; gambling was suppressed, along with dancing and singing and other forms of worldly pleasure. The most memorable event of Savonarola's turbulent years was the famous "Bonfire of the Vanities," when the friar's ardent followers went through the streets collecting sinful objects—mirrors, cosmetics, seductive clothing, songbooks, musical instruments, playing cards and other gambling paraphernalia, sculptures and paintings of pagan subjects, the works of ancient poets—and threw them onto an enormous blazing pyre in the Piazza della Signoria.

After a while, the city tired of its puritanical frenzy, and on May 23, 1498, Savonarola himself was hanged in chains, alongside two of his key associates, and burned to ashes on the spot where he had staged his cultural bonfire. But when his power was at its height and his words still filled the citizenry with pious fear and loathing, he devoted a series of his Lenten sermons to attacking ancient philosophers, singling out one group in particular for special ridicule. "Listen women," he preached to the crowd, "They say that this world was made of atoms, that is, those tiniest of particles that fly through the air." No doubt savoring the absurdity, he encouraged his listeners to express their derision out loud: "Now laugh, women, at the studies of these learned men."

By the 1490s, then, some sixty or seventy years after Lucretius' poem was returned to circulation, atomism was sufficiently present in Florence to make it worth ridiculing. Its presence did not mean that its positions were openly embraced as true. No prudent person stepped forward and said, "I think that the world is only atoms and void; that, in body and soul, we are only fantastically complex structures of atoms linked for a time and destined one day to come apart." No respectable citizen openly said, "The soul dies with the body. There is no judgment after death. The universe was not created for us by divine power, and the whole notion of the afterlife is a superstitious fantasy." No one who wished to live in peace stood up in public and said, "The preachers who tell us to live in fear and trembling are lying. God has no interest in our actions, and though nature is beautiful and intricate, there is no evidence of an underlying intelligent design. What should matter to us is the pursuit of pleasure, for pleasure is the highest goal of existence." No one said, "Death is nothing to us and no concern of ours." But these subversive, Lucretian thoughts percolated and surfaced wherever the Renaissance imagination was at its most alive and intense.

At the very time that Savonarola was urging his listeners to mock the foolish atomists, a young Florentine was quietly copying out for himself the whole of *On the Nature of Things*. Though its influence may be detected, he did not once mention the work directly in the famous books he went on to write. He was too cunning for that. But the handwriting was conclusively identified in 1961: the copy was made by Niccolò Machiavelli. Machiavelli's copy of Lucretius is preserved in the Vatican Library, MS Rossi 884. What better place for the progeny of Poggio, the apostolic secretary? In the wake of Poggio's friend, the humanist pope Nicholas V, classical texts had a place of honor in the Vatican Library.

Still, Savonarola's warnings corresponded to authentic concerns: the set of convictions articulated with such poetic power in Lucretius' poem was virtually a textbook—or, better still, an inquisitor's—definition of atheism. Its eruption into Renaissance intellectual life elicited an array of anxious responses precisely from those most powerfully responsive to it. One such response was that of the great mid-fifteenth-century Florentine Marsilio Ficino. In his twenties, Ficino was deeply shaken by *On the Nature of Things* and undertook to write a learned commentary on the poet he called "our brilliant Lucretius." But, coming to his senses—that is, returning to his faith—Ficino burned this commentary. He attacked those he called the "Lucretiani" and spent much of his life adapting Plato to construct an ingenious philosophical defense of Christianity. A second response was to separate Lucretius' poetic style from his ideas. This separation seems to have been Poggio's own tactic: he took pride in his discovery, as in the others he made, but he never associated himself or even grappled openly with Lucretian thought. In their Latin compositions Poggio and close friends like Niccoli could borrow elegant diction and turns of phrase from a wide range of pagan texts, but at the same time hold themselves aloof from their most dangerous ideas. Indeed, later in his career

Poggio did not hesitate to accuse his bitter rival, Lorenzo Valla, of a heretical adherence to Lucretius' master, Epicurus. It is one thing to enjoy wine, Poggio wrote, but quite another to sing its praises, as he claims Valla did, in the service of Epicureanism. Valla even went beyond Epicurus himself, Poggio adds, in attacking virginity and praising prostitution. "The stains of your sacrilegious speech will not be cleansed by means of words" Poggio added ominously, "but with fire, from which I hope you will not escape."

One might have expected Valla simply to turn the charge around and point out that it was after all Poggio who returned Lucretius to circulation. That Valla failed to do so suggests that Poggio had been successful in keeping a discreet distance from the implications of his own discovery. But it may suggest as well how limited the early circulation of On the Nature of Things was. When, in the early 1430s, in a work called On Pleasure (De voluptate), Valla was penning the praises of drink and sex that Poggio professed to find so shocking, the manuscript of Lucretius' poem was still being guarded by Niccoli. The fact of its existence, which had been gleefully announced in letters among the humanists, may have helped to stimulate a resurgent interest in Epicureanism, but Valla probably had to rely on other sources and on his own fertile imagination to construct his praise of pleasure.

Interest in a pagan philosophy radically at odds with fundamental Christian principles had its risks, as Poggio's attack suggests. Valla's reply to this attack allows us to glimpse a third type of response to the Epicurean ferment of the fifteenth century. The strategy is what might be called "dialogical disavowal." The ideas Poggio condemns were present in On Pleasure, Valla conceded, but they were not his own ideas but rather those of a spokesman for Epicureanism in a literary dialogue. At the dialogue's end, it is not Epicureanism but rather Christian orthodoxy, voiced by the monk Antonio Raudense, that is declared the clear victor: "When Antonio Raudense had thus concluded his speech, we did not get up immediately. We were caught in immense admiration for such pious and religious words."

And yet. At the center of his dialogue, Valla constructs a remarkably vigorous and sustained defense of key Epicurean principles: the wisdom of withdrawing from competitive striving into the tranquil garden of philosophy ("From the shore you shall laugh in safety at the waves, or rather at those who are wave-tossed"), the primacy of bodily pleasure, the advantages of moderation, the perverse unnaturalness of sexual abstinence, the denial of any afterlife. "It is plain," the Epicurean states, "that there are no rewards for the dead, certainly there are no punishments either." And lest this formulation allow an ambiguity, still setting human souls apart from all other created things, he returns to the point to render it unequivocal:

> According to my Epicurus . . . nothing remains after the dissolution of the living being, and in the term "living being" he included man just as much as he did the lion, the wolf, the dog, and all other things that breathe. With all this I agree. They eat, we eat; they drink, we drink; they sleep, and so do we. They engender, conceive, give birth, and nourish their young in no way different from ours. They possess some part of reason and memory, some more than others, and we a little more than they. We are like them in almost everything; finally, they die and we die—both of us completely.

If we grasp this end clearly—"finally, they die and we die—both of us completely"—then our determination should be equally clear: "Therefore, for as long as possible (would that it were longer!) let us not allow those bodily pleasures to slip away that cannot be doubted and cannot be recovered in another life."

It is possible to argue that Valla wrote these words only to show them crushed by the sober admonitions of the monkish Raudense:

> If you were to see the form of any angel next to your beloved, the beloved would seem so horrible and uncouth that you would turn away from her as from the countenance of a cadaver and direct all your attention to the angel's beauty—a beauty, I say, that does not inflame but extinguishes lust, and infuses a most sanctified religious awe.

If this interpretation is true, then *On Pleasure* is an attempt to contain subversion. Aware that he and his contemporaries had been exposed to the toxic allure of Lucretius, Valla decided not to suppress the contamination, as Ficino had tried to do, but to lance the imposthume by exposing Epicurean arguments to the purifying air of Christian faith.

But Valla's enemy Poggio reached the opposite conclusion: the Christian framework and the dialogic form of *On Pleasure* was, in his view, only a convenient cover to permit Valla to make public his scandalous and subversive assault on Christian doctrine. And if Poggio's venomous hatred calls this interpretation in question, Valla's celebrated proof of the fraudulence of the so-called "Donation of Constantine" suggests that he was by no means a safely orthodox thinker. *On Pleasure* would, from this perspective, be a comparably radical and subversive text, wearing a fig leaf designed to give its author, a priest who continued to jockey for the post of apostolic secretary that he eventually obtained, some protection.

How can the conflict between these two sharply opposed interpretations be resolved? Which is it: subversion or containment? It is exceedingly unlikely that at this distance anyone will discover the evidence that might definitively answer this question—if such evidence ever existed. The question itself implies a programmatic certainty and clarity that may bear little relation to the actual situation of intellectuals in the fifteenth and sixteenth centuries. A very small number of people may have fully embraced radical Epicureanism, as far as they understood it, in its entirety. Thus, for example, in 1484 the Florentine poet Luigi Pulci was denied Christian burial for denying miracles and describing the soul as "no more than a pine nut in hot white bread." But for many of the most daring speculative minds of the Renaissance, the ideas that surged up in 1417, with the recovery of Lucretius' poem and the renewed interest in Epicureanism, did not constitute a fully formed philosophical or ideological system. Couched in its beautiful, seductive poetry, the Lucretian vision was a profound intellectual and creative challenge.

What mattered was not adherence but mobility—the renewed mobility of a poem that had been resting untouched in one or at most two monastic libraries for many centuries, the mobility of Epicurean arguments that had been silenced first by hostile pagans and then by hostile Christians, the mobility of daydreams, half-formed speculations, whispered doubts, dangerous thoughts.

Poggio may have distanced himself from the content of *On the Nature of Things*, but he took the crucial first step in pulling the poem off the shelf, having it copied, and sending the copy to his friends in Florence. Once it began to circulate again, the difficulty was not in reading the poem (provided, of course, one had adequate Latin) but in discussing its content openly or taking its ideas seriously. Valla found a way to take one central Epicurean argument—the praise of pleasure as the ultimate good—and give it sympathetic articulation in a dialogue. That argument is detached from the full philosophical structure that gave it its original weight and finally repudiated. But the dialogue's Epicurean speaks in defense of pleasure with an energy, subtlety, and persuasiveness that had not been heard for more than a millennium.

In December 1516—almost a century after Poggio's discovery —the Florentine Synod, an influential group of high-ranking clergymen, prohibited the reading of Lucretius in schools. Its exquisite Latin may have tempted schoolteachers to assign it to their students, but it should be banned, the clerics said, as "a lascivious and wicked work, in which every effort is used to demonstrate the mortality of the soul." Violators of the edict were threatened with eternal damnation and a fine of 10 ducats.

The prohibition might have restricted circulation and it effectively halted the printing of Lucretius in Italy, but it was too late to close the door. An edition had already appeared in Bologna, another in Paris, another, from the great press of Aldus Manutius, in Venice. And in Florence the distinguished publisher Filippo Giunti had brought out an edition edited by the humanist Pier Candido, whom Poggio had known well at the court of Nicholas V.

The Giunti edition incorporated emendations proposed by the remarkable soldier, scholar, and poet of Greek origin Michele Tarchaniota Marullo. Marullo, whose portrait was painted by Botticelli, was well known in Italian humanist circles. He had, in the course of a restless career, written beautiful pagan hymns inspired by Lucretius, with whose work he engaged with remarkable intensity. In 1500 he was pondering the textual complexities of *On the Nature of Things* when, clad in armor, he rode out of Volterra to fight against Cesare Borgia's troops, then massing at the coast near Piombino. It was raining heavily, and the peasants advised him not to attempt to ford the swollen Cecina River. He supposedly replied that a gypsy had told him as a child that it was not Neptune but Mars whom he should fear. Halfway across the river, his horse slipped and fell on him, and it was said that he died cursing the gods. A copy of Lucretius' poem was found in his pocket.

The death of Marullo could be circulated as a cautionary tale—even the broad-minded Erasmus remarked that Marullo wrote as if he were a pagan—but it could not quell interest in Lucretius. And indeed the Church authorities themselves, many of whom had humanist sympathies, were not of one mind on its dangers. In 1549 it was proposed to include *On the Nature of Things* on the Index of Prohibited Books—the list, only abolished in 1966, of those works that Catholics were forbidden to read—but the proposal was dropped at the request of the powerful Cardinal Marcello Cervini, who was elected pope a few years later. (He served for less than one month, from April 9 to May 1, 1555.) The commissary general of the Inquisition, Michele Ghislieri, also opposed calls for the suppression of *On the Nature of Things*. He listed Lucretius as the author of one of those pagan books that could be read but only if they were read as fables. Ghislieri, who was himself elected pope in 1566, focused the attention of his pontificate on the struggle against heretics and Jews and did not further pursue the threat posed by pagan poets.

In fact, Catholic intellectuals could and did engage with Lucretian ideas through the medium of fables. Though he complained that Marullo sounded "just like a pagan," Erasmus wrote a fictional dialogue called *The Epicurean* in which one of the characters, Hedonius, sets out to show that "there are no people more Epicurean than godly Christians." Christians who fast, bewail their sins, and punish their flesh may look anything but hedonist, but they are seeking to live righteously, and "none live more enjoyably than those who live righteously."

If this paradox seems like little more than a sleight-of-hand, Erasmus' friend Thomas More took the engagement with Epicureanism much further in his most famous work, *Utopia*

A learned man, deeply immersed in the pagan Greek and texts that Poggio and his contemporaries had returned to circulation, More was also a pious Christian ascetic who wore a hair shirt under his clothes and whipped himself until the blood ran down his flesh. His speculative daring and his relentless intelligence enabled him to grasp the force of what had surged back from the ancient world and at the same time his ardent Catholic convictions led him to demarcate the boundaries beyond which he thought it was dangerous for him or anyone else to go. That is, he brilliantly explored the hidden tensions in the identity to which he himself subscribed: "Christian humanist."

Utopia begins with a searing indictment of England as a land where noblemen, living idly off the labor of others, bleed their tenants white by constantly raising their rents, where land enclosures for sheep-raising throw untold thousands of poor people into an existence of starvation or crime, and where the cities are ringed by gibbets on which thieves are hanged by the score without the slightest indication that the draconian punishment deters anyone from committing the same crimes.

That depiction of a ghastly reality—and the sixteenth-century chronicler Holinshed reports that in the reign of Henry VIII, 72,000 thieves were hanged—is set against an imaginary island, Utopia (the name means "No-place" in Greek), whose inhabitants are convinced that "either the whole or the most part of human happiness" lies in the pursuit of pleasure. This central Epicurean tenet, the work makes clear, lies at the heart of the opposition between the good society of the Utopians and the corrupt, vicious society of his own England. That is, More clearly grasped that the pleasure principle—the principle given its most powerful expression in Lucretius' spectacular hymn to Venus—is not a decorative enhancement of routine existence; it is a radical idea that, if taken seriously, would change everything.

More set his Utopia in the remotest part of the world. Its discoverer, More writes at the beginning of the work, was a man who "joined Amerigo Vespucci and was his constant companion in the last three of his four voyages, which are now universally read of, but on the final voyage he did not return with him." He was instead one of those left behind, at his own urging, in a garrison at the farthest point of the explorers' venture into the unknown.

Reading Amerigo Vespucci and reflecting on the newfound lands known, in his honor, as "America," More seized upon one of Vespucci's observations about the peoples he had encountered: "Since their life is so entirely given over to pleasure," Vespucci had written, "I should style it Epicurean." More must have realized with a jolt that he could use the amazing discoveries to explore some of the disturbing ideas that had returned to currency with Lucretius' *On the Nature of Things*. The link was not entirely surprising: the Florentine Vespucci was a part of the humanist circle in which *On the Nature of Things* circulated. The Utopians, More wrote, are inclined to believe "that no kind of pleasure is forbidden, provided no harm comes of it." And their behavior is not merely a matter of custom; it is a philosophical position: "They seem to lean more than they should to the school that espouses pleasure as the object by which to define either the whole or the chief part of human happiness." That "school" is the school of Epicurus and Lucretius.

The setting, in the remotest part of the remotest part of the world, enabled More to convey a sense that was extremely difficult for his contemporaries to articulate: that the pagan texts recovered by the humanists were at once compellingly vital and at the same time utterly weird. They had been reinjected into the intellectual bloodstream of Europe after long centuries in which they had been almost entirely forgotten, and they represented not continuity or recovery but rather a deep disturbance. They were in effect voices from another world, a

_ as different as Vespucci's Brazil was to England, and their power derived as much from their distance as their eloquent lucidity. ·

The invocation of the New World allowed More to articulate a second key response to the texts that fascinated the humanists. He insisted that these texts be understood not as isolated philosophical ideas but as expressions of a whole way of life lived in particular physical, historical, cultural, and social circumstances. The description of the Epicureanism of the Utopians only made sense for More in the larger context of an entire existence.

But that existence, More thought, would have to be for everyone. He took seriously the claim, so ardently made in *On the Nature of Things*, that Epicurus' philosophy would liberate all of mankind from its abject misery. Or rather, More took seriously the universality that is the underlying Greek meaning of the word "catholic." It would not be enough for Epicureanism to enlighten a small elite in a walled garden; it would have to apply to society as a whole. *Utopia* is a visionary, detailed blueprint for this application, from public housing to universal health care, from child care centers to religious toleration to the six-hour work day. The point of More's celebrated fable is to imagine those conditions that would make it possible for an entire society to make the pursuit of happiness its collective goal.

For More, those conditions would have to begin with the abolition of private property. Otherwise the avidity of human beings, their longing for "nobility, magnificence, splendor and majesty," would inevitably lead to the unequal distribution of wealth that consigns a large portion of the population to lives of misery, resentment, and crime. But communism was not enough. Certain ideas would have to be banned. Specifically, More wrote, the Utopians impose strict punishment, including

the harshest form of slavery, on anyone who denies the existence of divine providence or of the afterlife.

The denial of Providence and the denial of the afterlife were
the twin pillars of Lucretius' whole poem. Thomas More then
at once imaginatively embraced Epicureanism—the most sustained and intelligent embrace since Poggio recovered *De rerum
natura* a century earlier—and carefully cut its heart out. All citizens of his Utopia are encouraged to pursue pleasure; but those
who think that the soul dies with the body or who believe
that chance rules the universe, More writes, are arrested and
enslaved.

This harsh treatment was the only way More could conceive
of the pursuit of pleasure actually being realized by more than
a tiny privileged group of philosophers who have withdrawn
from public life. People would have to believe, at a bare minimum, that there was an overarching providential design—not
only in the state but in the very structure of the universe itself—
and they would have to believe as well that the norms by which
they are meant to regulate their pursuit of pleasure and hence
discipline their behavior were reinforced by this providential
design. The way that this reinforcement would work would be
through a belief in rewards and punishments in an afterlife.
Otherwise, in More's view, it would be impossible drastically
to reduce, as he wished, both the terrible punishments and the
extravagant rewards that kept his own unjust society in order.

By the standards of More's age, the Utopians are amazingly
tolerant: they do not prescribe a single official religious doctrine
and then apply thumbscrews to those who do not adhere to it.
Their citizens are permitted to worship any god they please
and even to share these beliefs with others, provided that they
do so in a calm and rational manner. But in Utopia there is no
tolerance at all for those who think that their souls will disintegrate at death along with their bodies or who doubt that the

gods, if they exist at all, concern themselves with the doings of mankind. These people are a threat, for what will restrain them from doing anything that they please? Utopians regard such unbelievers, More wrote, as less than human and certainly unfit to remain in the community. For no one, in their view, can be counted "among their citizens whose laws and customs he would treat as worthless if it were not for fear."

"If it were not for fear": fear might be eliminated in the philosopher's garden, among a tiny, enlightened elite, but it cannot be eliminated from an entire society, if that society is to be imagined as inhabited by the range of people who actually exist in the world as it has always been known. Even with the full force of Utopian social conditioning, human nature, More believed, would inevitably lead men to resort to force or fraud in order to get whatever they desire. More's belief was conditioned no doubt by his ardent Catholicism, but in this same period Machiavelli, who was considerably less pious than the saintly More, came to the same conclusion. Laws and customs, the author of *The Prince* thought, were worthless without fear.

More tried to imagine what it would take not for certain individuals to be enlightened but for a whole commonwealth to do away with cruelty and disorder, share the goods of life equitably, organize itself around the pursuit of pleasure, and tear down the gibbets. The gibbets, all but a few, could be dismantled, More concluded, if and only if people were persuaded to imagine gibbets (and rewards) in another life. Without these imaginary supplements the social order would inevitably collapse, with each individual attempting to fulfill his wishes: "Who can doubt that he will strive either to evade by craft the public laws of his country or to break them by violence in order to serve his private desires when he has nothing to fear but laws and no hope beyond the body?" More was fully prepared to countenance the public execution of anyone who thought and taught otherwise.

More's imaginary Utopians have a practical, instrumental motive for enforcing faith in Providence and in the afterlife: they are convinced that they cannot trust anyone who does not hold these beliefs. But More himself, as a pious Christian, had another motive: Jesus' own words. "Are not two sparrows sold for a penny? And not one of them will fall on the ground without your Father's will," Jesus tells his disciples, adding that "even the hairs of your head are all numbered" (Matthew 10:29–30). There is, as Hamlet paraphrased the verse, "a special providence in the fall of a sparrow." Who in Christendom would dare to argue with that?

One answer in the sixteenth century was a diminutive Dominican monk, Giordano Bruno. In the mid-1580s, the thirty-six-year-old Bruno, who had fled from his monastery in Naples and had wandered restlessly through Italy and France, found himself in London. Brilliant, reckless, at once charmingly charismatic and insufferably argumentative, he survived by cobbling together support from patrons, teaching the art of memory, and lecturing on various aspects of what he called the Nolan philosophy, named after the small town near Naples where he was born. That philosophy had several roots, tangled together in an exuberant and often baffling mix, but one of them was Epicureanism. Indeed, there are many indications that *De rerum natura* had unsettled and transformed Bruno's whole world.

During his stay in England, Bruno wrote and published a flood of strange works. The extraordinary daring of these works may be gauged by taking in the implications of a single passage from one of them, *The Expulsion of the Triumphant Beast*, printed in 1584. The passage—quoted here in Ingrid D. Rowland's fine translation—is long, but its length is very much part of the point. Mercury, the herald of the gods, is recounting to Sofia all the things Jove has assigned him to bring about. He has ordered

that today at noon two of the melons in Father Fran-
zino's melon patch will be perfectly ripe, but that they
won't be picked until three days from now, when they
will no longer be considered good to eat. He requests
that at the same moment, on the jujube tree at the base
of Monte Cicala in the house of Giovanni Bruno, thirty
perfect jujubes will be picked, and he says that several
shall fall to earth still green, and that fifteen shall be
eaten by worms. That Vasta, wife of Albenzio Savolino,
when she means to curl the hair at her temples, shall
burn fifty-seven hairs for having let the curling iron get
too hot, but she won't burn her scalp and hence shall
not swear when she smells the stench, but shall endure
it patiently. That from the dung of her ox two hundred
and fifty-two dung beetles shall be born, of which fourteen shall be trampled and killed by Albenzio's foot,
twenty-six shall die upside down, twenty-two shall live
in a hole, eighty shall make a pilgrim's progress around
the yard, forty-two shall retire to live under the stone by
the door, sixteen shall roll their ball of dung wherever
they please, and the rest shall scurry around at random.

This is by no means all that Mercury has to arrange.

Laurenza, when she combs her hair, shall lose seventeen
hairs and break thirteen, and of these, ten shall grow
back within three days and seven shall never grow back
at all. Antonio Savolino's bitch shall conceive five pup-
pies, of which three shall live out their natural lifespan
and two shall be thrown away, and of these three the first
shall resemble its mother, the second shall be mongrel,
and the third shall partly resemble the father and partly
resemble Polidoro's dog. In that moment a cuckoo shall

be heard from La Starza, cuckooing twelve times, no
more and no fewer, whereupon it shall leave and fly to
the ruins of Castle Cicala for eleven minutes, and then
shall fly off to Scarvaita, and as for what happens next,
we'll see to it later.

Mercury's work in this one tiny corner of a tiny corner of the
Campagna is still not done.

That the skirt Mastro Danese is cutting on his board
shall come out crooked. That twelve bedbugs shall
leave the slats of Costantino's bed and head toward the
pillow: seven large ones, four small, and one middle-
sized, and as for the one who shall survive until this
evening's candlelight, we'll see to it. That fifteen minutes thereafter, because of the movement of her tongue,
which she has passed over her palate four times, the old
lady of Fiurulo shall lose the third right molar in her
lower jaw, and it shall fall without blood and without
pain, because that molar has been loose for seventeen
months. That Ambrogio on the one hundred twelfth
thrust shall finally have driven home his business with
his wife, but shall not impregnate her this time, but
rather another, using the sperm into which the cooked
leek that he has just eaten with millet and wine sauce
shall have been converted. Martinello's son is beginning to grow hair on his chest, and his voice is beginning to crack. That Paulino, when he bends over to pick
up a broken needle, shall snap the red drawstring of his
underpants. . . .

Conjuring up in hallucinatory detail the hamlet where he
was born, Bruno staged a philosophical farce, designed to show

that divine providence, at least as popularly understood, is rubbish. The details were all deliberately trivial but the stakes were
extremely high: to mock Jesus' claim that the hairs on one's head
are all numbered risked provoking an unpleasant visit from the
thought police. Religion was not a laughing matter, at least for
the officials assigned to enforce orthodoxy. They did not treat
even trivial jokes lightly. In France, a villager named Isambard
was arrested for having exclaimed, when a friar announced
after mass that he would say a few words about God, "The
fewer the better." In Spain, a tailor named Garcia Lopez, coming out of church just after the priest had announced the long
schedule of services for the coming week, quipped that "When
we were Jews, we were bored stiff by one Passover each year,
and now each day seems to be a Passover and feast-day." Garcia
Lopez was denounced to the Inquisition.

But Bruno was in England. Despite the vigorous efforts that
Thomas More made, during his time as chancellor, to establish
one, England had no Inquisition. Though it was still quite possible to get into serious trouble for unguarded speech, Bruno
may have felt more at liberty to speak his mind, or, in this case,
to indulge in raucous, wildly subversive laughter. That laughter
had a philosophical point: once you take seriously the claim
that God's providence extends to the fall of a sparrow and the
number of hairs on your head, there is virtually no limit, from
the agitated dust motes in a beam of sunlight to the planetary
conjunctions that are occurring in the heavens above. "O Mercury," Sofia says pityingly. "You have a lot to do."

Sofia grasps that it would take billions of tongues to describe
all that must happen even in a single moment in a tiny village
in the Campagna. At this rate, no one could envy poor Jove. But
then Mercury admits that the whole thing does not work that
way: there is no artificer god standing outside the universe,
barking commands, meting out rewards and punishments,

determining everything. The whole idea is absurd. There is an order in the universe, but it is one built into the nature of things, into the matter that composes everything, from stars to men to bedbugs. Nature is not an abstract capacity, but a generative mother, bringing forth everything that exists. We have, in other words, entered the Lucretian universe.

That universe was not for Bruno a place of melancholy disenchantment. On the contrary, he found it thrilling to realize that the world has no limits in either space or time, that the grandest things are made of the smallest, that atoms, the building blocks of all that exists, link the one and the infinite. "The world is fine as it is," he wrote, sweeping away as if they were so many cobwebs innumerable sermons on anguish, guilt, and repentance. It was pointless to search for divinity in the bruised and battered body of the Son and pointless to dream of finding the Father in some far-off heaven. "We have the knowledge," he wrote, "not to search for divinity removed from us if we have it near; it is within us more than we ourselves are." And his philosophical cheerfulness extended to his everyday life. He was, a Florentine contemporary observed, "a delightful companion at the table, much given to the Epicurean life."

Like Lucretius, Bruno warned against focusing all of one's capacity for love and longing on a single object of obsessive desire. It was perfectly good, he thought, to satisfy the body's sexual cravings, but absurd to confuse those cravings with the search for ultimate truths, the truths that only philosophy—the Nolan philosophy, of course—could provide. It is not that those truths were abstract and bodiless. On the contrary, Bruno might have been the first person in more than a millennium to grasp the full force, at once philosophical and erotic, of Lucretius' hymn to Venus. The universe, in its ceaseless process of generation and destruction and regeneration, is inherently sexual.

Bruno found the militant Protestantism he encountered in

England and elsewhere as bigoted and narrow-minded as the Counter-Reformation Catholicism from which he had fled. The whole phenomenon of sectarian hatred filled him with contempt. What he prized was the courage to stand up for the truth against the belligerent idiots who were always prepared to shout down what they could not understand. That courage he found preeminently in the astronomer Copernicus, who was, as he put it, "ordained by the gods to be the dawn which must precede the rising of the sun of the ancient and true philosophy, for so many centuries entombed in the dark caverns of blind, spiteful, arrogant, and envious ignorance."

Copernicus's assertion that the earth was not the fixed point at the center of the universe but a planet in orbit around the sun was still, when Bruno championed it, a scandalous idea, anathema both to the Church and to the academic establishment. And Bruno managed to push the scandal of Copernicanism still further: there was no center to the universe at all, he argued, neither earth nor sun. Instead, he wrote, quoting Lucretius, there were multiple worlds, where the seeds of things, in their infinite numbers, would certainly combine to form other races of men, other creatures. Each of the fixed stars observed in the sky is a sun, scattered through limitless space. Many of these are accompanied by satellites that revolve around them as the earth revolves around our sun. The universe is not all about us, about our behavior and our destiny; we are only a tiny piece of something inconceivably larger. And that should not make us shrink in fear. Rather, we should embrace the world in wonder and gratitude and awe.

These were extremely dangerous views, every one of them, and it did not improve matters when Bruno, pressed to reconcile his cosmology with Scripture, wrote that the Bible was a better guide to morality than to charting the heavens. Many people may have quietly agreed, but it was not prudent to say so in public, let alone in print.

Bruno was hardly the only brilliant scientific mind at work in Europe, rethinking the nature of things: in London he would almost certainly have met Thomas Harriot, who constructed the largest telescope in England, observed sun spots, sketched the lunar surface, observed the satellites of planets, proposed that planets moved not in perfect circles but in elliptical orbits, worked on mathematical cartography, discovered the sine law of refraction, and achieved major breakthroughs in algebra. Many of these discoveries anticipated ones for which Galileo, Descartes, and others became famous. But Harriot is not credited with any of them: they were found only recently in the mass of unpublished papers he left at his death. Among those papers was a careful list that Harriot, an atomist, kept of the attacks upon him as a purported atheist. He knew that the attacks would only intensify if he published any of his findings, and he preferred life to fame. Who can blame him?

Bruno, however, could not remain silent. "By the light of his senses and reason," he wrote about himself, "he opened those cloisters of truth which it is possible for us to open with the key of most diligent inquiry, he laid bare covered and veiled nature, gave eyes to the moles and light to the blind . . . he loosed the tongues of the dumb who could not and dared not express their entangled opinions." As a child, he recalled in *On the Immense and the Numberless*, a Latin poem modeled on Lucretius, he had believed that there was nothing beyond Vesuvius, since his eye could not see beyond the volcano. Now he knew that he was part of an infinite world, and he could not enclose himself once again in the narrow mental cell his culture insisted that he inhabit.

Perhaps if he had stayed in England—or in Frankfurt or Zurich, Prague or Wittenberg, where he had also wandered—he could, though it would have been difficult, have found a way to remain at liberty. But in 1591 he made a fateful decision to return to Italy, to what seemed to him the safety of famously independent Padua and Venice. The safety proved illusory: denounced by his patron to the Inquisition, Bruno was arrested in Venice and then extradited to Rome, where he was imprisoned in a cell of the Holy Office near St. Peter's Basilica.

Bruno's interrogation and trial lasted for eight years, much of his time spent endlessly replying to charges of heresy, reiterating his philosophical vision, rebutting wild accusations, and drawing on his prodigious memory to delineate his precise beliefs again and again. Finally threatened with torture, he denied the right of the inquisitors to dictate what was heresy and what was orthodox belief. That challenge was the last straw. The Holy Office acknowledged no limits to its supreme jurisdiction—no limits of territory and, apart from the pope and the cardinals, no limits of person. It claimed the right to judge and, if necessary, to persecute anyone, anywhere. It was the final arbiter of orthodoxy.

Before an audience of spectators, Bruno was forced to his knees and sentenced as "an impenitent, pernicious, and obstinate heretic." He was no Stoic; he was clearly terrified by the grisly fate that awaited him. But one of the spectators, a German Catholic, jotted down strange words that the obstinate heretic had spoken at the moment of his conviction and excommunication: "He made no other reply than, in a menacing tone, 'You may be more afraid to bring that sentence against me than I am to accept it.'"

On February 17, 1600, the defrocked Dominican, his head shaved, was mounted on a donkey and led out to the stake that had been erected in the Campo dei Fiori. He had steadfastly refused to repent during the innumerable hours in which he had been harangued by teams of friars, and he refused to repent or simply to fall silent now at the end. His words are unrecorded, but they must have unnerved the authorities, since they ordered that his tongue be bridled. They meant it literally: according to one account, a pin was driven into his cheek, through his tongue, and out the other side; another pin sealed his lips, forming a cross. When a crucifix was held up to his face, he turned his head away. The fire was lit and did its work. After he was burned alive, his remaining bones were broken into pieces and his ashes—the tiny particles that would, he believed, reenter the great, joyous, eternal circulation of matter—were scattered.

CHAPTER ELEVEN

AFTERLIVES

S ILENCING BRUNO PROVED far easier than returning *On the Nature of Things* to the darkness. The problem was that, once Lucretius' poem reentered the world, the words of this visionary poet of human experience began to resonate powerfully in the works of Renaissance writers and artists, many of whom thought of themselves as pious Christians. This resonance—the trace of an encounter in painting or in epic romance—was less immediately disturbing to the authorities than it was in the writings of scientists or philosophers. The ecclesiastical thought police were only rarely called to investigate works of art for their heretical implications. But just as Lucretius' gifts as a poet had helped to diffuse his radical ideas, so too those ideas were transmitted, in ways extremely difficult to control, by artists who were in contact directly or indirectly with Italian humanist circles: painters like Sandro Botticelli, Piero di Cosimo, and Leonardo da Vinci; poets like Matteo Boiardo, Ludovico Ariosto, and Torquato Tasso. And before long the ideas surfaced as well far from Florence and Rome.

On the London stage in the mid-1590s, Mercutio teased Romeo with a fantastical description of Queen Mab:

> She is the fairies' midwife, and she comes
> In shape no bigger than an agate stone
> On the forefinger of an alderman,
> Drawn with a team of little atomi
> Athwart men's noses as they lie asleep . . .
>
> (*Romeo and Juliet*, I.iv.55–59)

". . . a team of little atomi": Shakespeare expected then that his popular audience would immediately understand that Mercutio was comically conjuring up an unimaginably small object. That is interesting in itself, and still more interesting in the context of a tragedy that broods upon the compulsive power of desire in a world whose main characters conspicuously abjure any prospect of life after death:

> Here, here will I remain
> With worms that are thy chambermaids. O, here
> Will I set up my everlasting rest . . .
>
> (V.iii.108–10)

Bruno's years in England had not been in vain. The author of *Romeo and Juliet* shared his interest in Lucretian materialism with Spenser, Donne, Bacon, and others. Though Shakespeare had not attended either Oxford or Cambridge, his Latin was good enough to have enabled him to read Lucretius' poem for himself. In any case, he seems to have personally known John Florio, Bruno's friend, and he could also have discussed Lucretius with his fellow playwright Ben Jonson, whose own signed copy of *On the Nature of Things* has survived and is today in the Houghton Library at Harvard.

Shakespeare would certainly have encountered Lucretius from one of his favorite books: Montaigne's *Essays*. The *Essays*, first published in French in 1580 and translated into English by Florio in 1603, contains almost a hundred direct quotations from *On the Nature of Things*. It is not a matter of quotations alone: there is a profound affinity between Lucretius and Montaigne, an affinity that goes beyond any particular passage.

Montaigne shared Lucretius' contempt for a morality enforced by nightmares of the afterlife; he clung to the importance of his own senses and the evidence of the material world; he intensely disliked ascetic self-punishment and violence against the flesh; he treasured inward freedom and content. In grappling with the fear of death, he was influenced by Stoicism as well as Lucretian materialism, but it is the latter that proves the dominant guide, leading him toward a celebration of bodily pleasure.

Lucretius' impersonal philosophical epic offered no guidance at all in Montaigne's great project of representing the particular twists and turns of his physical and mental being:

> I am not excessively fond of either salads or fruits, except melons. My father hated all kinds of sauces; I love them all. . . . There are changes that take place in us, irregular and unknown. Radishes, for example, I first found to agree with me, and then to disagree, now to agree again.

But this sublimely eccentric attempt to get his whole self into his text is built upon the vision of the material cosmos that Poggio awoke from dormancy in 1417.

"The world is but a perennial movement," Montaigne writes in "Of Repentance,"

> All things in it are in constant motion—the earth, the rocks of the Caucasus, the pyramids of Egypt—both with the common motion and with their own. Stability itself is nothing but a more languid motion. (610)

And humans, however much they may think they choose whether to move or to stand still, are no exception: "Our ordinary practice," Montaigne reflects in an essay on "The Inconsistency of our actions," "is to follow the inclinations of our appetite, to the left, to the right, uphill and down, as the wind of circumstance carries us."

As if that way of putting things still gives humans too much control, he goes on to emphasize, with a quotation from Lucretius, the entirely random nature of human swerves: "We do not go; we are carried away, like floating objects, now gently, now violently, according as the water is angry or calm: 'Do we not see all humans unaware/Of what they want, and always searching everywhere,/And changing place, as if to drop the load they bear?'" (240). And the volatile intellectual life in which his essays participate is no different: "Of one subject we make a thousand, and, multiplying and subdividing, fall back into Epicurus' infinity of atoms" (817). Better than anyone—including Lucretius himself—Montaigne articulates what it feels like from the inside to think, write, live in an Epicurean universe.

In doing so, Montaigne found that he had to abandon altogether one of Lucretius' most cherished dreams: the dream of standing in tranquil security on land and looking down at a shipwreck befalling others. There was, he grasped, no stable cliff on which to stand; he was already on board the ship. Montaigne fully shared Lucretius' Epicurean skepticism about the restless striving for fame, power, and riches, and he cherished his own withdrawal from the world into the privacy of his book-lined study in the tower of his château. But the withdrawal seems only to have intensified his awareness of the perpetual motion, the instability of forms, the plurality of worlds, the random swerves to which he himself was as fully prone as everyone else.

Montaigne's skeptical temper kept him from the dogmatic

certainty of Epicureanism. But his immersion in *On the Nature of Things*, in its style as well as its ideas, helped him to account for his experience of lived life and to describe that experience, along with the fruits of his reading and reflection, as faithfully as he could. It helped him articulate his rejection of pious fear, his focus on this world and not on the afterlife, his contempt for religious fanaticism, his fascination with supposedly primitive societies, his admiration for the simple and the natural, his loathing of cruelty, his deep understanding of humans as animals and his correspondingly deep sympathy with other species of animals.

It was in the spirit of Lucretius that Montaigne wrote, in "Of Cruelty," that he willingly resigned "that imaginary kingship that people give us over the other creatures," admitted that he could barely watch the wringing of a chicken's neck, and confessed that he "cannot well refuse my dog the play he offers me or asks of me outside the proper time." It is in the same spirit in "Apology for Raymond Sebond" that he mocked the fantasy that humans are the center of the universe:

> Why shall a gosling not say thus: "All the parts of the universe have me in view; the earth serve for me to walk on, the sun to give me light, the stars to breathe their influences into me; I gain this advantage from the winds, that from the waters; there is nothing that the heavenly vault regards so favorably as me; I am the darling of nature."

And when Montaigne reflected on the noble end of Socrates, it was in the spirit of Lucretius that he focused on the most implausible—and the most Epicurean—of details, as in "Of Cruelty," "the quiver of pleasure" that Socrates felt "in scratching his leg after the irons were off."

Above all, Lucretius' fingerprints are all over Montaigne's reflections on two of his favorite subjects: sex and death. Recalling that "the courtesan Flora used to say that she had never lain with Pompey without making him carry away the marks of her bites," Montaigne immediately recalls lines from Lucretius: "They hurt the longed-for body with their viselike grip,/And with their teeth they lacerate the tender lip" ("That our desire is increased by difficulty"). Urging those whose sexual passion is too powerful to "disperse it," Montaigne in "Of Diversion" quotes Lucretius' scabrous advice—"Eject the gathered sperm in anything at all"—and then adds, "I have often tried it with profit." And attempting to conquer any bashfulness and capture the actual experience of intercourse, he finds that no description ever written is more wonderful—more ravishing, as he puts it—than Lucretius' lines on Venus and Mars cited in "On some verses of Virgil":

> He who rules the savage things
> Of war, the mighty Mars, oft on thy bosom flings
> Himself; the eternal wound of love drains all his powers
> Wide-mouthed, with greedy eyes thy person he devours,
> Head back, his very soul upon thy lips suspended:
> Take him in thy embrace, goddess, let him be blended
> With thy holy body as he lies; let sweet words pour
> Out of thy mouth.

Citing the Latin, Montaigne does not attempt to match this description in his own French; he simply stops to savor its perfection, "so alive, so profound."

There are moments, rare and powerful, in which a writer, long vanished from the face of the earth, seems to stand in your presence and speak to you directly, as if he bore a message meant for you above all others. Montaigne seems to have felt this intimate link with Lucretius, a link that helped him come to terms with the prospect of his own extinction. He once saw a man die, he recalled, who complained bitterly in his last moments that destiny was preventing him from finishing the book he was writing. The absurdity of the regret, in Montaigne's view, is best conveyed by lines from Lucretius: "But this they fail to add: that after you expire/Not one of all these things will fill you with desire." As for himself, Montaigne wrote, "I want death to find me planting my cabbages, but careless of death, and still more of my unfinished garden" ("That to philosophize is to learn to die").

To die "careless of death," Montaigne understood, was a far more difficult goal than it sounded: he had to marshal all of the resources of his capacious mind in order to hear and to obey what he took to be the voice of Nature. And that voice, he understood, spoke above all others the words of Lucretius. "Go out of this world," Montaigne imagined Nature to say,

> as you entered it. The same passage that you made from death to life, without feeling or fright, make it again from life to death. Your death is part of the order of the universe; it is part of the life of the world.
>
> Our lives we borrow from each other . . .
> And men, like runners, pass along the torch of life.
> (Lucretius)
>
> ("That to philosophize")

Lucretius was for Montaigne the surest guide to understanding the nature of things and to fashioning the self to live life with pleasure and to meet death with dignity.

In 1989, Paul Quarrie, then the librarian at Eton College, bought a copy of the splendid 1563 *De rerum natura,* edited by

Denys Lambin, at auction for £250. The catalogue entry noted that the endpapers of the copy were covered with notes and that there were many marginalia in both Latin and French, but the owner's name was lost. Scholars quickly confirmed what Quarrie suspected, as soon as he had the book in his hands: this was Montaigne's personal copy of Lucretius, bearing the direct marks of the essayist's passionate engagement with the poem. Montaigne's name on his copy of Lucretius was overwritten— that is why it took so long to realize who had owned it. But in a wildly heterodox comment penned in Latin on the verso of the third flyleaf, he did leave an odd proof that the book was his. "Since the movements of the atoms are so varied," he wrote, "it is not unbelievable that the atoms once came together in this way, or that in the future they will come together like this again, giving birth to another Montaigne."

Montaigne took pains to mark the many passages in the poem that seemed to him "against religion" in denying the fundamental Christian principles of creation *ex nihilo*, divine providence, and judgment after death. Fear of death, he wrote in the margin, is the cause of all our vices. Above all, he noted again and again, the soul is corporeal: "The soul is bodily" (296); "The soul and the body have an extreme conjunction" (302); "the soul is mortal" (306); "The soul, like the foot, is part of the body" (310); "the body and the soul are inseparably joined." (311) These are reading notes, not assertions of his own. But they suggest a fascination with the most radical conclusions to be drawn from Lucretian materialism. And though it was prudent to keep that fascination hidden, it is clear that Montaigne's response was by no means his alone.

Even in Spain, where the vigilance of the Inquisition was high, Lucretius' poem was being read, in printed copies carried across the border from Italy and France and in manuscripts that quietly passed from hand to hand. In the early seventeenth

century Alonso de Olivera, doctor to Princess Isabel de Bor-
bón, owned a French edition printed in 1565. At a book sale in
1625, the Spanish poet Francisco de Quevedo acquired a manuscript copy of the work for only one *real*. The writer and anti-
quary Rodrigo Caro, from Seville, had two copies, printed in
Antwerp in 1566, in his library inventoried in 1647; and in the
monastery of Guadalupe an edition of Lucretius, printed in
Amsterdam in 1663, was kept in his cell, it would appear, by
Padre Zamora. As Thomas More discovered when he tried to
buy up and burn Protestant translations of the Bible, the printing press had made it maddeningly difficult to kill a book. And
to suppress a set of ideas that were vitally important in enabling
new scientific advances in physics and astronomy proved to be
even more difficult.

It was not for want of trying. Here is an attempt from the
seventeenth century to accomplish what the killing of Bruno
had failed to do:

> Nothing comes from atoms.
> All the bodies of the world shine with the beauty of
> their forms.
> Without these the globe would only be an immense
> chaos.
> In the beginning God made all things, so that they
> might generate something.
> Consider to be nothing that from which nothing can
> come.
> You, O Democritus, form nothing different starting
> from atoms.
> Atoms produce nothing; therefore, atoms are nothing.

These are the words of a Latin prayer that young Jesuits at the
University of Pisa were assigned to recite every day to ward off

what their superiors regarded as a particularly noxious temptation. The aim of the prayer was to exorcise atomism and to claim the form, structure, and beauty of things as the work of God. The atomists had found joy and wonder in the way things are: Lucretius saw the universe as a constant, intensely erotic hymn to Venus. But the obedient young Jesuit was to tell himself every day that the only alternative to the divine order he could see celebrated all around him in the extravagance of Baroque art was a cold, sterile, chaotic world of meaningless atoms.

Why did it matter? As More's *Utopia* had made clear, divine providence and the soul's postmortem rewards and punishments were non-negotiable beliefs, even in playful fantasies about non-Christian peoples at the edge of the known world. But the Utopians did not base their doctrinal insistence on their understanding of physics. Why would the Jesuits, at once the most militant and the most intellectually sophisticated Catholic order in this period, commit themselves to the thankless task of trying to eradicate atoms? After all, the notion of the invisible seeds of things had never completely vanished during the Middle Ages. The core idea of the universe's basic material building blocks—atoms—had survived the loss of the ancient texts. Atoms could even be spoken of without substantial risk, provided that they were said to be set in motion and ordered by divine providence. And there remained within the highest reaches of the Catholic Church daring speculative minds eager to grapple with the new science. Why should atoms in the High Renaissance have come to seem, in some quarters at least, so threatening?

The short answer is that the recovery and recirculation of Lucretius' *On the Nature of Things* had succeeded in linking the very idea of atoms, as the ultimate substrate of all that exists, with a host of other, dangerous claims. Detached from any context, the idea that all things might consist of innumerable invisible particles did not seem particularly disturbing. After all, the world had to consist of *something*. But Lucretius' poem restored to atoms their missing context, and the implications—for morality, politics, ethics, and theology—were deeply upsetting.

Those implications were not immediately apparent to everyone. Savonarola may have mocked the pointy-headed intellectuals who thought the world was made up out of invisible particles, but on this issue at least he was playing for laughs, not yet calling for an auto-da-fé. Catholics like Erasmus and More could, as we have seen, think seriously about how to integrate elements of Epicureanism with the Christian faith. And in 1509, when Raphael painted the *School of Athens* in the Vatican—his magnificent vision of Greek philosophy—he seems to have been sublimely confident that the whole classical inheritance, not simply the work of a select few, could live in harmony with the Christian doctrine being earnestly debated by the theologians depicted on the opposite wall. Plato and Aristotle have pride of place in Raphael's luminous scene, but there is room under the capacious arch for all of the major thinkers, including—if traditional identifications are correct—Hypatia of Alexandria and Epicurus.

But by midcentury, this confidence was no longer possible. In 1551 the theologians at the Council of Trent had, to their satisfaction at least, resolved once and for all the debates that had swirled around the precise nature of the central Christian mystery. They had confirmed as Church dogma the subtle arguments with which Thomas Aquinas in the thirteenth century, drawing on Aristotle, had attempted to reconcile transubstantiation—the metamorphosis of the consecrated water and wine into the body and blood of Jesus Christ—with the laws of physics. Aristotle's distinction between the "accidents" and the "substance" of matter made it possible to explain how something that looked and smelled and tasted exactly like a piece of bread could actually (and not merely symbolically) be Christ's flesh. What the human senses experienced was merely the accidents of bread; the substance of the consecrated wafer was God.

The theologians at Trent presented these ingenious arguments not as a theory but as the truth, a truth utterly incompatible with Epicurus and Lucretius. The problem with Epicurus and Lucretius was not their paganism—after all, Aristotle too was a pagan—but rather their physics. Atomism absolutely denied the key distinction between substance and accidents, and therefore threatened the whole magnificent intellectual edifice resting on Aristotelian foundations. And this threat came at exactly the moment when Protestants had mounted their most serious assault on Catholic doctrine. That assault did not depend on atomism—Luther and Zwingli and Calvin were not Epicureans, any more than Wycliffe and Hus had been—but for the militant, embattled forces of the Counter-Reformation Catholic Church, it was as if the resurgence of ancient materialism had opened a dangerous second front. Indeed, atomism seemed to offer the Reformers access to an intellectual weapon of mass destruction. The Church was determined not to allow anyone to lay hands on this weapon, and its ideological arm, the Inquisition, was alerted to detect the telltale signs of proliferation.

"Faith must take first place among all the other laws of philosophy," declared a Jesuit spokesman in 1624, "so that what, by established authority, is the word of God may not be exposed to falsity." The words were a clear warning to curb unacceptable speculation: "The only thing necessary to the Philosopher, in order to know the truth, which is one and simple, is to oppose whatever is contrary to Faith and to accept that which is contained in Faith." The Jesuit did not specify a specific target of this warning, but contemporaries would have easily understood that his words were particularly directed at the writer of a recently published scientific work called *The Assayer.* That writer was Galileo Galilei.

Galileo had already been in trouble for using his astronomical observations to support the Copernican claim that the earth was in orbit around the sun. Under pressure from the Inquisition, he had pledged not to continue to advance this claim. But *The Assayer,* published in 1623, demonstrated that the scientist was continuing to tread on extremely dangerous ground. Like Lucretius, Galileo defended the oneness of the celestial and terrestrial world: there was no essential difference, he claimed, between the nature of the sun and the planets and the nature of the earth and its inhabitants. Like Lucretius, he believed that everything in the universe could be understood through the same disciplined use of observation and reason. Like Lucretius, he insisted on the testimony of the senses, against, if necessary, the orthodox claims of authority. Like Lucretius, he sought to work through this testimony toward a rational comprehension of the hidden structures of all things. And like Lucretius, he was convinced that these structures were by nature constituted by what he called "minims" or minimal particles, that is, constituted by a limited repertory of atoms combined in innumerable ways.

Galileo had friends in the highest places: *The Assayer* was dedicated to none other than the enlightened new pope, Urban VIII, who as Cardinal Maffeo Barbarini had warmly supported the great scientist's research. As long as the pope was willing to protect him, Galileo could hope to get away with the expression of his views and with the scientific investigations that they helped to generate. But the pope himself was under growing pressure to suppress what many in the Church, the Jesuits above all, regarded as particularly noxious heresies. On August 1, 1632, the Society of Jesus strictly prohibited and condemned the doctrine of atoms. That prohibition in itself could not have precipitated a move against Galileo, since *The Assayer* had been cleared eight years earlier for publication. But Galileo's publication, also in 1632, of the *Dialogue Concerning the Two Chief World Systems* gave his enemies the opportunity that they had been looking for: they promptly denounced him to the Congregation of the Holy Office, as the Inquisition was called.

On June 22, 1633, the Inquisition delivered its verdict: "We say, sentence, and declare that you, Galileo, by reason of the evidence arrived at in the trial, and by you confessed as above, have rendered yourself in the judgment of this Holy Office vehemently suspected of heresy." Still protected by powerful friends and hence spared torture and execution, the convicted scientist was sentenced to life imprisonment, under house arrest. The heresy officially specified in the verdict was "having believed and held the doctrine, false and contrary to sacred and divine Scripture, that the Sun is the center of the world and does not move from east to west and that the Earth moves and is not the center of the world." But in 1982 an Italian scholar, Pietro Redondi, uncovered a document in the archives of the Holy Office that altered the picture. The document was a memorandum detailing heresies found in *The Assayer*. Specifically, the inquisitor found evidence of atomism. Atomism, explained the inquisitor, is incompatible with the second canon of the thirteenth session of the Council of Trent, the session that spelled out the dogma of the Eucharist. If you accept Signor Galileo Galilei's theory, the document observes, then when you find in the Most Holy Sacrament "the objects of touch, sight, taste, etc.," characteristic of bread and wine, you will also have to say, according to the same theory, that these characteristics are produced on our senses by "very tiny particles." And from this you will have to conclude "that in the Sacrament there must be substantial parts of bread and wine," a conclusion that is flat-out heresy. Thirty-three years after the execution of Bruno, atomism remained a belief that the vigilant forces of orthodoxy were determined to suppress.

If complete suppression proved impossible, there was some consolation for the enemies of Lucretius in the fact that most printed editions carried disclaimers. One of the most interesting of these is in the text used by Montaigne, the 1563 edition annotated by Denys Lambin. It is true, Lambin concedes, that Lucretius denies the immortality of the soul, rejects divine providence, and claims that pleasure is the highest good. But "even though the poem itself is alien to our religion because of its beliefs," Lambin writes, "it is no less a poem." Once the distinction has been drawn between the work's beliefs and its artistic merit, the full force of that merit can be safely acknowledged: "Merely a poem? Rather it is an elegant poem, a magnificent poem, a poem highlighted, recognized and praised by all wise men." What about the content of the poem, "these insane and frenzied ideas of Epicurus, those absurdities about a fortuitous conjunction of atoms, about innumerable worlds, and so on"? Secure in their faith, Lambin writes, good Christians do not have to worry: "neither is it difficult for us to refute them, nor indeed is it necessary, certainly when they are most easily disproved by the voice of truth itself or by everyone remaining silent about them." Disavowal shades into a reassurance subtly conjoined with a warning: sing the praises of the poem, but remain silent about its ideas.

The aesthetic appreciation of Lucretius depended on the possession of very good Latin, and hence the poem's circulation was limited to a relatively small, elite group. Everyone grasped that any attempt to make it more broadly accessible to the literate public would arouse the deepest suspicion and hostility from the authorities. More than two hundred years apparently passed, after Poggio's discovery in 1417, before an attempt was actually made.

But by the seventeenth century the pressure of the new science, growing intellectual speculation, and the lure of the great poem itself became too great to contain. The brilliant French astronomer, philosopher, and priest Pierre Gassendi (1592–1655) devoted himself to an ambitious attempt to reconcile Epicureanism and Christianity, and one of his most remarkable students, the playwright Molière (1622–1673), undertook to produce a verse translation (which does not, unfortunately, survive) of *De rerum natura.* Lucretius had already appeared in a prose translation in French by the abbé Michel de Marolles (1600–1681). Not long afterwards, an Italian translation by the mathematician Alessandro Marchetti (1633–1714) began to circulate in manuscript, to the dismay of the Roman Church, which successfully banned it from print for decades. In England, the wealthy diarist John Evelyn (1620–1706) translated the first book of Lucretius' poem; a complete version in heroic couplets was published in 1682 by the young Oxford-educated scholar Thomas Creech.

Creech's Lucretius was greeted as an astonishing achievement when it appeared in print, but an English translation of almost the entire poem, also in couplets, was already in very limited circulation, and from a surprising source. This translation, which was not printed until the twentieth century, was by the Puritan Lucy Hutchinson, the wife of Colonel John Hutchinson, parliamentarian and regicide. What is most striking perhaps about this remarkable accomplishment is that, by the time the learned translator presented the text to Arthur Annesley, first Earl of Anglesey, on June 11, 1675, she had come to detest its central principles—or so she claimed—and to hope that they would vanish from the face of the earth.

She would certainly have consigned these verses to the fire, she wrote in her autograph dedicatory letter, "had they not by misfortune been gone out of my hands in one lost copy." This sounds, of course, like the familiar gesture of feminine modesty. It is a gesture she reinforces by refusing to translate several hundred sexually explicit lines in book 4, noting in the margin that "much here was left out for a midwife to translate whose obscene art it would better become than a nicer pen." But in fact Hutchinson made no apology for what she called her "aspiring Muse." Rather, she abhorred "all the atheism and impieties" in Lucretius' work.

The "lunatic" Lucretius, as Hutchinson called him, is no better than the other pagan philosophers and poets routinely commended to pupils by their tutors, an educational practice that is "one great means of debauching the learned world, at least of confirming them in that debauchery of soul, which their first sin led them into, and of hindering their recovery, while they puddle all the streams of Truth, that flow down to them from divine grace, with this pagan mud." It is a lamentation and a horror, Hutchinson wrote, that now, in these days of the Gospel, men should study Lucretius and adhere to his "ridiculous, impious, execrable doctrines, reviving the foppish, casual dance of atoms."

Why, then, when she earnestly hopes that this wickedness will disappear, did she painstakingly prepare a verse translation, pay a professional scribe to write out the first five books, and carefully copy out book 6, along with the Arguments and the marginalia, in her own hand?

Her answer is a revealing one. She had not initially realized, she confessed, how dangerous Lucretius was. She undertook the translation "out of youthful curiosity, to understand things I heard so much discourse of at second hand." We have, through this remark, a glimpse of those quiet conversations, conducted not in the lecture hall or from the pulpit, but away from the prying ears of the authorities, in which Lucretius' ideas were weighed and debated. This gifted, learned woman wanted to know for herself what the men in her world were arguing about.

When her religious convictions matured, Hutchinson wrote, when she "grew in Light and Love," this curiosity and the pride she felt and in some sense continued to feel in her accomplishment began to sour:

> The little glory I had among some few of my intimate friends, for understanding this crabbed poet, became my shame, and I found I never understood him till I learned to abhor him, and dread a wanton dalliance with impious books.

But why, in that case, should she have wished to make this wanton dalliance available to others?

Hutchinson said that she was simply obeying Anglesey, who had asked to see this book that she now beseeched him to conceal. To conceal, not to destroy. Something restrained her from urging that it be consigned to the fire, something more than the copy that had already gone out of her hands—for why should that have held her back?—and more even than her pride in her own accomplishment. An ardent Puritan, she echoed Milton's principled opposition to censorship. She had, after all, "reaped some profit by it, for it showed me that senseless superstitions drive carnal reason into atheism." That is, she learned from Lucretius that childish "fables" meant to enhance piety have the effect of leading rational intelligence toward disbelief.

Perhaps too Hutchinson found the manuscript strangely difficult to destroy. "I turned it into English," she wrote, "in a room where my children practiced the several qualities they were taught with their tutors, and I numbered the syllables of my translation by the threads of the canvas I wrought in, and set them down with a pen and ink that stood by me."

Lucretius insisted that those things that seemed completely detached from the material world—thoughts, ideas, fantasies, souls themselves—were nonetheless inseparable from the atoms that constituted them, including in this instance the pen, the ink, and the threads of the needlework Hutchinson used to count the syllables in her lines of verse. In his theory, even vision, so seemingly immaterial, depended on tiny films of atoms that constantly emanated from all things and, as images or simulacra, floated through the void until they struck the perceiving eye. Thus it was, he explained, that people who saw what they thought to be ghosts were falsely persuaded of the existence of an afterlife. Such apparitions were not in reality the souls of the dead but films of atoms still floating through the world after the death and dissolution of the person from whom they had emanated. Eventually, the atoms in these films too would be dispersed, but for the moment they could astonish and frighten the living.

The theory now only makes us smile, but perhaps it can serve as an image of the strange afterlife of Lucretius' poem, the poem that almost disappeared forever, dispersed into random atoms, but that somehow managed to survive. It survived because a succession of people, in a range of places and times and for reasons that seem largely accidental, encountered the material object—the papyrus or parchment or paper, with its inky marks attributed to Titus Lucretius Carus—and then sat down to make material copies of their own. Sitting in the room with her children, counting the syllables of translated verses on the threads of her canvas, the Puritan Lucy Hutchinson was serving in effect as one of the transmitters of the atomic particles that Lucretius had set in motion centuries and centuries earlier.

By the time Hutchinson reluctantly sent her translation to Anglesey, the idea of what she called "the foppish, casual dance of atoms" had already long penetrated the intellectual imagination of England. Edmund Spenser had written an ecstatic and

strikingly Lucretian hymn to Venus; Francis Bacon had ventured that "In nature nothing really exists besides individual
bodies"; Thomas Hobbes had reflected wryly on the relationship between fear and religious delusions.

In England, as elsewhere in Europe, it had proved possible,
though quite difficult, to retain a belief in God as the creator
of atoms in the first place. Thus Isaac Newton, in what has
been called one of the most influential pieces of writing in the
history of science, declared himself an atomist, making what
appears to be a direct allusion to the title of Lucretius' poem.
"While the Particles continue entire," he remarked, "they may
compose Bodies of one and the same Nature and Texture in all
Ages: But should they wear away, or break in pieces, the Nature
of Things depending on them, would be changed." At the same
time, Newton was careful to invoke a divine maker. "It seems
probable to me," Newton wrote in the second edition of the
Opticks (1718),

> That God in the Beginning form'd Matter in solid,
> massy, hard, impenetrable, moveable Particles, of such
> Sizes and Figures, and with such other Properties, and
> in such Proportions to Space, as most conduced to the
> End for which he form'd them; and that these primitive
> Particles being Solids, are incomparably harder than
> any porous Bodies compounded of them; even so very
> hard, as never to wear or break in pieces; no ordinary
> Power being able to divide what God himself made one
> in the first creation.

For Newton, as for other scientists from the seventeenth
century to our own time, it remained possible to reconcile
atomism with Christian faith. But Hutchinson's fears proved
well grounded. Lucretius' materialism helped to generate and

support the skepticism of the likes of Dryden and Voltaire and the programmatic, devastating disbelief expressed in Diderot, Hume, and many other Enlightenment figures.

What lay ahead, beyond the horizon of even these farsighted figures, were the astonishing empirical observations and experimental proofs that put the principles of ancient atomism on a whole different plane. When in the nineteenth century he set out to solve the mystery of the origin of human species, Charles Darwin did not have to draw on Lucretius' vision of an entirely natural, unplanned process of creation and destruction, endlessly renewed by sexual reproduction. That vision had directly influenced the evolutionary theories of Darwin's grandfather, Erasmus Darwin, but Charles could base his arguments on his own work in the Galápagos and elsewhere. So too when Einstein wrote of atoms, his thought rested on experimental and mathematical science, not upon ancient philosophical speculation. But that speculation, as Einstein himself knew and acknowledged, had set the stage for the empirical proofs upon which modern atomism depends. That the ancient poem could now be safely left unread, that the drama of its loss and recovery could fade into oblivion, that Poggio Bracciolini could be forgotten almost entirely—these were only signs of Lucretius' absorption into the mainstream of modern thought.

Among those for whom Lucretius was still a crucial guide, before this absorption had become complete, was a wealthy Virginia planter with a restless skeptical intelligence and a scientific bent. Thomas Jefferson owned at least five Latin editions of *On the Nature of Things*, along with translations of the poem into English, Italian, and French. It was one of his favorite books, confirming his conviction that the world is nature alone and that nature consists only of matter. Still more, Lucretius helped to shape Jefferson's confidence that ignorance and fear were not necessary components of human existence.

Jefferson took this ancient inheritance in a direction that Lucretius could not have anticipated but of which Thomas More, back in the early sixteenth century, had dreamed. Jefferson had not, as the poet of *On the Nature of Things* urged, withdrawn from the fierce conflicts of public life. Instead, he had given a momentous political document, at the founding of a new republic, a distinctly Lucretian turn. The turn was toward a government whose end was not only to secure the lives and the liberties of its citizens but also to serve "the pursuit of Happiness." The atoms of Lucretius had left their traces on the Declaration of Independence.

On August 15, 1820, the seventy-seven-year-old Jefferson wrote to another former president, his friend John Adams. Adams was eighty-five, and the two old men were in the habit of exchanging views on the meaning of life, as they felt it ebb away. "I [am] obliged to recur ultimately to my habitual anodyne," Jefferson wrote:

> "I feel: therefore I exist." I feel bodies which are not myself: there are other existencies then. I call them *matter*. I feel them changing place. This gives me *motion*. Where there is an absence of matter, I call it *void*, or *nothing*, or *immaterial space*. On the basis of sensation, of matter and motion, we may erect the fabric of all the certainties we can have or need.

These are the sentiments that Lucretius had most hoped to instill in his readers. "I am," Jefferson wrote to a correspondent who wanted to know his philosophy of life, "an Epicurean."

ACKNOWLEDGMENTS

THE ANCIENT PHILOSOPHER whose work gave rise to the story that I trace in these pages believed that life's highest end was pleasure, and he took particular pleasure in the community of his friends. It is only fitting then that I acknowledge the rich and sustaining network of friends and colleagues who have enhanced the writing of this book. Over the course of a year at the Wissenschaftskolleg in Berlin I spent many pleasurable hours discussing Lucretius with the late Bernard Williams, whose marvelous intelligence illuminated everything that it touched. And some years later at the same wonderful Berlin institution I participated in an extraordinary Lucretius reading group that gave me the critical impetus I needed. Generously guided by two philosophers, Christoph Horn and Christof Rapp, the group, which included Horst Bredekamp, Susan James, Reinhard Meyer-Kalkus, Quentin Skinner, and Ramie Targoff, along with more occasional visitors, worked its way with exemplary care and contentiousness through the poem.

A second wonderful institution—the American Academy in Rome—provided the perfect setting for the bulk of the book's writing: Nowhere else in my experience is the precious opportunity to sit quietly and work so exquisitely braided together with Epicurean pleasure. To the Academy's director, Carmela Vircillo Franklin, and its capable staff, along with a host of fellows and visitors, I owe a deep debt of gratitude. My agent, Jill Kneerim, and my editor, Alane Salierno Mason, have been extraordinarily helpful, generous, and acute readers. Among the many others who have given me advice and assistance, I want to single out Albert Ascoli, Homi Bhabha, Alison Brown, Gene Brucker, Joseph Connors, Brian Cummings, Trevor Dadson, James H. Dee, Kenneth Gouwens, Jeffrey Hamburger, James Hankins, Philip Hardie, Bernard Jussen, Joseph Koerner, Thomas Laqueur, George Logan, David Norbrook, William O'Connell, Robert Pinsky, Oliver Primavesi, Steven Shapin, Marcello Simonetta, James Simpson, Pippa Skotnes, Nick Wilding, and David Wootton.

My students and colleagues at Harvard have been a source of constant intellectual stimulation and challenge, and the stupendous library resources of this university have never ceased to amaze me. I owe particular thanks for research assistance to Christine Barrett, Rebecca Cook, Shawon Kinew, Ada Palmer, and Benjamin Woodring.

My deepest debt of gratitude—for wise advice and for inexhaustible pleasure—is to my wife, Ramie Targoff.

NOTES

PREFACE

2 **"First, goddess"**: Lucretius, *On the Nature of Things*, trans. Martin Ferguson Smith (London: Sphere Books, 1969; rev. edn., Indianapolis: Hackett, 2001), 1:12–20. I have consulted the modern English translations of H. A. J. Munro (1914), W. H. D. Rouse, rev. Martin Ferguson Smith (1975, 1992), Frank O. Copley (1977), Ronald Melville (1997), A. E. Stallings (2007), and David Slavitt (2008). Among earlier English translations I have consulted those of John Evelyn (1620–1706), Lucy Hutchinson (1620–1681), John Dryden (1631–1700), and Thomas Creech (1659–1700). Of these translations Dryden's is the best, but, in addition to the fact that he only translated small portions of the poem (615 lines in all, less than 10 percent of the total), his language often renders Lucretius difficult for the modern reader to grasp. For ease of access, unless otherwise indicated, I have used Smith's 2001 prose translation, and I have cited the lines in the Latin text given in the readily available Loeb edition—Cambridge, MA: Harvard University Press, 1975.

10 **"Spring comes"**: *On the Nature of Things* 5:737–40. Venus' "winged harbinger" is Cupid, whom Botticelli depicts blindfolded and aiming his winged arrow; Flora, the Roman goddess of flowers, strews blossoms gathered in the folds of her exquisite dress; and Zephyr, the god of the fecundating west wind, is reaching for the nymph Chloris. On Lucretius' influence on Botticelli, mediated by the humanist Poliziano, see Charles Dempsey, *The Portrayal of Love: Botticelli's "Primavera" and Humanist Culture at the Time of Lorenzo the Magnificent* (Princeton: Princeton University Press, 1992), esp. pp. 36–49; Horst Bredekamp, *Botticelli: Primavera. Florenz als Garten der Venus* (Frankfurt am Main: Fischer Verlag GmbH, 1988); and Aby Warburg's seminal 1893 essay,

"Sandro Botticelli's *Birth of Venus* and *Spring*: An Examination of Concepts of Antiquity in the Italian Early Renaissance," in *The Revival of Pagan Antiquity*, ed. Kurt W. Forster, trans. David Britt (Los Angeles: Getty Research Institute for the History of Art and the Humanities, 1999), pp. 88–156.

13 **an avid letter writer:** A total of 558 letters by Poggio, addressed to 172 different correspondents, survive. In a letter written in July 1417 congratulating Poggio on his discoveries, Francesco Barbaro refers to a letter about the journey of discovery that Poggio had sent to "our fine and learned friend Guarinus of Verona"—*Two Renaissance Book Hunters: The Letters of Poggius Bracciolini to Nicolaus de Nicolis*, trans. Phyllis Walter Goodhart Gordan (New York: Columbia University Press, 1974), p. 201. For Poggio's letters, see Poggio Bracciolini, *Lettere*, ed. Helene Harth, 3 vols. (Florence: Olschki, 1984).

CHAPTER ONE: THE BOOK HUNTER

14 **Slight of build:** On Poggio's appearance, see *Poggio Bracciolini 1380–1980: Nel VI centenario della nascita*, Instituto Nazionale di Studi Sul Rinascimento, vol. 7 (Florence: Sansoni, 1982) and *Un Toscano del '400 Poggio Bracciolini, 1380–1459*, ed. Patrizia Castelli (Terranuova Bracciolini: Administrazione Comunale, 1980). The principal biographical source is Ernst Walser, *Poggius Florentinus: Leben und Werke* (Hildesheim: George Olms, 1974).

16 **Indeed, curiosity was said:** On curiosity as a sin and the complex process of rehabilitating it, see Hans Blumenberg, *The Legitimacy of the Modern Age*, trans. Robert M. Wallace (Cambridge, MA: MIT Press, 1983; orig. German edn. 1966), pp. 229–453.

19 **his "detestable and unseemly life":** Eustace J. Kitts, *In the Days of the Councils: A Sketch of the Life and Times of Baldassare Cossa (Afterward Pope John the Twenty-Third)* (London: Archibald Constable & Co., 1908), p. 359.

21 **George of Trebizond had salted:** Peter Partner, *The Pope's Men: The Papal Civil Service in the Renaissance* (Oxford: Clarendon Press, 1990), p. 54.

22 **By the 1450s:** Lauro Martines, *The Social World of the Florentine Humanists, 1390–1460* (Princeton: Princeton University Press, 1963), pp. 123–27.

22 **in this difficult period:** In 1416 he evidently tried, with the others in the curia, to secure a benefice for himself, but the grant was controversial and in the end was not awarded. Apparently, he could also have taken a position as Scriptor in the new papacy of Martin V, but he refused, regarding it as a demotion from his position as secretary— Walser, *Poggius Florentinus*, pp. 42ff.

CHAPTER TWO: THE MOMENT OF DISCOVERY

23 **Petrarch brought glory:** Nicholas Mann, "The Origins of Humanism," in *The Cambridge Companion to Renaissance Humanism*, ed. Jill Kraye (Cambridge: Cambridge University Press, 1996), p. 11. On Poggio's response to Petrarch, see Riccardo Fubini, *Humanism and Secularization: From Petrarch to Valla*, Duke Monographs in Medieval and Renaissance Studies, 18 (Durham, NC, and London: Duke University Press, 2003). On the development of Italian humanism, see John Addington Symonds, *The Revival of Learning* (New York: H. Holt, 1908; repr. 1960); Wallace K. Ferguson, *The Renaissance in Historical Thought: Five Centuries of Interpretation* (Cambridge, MA: Harvard University Press, 1948); Paul Oskar Kristeller, "The Impact of Early Italian Humanism on Thought and Learning," in Bernard S. Levy, ed. *Developments in the Early Renaissance* (Albany: State University of New York Press, 1972), pp. 120–57; Charles Trinkaus, *The Scope of Renaissance Humanism* (Ann Arbor: University of Michigan Press, 1983); Anthony Grafton and Lisa Jardine, *From Humanism to the Humanities: Education and the Liberal Arts in Fifteenth- and Sixteenth-Century Europe* (Cambridge, MA: Harvard University Press, 1986); Peter Burke, "The Spread of Italian Humanism," in Anthony Goodman and Angus Mackay, eds., *The Impact of Humanism on Western Europe* (London: Longman, 1990), pp. 1–22; Ronald G. Witt, *"In the Footsteps of the Ancients": The Origins of Humanism from Lovato to Bruni*, Studies in Medieval and Reformation Thought, ed. Heiko A. Oberman, vol. 74 (Leiden: Brill, 2000); and Riccardo, Fubini, *L'Umanesimo Italiano e I Suoi Storici* (Milan: Franco Angeli Storia, 2001).

23 **"Macer and Lucretius are certainly":** Quintilian, *Institutio Oratoria (The Orator's Education)*, ed. and trans. Donald A. Russell, Loeb Classical Library, 127 (Cambridge, MA: Harvard University Press, 2001), 10.1, pp. 299ff. Though a complete (or nearly complete) copy of Quintilian was only found—by Poggio Bracciolini—in 1516, book X, with its lists of Greek and Roman writers, circulated throughout the Middle

Ages. Quintilian remarks of Macer and Lucretius that "Each is elegant on his own subject, but the former is prosaic and the latter difficult," p. 299.

24 **literacy rates, by our standards:** Robert A. Kaster, *Guardians of Language: The Grammarian and Society in Late Antiquity* (Berkeley and London: University of California Press, 1988). Estimates of literacy rates in earlier societies are notoriously unreliable. Kaster, citing the research of Richard Duncan-Jones, concludes: "the great majority of the empire's inhabitants were illiterate in the classical languages." The figures for the first three centuries CE suggest upwards of 70 percent illiteracy, though with many regional differences. There are similar figures in Kim Haines-Eitzen, *Guardians of Letters: Literacy, Power, and the Transmitters of Early Christian Literature* (Oxford: Oxford University Press, 2000), though Haines-Eitzen has even lower literacy levels (10 percent perhaps). See also Robin Lane Fox, "Literacy and Power in Early Christianity," in Alan K. Bowman and Greg Woolf, eds., *Literacy and Power in the Ancient World* (Cambridge: Cambridge University Press, 1994).

24 **"they shall give him twenty":** Cited in Fox, "Literacy and Power," p. 147.

25 **"Above all, one or two seniors":** The Rule does include a provision for those who simply cannot abide reading: "If anyone is so remiss and indolent that he is unwilling or unable to study or to read, he is to be given some work in order that he may not be idle"—*The Rule of Benedict*, trans. by Monks of Glenstal Abbey (Dublin: Four Courts Press, 1982), 48:223.

26 **"He looks about anxiously":** John Cassian, *The Institutes*, trans. Boniface Ramsey (New York: Newman Press, 2000), 10:2.

26 **"If such a monk":** *The Rule of Benedict*, 48:19–20. I have amended the translation given, "as a warning to others," to capture what I take to be the actual sense of the Latin: *ut ceteri timeant*.

27 **"the feeling of elation":** *Spiritum elationis*: the translators render these words as "spirit of vanity" but I believe that "elation" or "exaltation" is the principal sense here.

27 **"Let there be":** *The Rule of Benedict*, 38:5–7.

27 **"No one should presume":** Ibid., 38:8.

27 **"The superior"**: Ibid., 38:9.

30 **"For him that stealeth"**: Leila Avrin, *Scribes, Script and Books: The Book Arts from Antiquity to the Renaissance* (Chicago and London: American Library Association and the British Library: 1991), p. 324. The manuscript is in Barcelona.

32 **the beautiful handwriting**: On the larger context of Poggio's handwriting, see Berthold L. Ullman, *The Origin and Development of Humanistic Script* (Rome: Edizioni di Storia e Letteratura, 1960). For a valuable introduction, see Martin Davies, "Humanism in Script and Print in the Fifteenth Century," in *The Cambridge Companion to Renaissance Humanism*, pp. 47–62.

34 **to serve as apostolic secretaries**: Bartolomeo served as secretary in 1414; Poggio the following year—Partner, *The Pope's Men*, pp. 218, 222.

34 **"I hate all boastful conversation"**: Gordan, *Two Renaissance Book Hunters*, pp. 208–9 (letter to Ambrogio Traversari).

35 **"I shall set out"**: Ibid, p. 210.

36 **he was brought to the armory**: Eustace J. Kitts, *In the Days of the Councils: A Sketch of the Life and Times of Baldassare Cossa* (London: Archibald Constable & Co., 1908), p. 69.

37 **"I cannot find that they do anything"**: Cited in W. M. Shepherd, *The Life of Poggio Bracciolini* (Liverpool: Longman et al., 1837), p. 168.

40 **"The parchment is hairy"**: Avrin, *Scribes, Script and Books*, p. 224. The scribe in question actually used "vellum," not parchment, but it must have been a particularly miserable vellum.

40 **"Now I've written"**: Ibid.

41 **"Vouchsafe, O Lord"**: Quoted in George Haven Putnam, *Books and Their Makers During the Middle Ages*, 2 vols. (New York: Hillary House, 1962; repr. of 1896–98 edn.) 1:61.

43 **Working with knives**: The great monastery at Bobbio, in the north of Italy, had a celebrated library: a catalogue drawn up at the end of the ninth century includes many rare ancient texts, including a copy of Lucretius. But most of these have disappeared, presumably scraped away to make room for the gospels and psalters that served the community. Bernhard Bischhoff writes: "Many ancient texts were buried

when their codices were palimsested at Bobbio, which had abandoned the rule of Columbanus for the rule of Benedict. A catalogue from the end of the ninth century informs us that Bobbio possessed at that time one of the most extensive libraries in the West, including many grammatical treatises as well as rare poetical works. The sole copy of Septimius Serenus' *De runalibus*, an elaborate poem from the age of Hadrian, was lost. Copies of Lucretius and Valerius Flaccus seem to have disappeared without Italian copies having been made. Poggio eventually discovered these works in Germany"—*Manuscripts and Libraries in the Age of Charlemagne* (Cambridge: Cambridge University Press, 1994), p. 151.

44 **Abbey of Fulda:** A strong alternative candidate is the Abbey of Murbach, in southern Alsace. By the middle of the ninth century, Murbach, founded in 727, had become an important center of scholarship and is known to have possessed a copy of Lucretius. The challenge facing Poggio would have been roughly the same in any monastic library he approached.

47 **Rabanus, who as a young man:** In the context of the current book, the most intriguing comment comes in Rabanus's prose preface to his fascinating collection of acrostic poems in praise of the Cross, composed in 810. Rabanus writes that his poems include the rhetorical figure of *synalepha*, the contraction of two syllables into one. This is a figure, he explains, *Quod et Titus Lucretius non raro fecisse invenitur*—"which is frequently found in Titus Lucretius." Quoted in David Ganz, "Lucretius in the Carolingian Age: The Leiden Manuscripts and Their Carolingian Readers," in Claudine A. Chavannes-Mazel and Margaret M. Smith, eds., *Medieval Manuscripts of the Latin Classics: Production and Use*, Proceedings of the Seminar in the History of the Book to 1500, Leiden, 1993 (Los Altos Hills, CA: Anderson-Lovelace, 1996), 99.

48 **"obliterated by the praiseworthy use":** Pliny the Younger, *Letters*, 3.7.

50 **neither he nor anyone in his circle:** The humanists might have picked up shadowy signs of the poem's continued existence. Macrobius, in the early fifth century CE, quotes a few lines in his *Saturnalia* (see George Hadzsits, *Lucretius and His Influence* [New York: Longmans, Green & Co., 1935]), as does Isidore of Seville's vast *Etymologiae* in the early seventh century. Other moments in which the work surfaced briefly will be mentioned below, but it would have been rash for anyone in

the early fifteenth century to believe that the entire poem would be found.

CHAPTER THREE: IN SEARCH OF LUCRETIUS

51 **and it continued to be read:** "Send me some piece by Lucretius or Ennius," the highly cultivated emperor Antoninus Pius (86–161 CE) wrote to a friend; "something harmonious, powerful, and expressive of the state of the spirit." (Apart from fragments, Ennius, the greatest early Roman poet, has never been recovered.)

51 **"The poetry of Lucretius":** "Lucreti poemata, ut scribis, ita sunt, multis luminibus ingenii, multae tamen artis"—Cicero, *Q.Fr.* 2.10.3.

51 **"Blessed is he":** *Georgics*, 2.490–92:

> *Felix, qui potuit rerum cognoscere causas,*
> *atque metus omnis et inexorabile fatum*
> *subiecit pedibus strepitumque Acherontis avari.*

Acheron, a river of the underworld, is used by Virgil and Lucretius as a symbol of the whole realm of the afterlife. For Lucretius' presence in the *Georgics*, see especially Monica Gale, *Virgil on the Nature of Things: The Georgics, Lucretius, and the Didactic Tradition* (Cambridge: Cambridge University Press, 2000).

52 **But Virgil did not mention:** The author of the *Aeneid*, with his somber sense of the burden of imperial power and the stern necessity of renouncing pleasures, was clearly more skeptical than he had been in the *Georgics* about anyone's ability to grasp with serene clarity the hidden forces of the universe. But Lucretius' vision and the tough elegance of his poetry are present throughout Virgil's epic, if only as glimpses of an achieved security that now constantly and forever eludes the poet and his hero. On the deep presence of Lucretius in the *Aeneid* (and in other works of Virgil, as well as those of Ovid and Horace), see Philip Hardie, *Lucretian Receptions: History, The Sublime, Knowledge* (Cambridge: Cambridge University Press, 2009).

52 **"The verses of sublime Lucretius":** *Amores*, 1.15.23–24. See Philip Hardie, *Ovid's Poetics of Illusion* (Cambridge: Cambridge University Press, 2002) esp. pp. 143–63, 173–207.

53 **Memmius had a relatively successful:** Son-in-law for a time of the merciless patrician dictator Sulla, Memmius' political career came to an end

in 54 BCE, when, as a candidate for the office of consul, he was forced to disclose his involvement in a financial scandal that lost him the crucial support of Julius Caesar. As an orator, in Cicero's view, Memmius was lazy. He was, Cicero conceded, extremely well read, though more in Greek than in Latin literature. Perhaps this immersion in Greek culture helps to explain why, after his political fortunes fell, Memmius moved to Athens, where he apparently bought land on which stood the ruins of the house of the philosopher Epicurus, who died more than two hundred years earlier. In 51 BCE, Cicero wrote a letter to Memmius in which he asked him as a personal favor to give these ruins to "Patro the Epicurean." (The ruins were evidently threatened by a building project that Memmius had in mind.) Patro pleads, Cicero reports, "that he owes a responsibility to his office and duty, to the sanctity of testaments, to the prestige of Epicurus' name . . . to the abode, domicile, and memorials of great men"—Letter 63 (13:1) in *Cicero's Letters to Friends* (Loeb edn.), 1:271. With Epicurus, we close the circle back to Lucretius, for Lucretius was Epicurus' most passionate, intelligent, and creative disciple.

53 **These lurid details:** On the creation of the legend, see esp. Luciano Canfora's *Vita di Lucrezio* (Palermo: Sellerio, 1993). The greatest evocation of it is Tennyson's "Lucretius."

54 **Lucretius remains almost:** Canfora's fascinating *Vita di Lucrezio* is not a biography in any conventional sense, but rather a brilliant exercise in dismantling the mythic narrative launched by Jerome. In a work in progress, Ada Palmer shows that Renaissance scholars assembled what they thought were clues to Lucretius' life, but that most of those clues turn out to have been comments about other, unrelated people.

55 **"This man":** Johann Joachim Winkelmann, cited in David Sider, *The Library of the Villa dei Papiri at Herculaneum* (Los Angeles: J. Paul Getty Museum, 2005). Winkelmann's colorful phrase is an Italian proverb.

55 **"about half a palm long":** Camillo Paderni, director of the Museum Herculanense in the Royal Palace at Portici, in a letter written on February 25, 1755, quoted in Sider, *The Library*, p. 22.

56 **Rolls of papyrus:** Avrin, *Scribes, Script and Books*, pp. 83ff.

57 **The room unearthed:** At this point, by rare good fortune, the investigation of the site was under the supervision of a Swiss army engineer, Karl Weber, who took a more responsible and scholarly interest in what lay underground.

59 **It prided itself on being:** This way of viewing themselves had a long life. When Scipio sacked Carthage in 146 BCE, the library collections of that great North African city fell into his hands, along with all the other plunder. He wrote to the Senate and asked what to do with the books now in his possession. Answer came back that a single book, a treatise on agriculture, was worth returning to be translated into Latin; the rest of the books, the senators wrote, Scipio should distribute as gifts to the petty kings of Africa—Pliny the Elder, *Natural History*, 18:5.

60 **the captive monarch's library:** The seizing of Greek libraries as spoils became a fairly common practice, though rarely as the conqueror's sole prize. In 67 BCE, Lucullus, an ally of Sulla, brought home from his eastern conquests a very valuable library, along with other riches, and in retirement he devoted himself to the study of Greek literature and philosophy. At his villa and gardens in Rome and in Tusculum, near Naples, Lucullus was the generous patron of Greek intellectuals and poets, and he figures in Cicero's dialogue *Academica* as one of the principal interlocutors.

61 **Rome's first public library:** Appointed to administer northern Italy (Gallia Transpadana), Pollio used his influence to save Virgil's property from confiscation.

61 **The library established by Pollio:** Augustus' two libraries were known as the Octavian and the Palatine. The former, founded in honor of his sister (33 BC), was situated in the Porticus Octaviae and combined a magnificent promenade on the lower story with the reading room and book collection on the upper. The other library, attached to the Temple of Apollo on the Palatine Hill, seems to have had two separately administered departments, a Greek and a Latin one. Both libraries were subsequently destroyed by fire. Augustus' successors maintained the tradition of establishing libraries: Tiberius founded the Tiberian Library in his house on the Palatine (according to Suetonius, he caused the writings and images of his favorite Greek poets to be placed in the public libraries). Vespasian established a library in the Temple of Peace erected after the burning of the city under Nero. Domitian restored the libraries after the same fire, even sending to Alexandria for copies. The most important imperial library was the Ulpian Library, created by Ulpius Trajanus—first established in the Forum of Trajan but afterwards removed to the Baths of Diocletian. See Lionel Casson, *Libraries in the Ancient World* (New Haven: Yale University Press, 2002).

62 **Many other cities:** Among them: Athens, Cyprus, Como, Milan, Smyrna, Patrae, Tibur—from which books could even be borrowed. But see the inscription found in the Agora of Athens, on the wall of the Library of Pantainos (200 CE): "No book shall be removed, since we have sworn thus. Opening hours are from six in the morning until noon" (quoted in Sider, *The Library of the Villa dei Papiri at Herculaneum*, p. 43).

62 **throughout their territories the Romans:** Clarence E. Boyd, *Public Libraries and Literary Culture in Ancient Rome* (Chicago: University of Chicago Press, 1915), pp. 23–24.

63 **houses of cultivated men and women:** Cf. Arnaldo Momigliano, *Alien Wisdom: The Limits of Hellenization* (Cambridge: Cambridge University Press, 1975).

63 **At the games in the Colosseum:** Erich Auerbach, *Literary Language and Its Public in Late Latin Antiquity and in the Middle Ages*, trans. Ralph Manheim (Princeton: Princeton University Press, 1965), p. 237.

64 ***"De rerum natura* has been rediscovered":** Knut Kleve, "Lucretius in Herculaneum," in *Cronache Ercolanesi* 19 (1989), p. 5.

65 **"amid his tipsy":** *In Pisonem* ("Against Piso"), in Cicero, *Orations*, trans. N. H. Watts, Loeb Classical Library, vol. 252 (Cambridge, MA: Harvard University Press, 1931), p. 167 ("in suorum Gaecorum foetore atque vino").

66 **"Tomorrow, friend Piso":** *The Epigrams of Philodemos*, ed. and trans. David Sider (New York: Oxford University Press, 1997), p. 152.

67 **Staring up idly:** Though there had been a serious recent earthquake, the last major eruption had taken place ca. 1200 BCE, so the source of queasiness, if there was one, was not the volcano.

69 **"This has often struck me":** Cicero, *De natura deorum* ("On the Nature of the Gods"), trans. H. Rackham, Loeb Classical Library, 268 (Cambridge, MA: Harvard University Press, 1933), 1.6, pp. 17–19.

70 **"Here the conversation ended":** Ibid., p. 383.

70 **"The one who engages":** Cicero, *De officiis* ("On Duties"), trans. Walter Miller, Loeb Classical Library, 30. (Cambridge, MA: Harvard University Press, 1913), 1.37, p. 137.

72 **When "human life":** As I will discuss below, the word translated here as "superstitition" is in Latin *religio*, that is, "religion."

72 **Epicurus:** Diogenes Laertius, *Lives of the Eminent Philosophers*, 2 vols., Loeb Classical Library, 184–85 (Cambridge, MA: Harvard University Press, 1925), 2:531–33.

75 **Epicurus' philosophy:** Epicurus' *epilogismos* was a term frequently used to suggest "reasoning based on empirical data," but according to Michael Schofield, it conveys "our everyday procedures of assessment and appraisal"—Schofield, in *Rationality in Greek Thought*, ed. Michael Frede and Gisele Striker (Oxford: Clarendon Press, 1996). Schofield suggests that these procedures are linked to a famous passage by Epicurus on time: "We must not adopt special expressions for it, supposing that this will be an improvement; we must use just the existing ones," p. 222. The thinking that Epicurus urged upon his followers was "a perfectly ordinary kind of activity available to all, not a special intellectual accomplishment restricted to, for example, mathematicians or dialecticians," p. 235.

76 **"Do you suppose":** Cicero, *Tusculanae disputationes* ("Tusculan Disputations"), trans. J. E. King. Loeb Classical Library, 141 (Cambridge, MA: Harvard University Press, 1927), 1.6.10.

76 **it is difficult to understand:** Ibid., 1.21.48–89.

76 **He "vomited twice a day":** The charge was made by "Timocrates, the brother of Metrodorus, who was his [Epicurus'] disciple and then left the school," in Diogenes Laertius, *Lives of Eminent Philosophers*, trans. R. D. Hicks, 2 vols., Loeb Classical Library, 185 (Cambridge, MA: Harvard University Press, 1925), 2:535.

77 **the passerby who entered:** Seneca, *Ad Lucilium Epistulae Morales*, trans. Richard Gummere, 3 vols. (Cambridge: Cambridge University Press, 1917), 1:146.

77 **"When we say, then":** Letter to Menoeceus, in Laertius, *Lives*, 2:657.

77 **"Men suffer the worst evils":** Philodemus, *On Choices and Avoidances*, trans. Giovanni Indelli and Voula Tsouna-McKirahan, La Scuola di Epicuro, 15 (Naples: Bibliopolis, 1995), pp. 104–6.

77 **"I'll have all my beds":** Ben Jonson, *The Alchemist*, ed. Alvin B. Kernan, 2 vols. (New Haven: Yale University Press, 1974), II.ii.41–42; 72–87. Jonson is participating in a tradition of representing Epicurus as the patron saint of the inn and the brothel, a tradition that includes Chau-

cer's well-fed Franklin, who is described in the *Canterbury Tales* as "Epicurus owene sone."

79 **"Some men have sought"**: Maxim #7, in Diogenes Laertius, *Lives of Eminent Philosophers*, trans. R. D. Hicks, 2 vols. Loeb Classical Library, 185 (Cambridge, MA: Harvard University Press, 1925; rev. ed. 1931), 1:665.

80 **"Against other things"**: Vatican sayings 31, in A. A. Long and D. N. Sedley, *The Hellenistic Philosophers*, 2 vols. (Cambridge: Cambridge University Press, 1987), 1:150.

CHAPTER FOUR: THE TEETH OF TIME

81 **The indefatigable scholar Didymus of Alexandria**: Cf. Moritz W. Schmidt, *De Didymo Chalcentero* (Oels: A. Ludwig, 1851) and *Didymi Chalcenteri fragmenta* (Leipzig: Teubner, 1854).

82 **an ambitious literary editor**: Cf. David Diringer, *The Book Before Printing* (New York: Dover Books, 1982), pp. 241ff.

82 **extraordinarily prolific**: Diogenes Laertius: "Epicurus was a most prolific author and eclipsed all before him in the number of his writings: for they amount to about three hundred rolls, and contain not a single citation from other authors; it is Epicurus himself who speaks throughout"—*Lives of Eminent Philosophers*, 2:555. Diogenes Laertius lists the titles of thirty-seven books by Epicurus, all of which have been lost.

82 **On that wall**: Cf. Andrew M. T. Moore, "Diogenes's Inscription at Oenoanda," in Dane R. Gordon and David B. Suits, eds., *Epicurus: His Continuing Influence and Contemporary Relevance* (Rochester, NY: Rochester Institute of Technology Cary Graphic Arts Press, 2003), pp. 209–14. See *The Epicurean Inscription* [*of Diogenes of Oinoanda*], ed. and trans. Martin Ferguson Smith (Naples: Bibliopolis, 1992).

83 **"Others are found"**: Aristotle, *Historia animalium*, trans. A. L. Peck, Loeb Classical Library, 438 (Cambridge, MA: Harvard University Press, 1965–91), 5:32.

83 **"a small white silver-shining"**: Quoted in William Blades, *The Enemies of Books* (London: Elliot Stock, 1896), pp. 66–67.

84 **"constant gnawing"**: Ovid, *Ex ponto*, trans. A. L. Wheeler, rev. G. P. Goold, 2nd edn. (Cambridge, MA: Harvard University Press, 1924), 1.1.73.

84 "food for vandal moths": Horace, *Satires. Epistles. The Art of Poetry*, trans. H. Rushton Fairclough, Loeb Classical Library, 194 (Cambridge, MA: Harvard University Press, 1926), Epistle 1.20.12.

84 "Page-eater": In *Greek Anthology*, trans. W. R. Paton, Loeb Classical Library, 84 (Cambridge, MA: Harvard University Press, 1917), 9:251. (Evenus of Ascalon, fl. between 50 BCE and 50 CE).

84 many, perhaps most, Greek scribes: Kim Haines-Eitzen, *Guardians of Letters: Literacy, Power, and the Transmitters of Early Christian Literature* (Oxford: Oxford University Press, 2000), p. 4.

85 "I have received the book": Quoted in Lionel Casson, *Libraries in the Ancient World* (New Haven: Yale University Press, 2001), p. 77.

85 Publishers had to contend: Leila Avrin, *Scribes, Script and Books: The Book Arts from Antiquity to the Renaissance* (Chicago: American Library Association, 1991), p. 171. See also pp. 149–53.

85 female as well as male copyists: On women copyists, see Haines-Eitzen.

86 The invention of movable type: It is estimated that the number of books that had been produced cumulatively in the history of the world before 1450 was equaled by the number produced between 1450 and 1500; that this number was produced again between 1500 and 1510; and that twice this number was produced in the next decade.

86 a roomful of well-trained scribes: On scribes, see L. D. Reynolds and N. G. Wilson, *Scribes and Scholars: A Guide to the Transmission of Greek and Latin Literature*, 2nd edn. (London: Oxford University Press, 1974); Avrin, *Scribes, Script and Books*; Rosamond McKitterick, *Books, Scribes and Learning in the Frankish Kingdoms, 6th–9th Centuries* (Aldershot, UK: Variorum, 1994); M. B. Parkes, *Scribes, Scripts, and Readers* (London: Hambledon Press, 1991). On the symbolic significance of the scribe, cf. Giorgio Agamben, *Potentialities: Collected Essays in Philosophy*, ed. Daniel Heller-Roazen (Stanford: Stanford University Press, 2000), pp. 246ff. Avicenna's figure of "perfect potentiality," for example, is the scribe in the moment in which he does not write.

87 in Alexandria: Huge granaries south of Alexandria received endless bargeloads of grain, harvested from the rich flood plains along the river. These had been scrutinized by lynx-eyed officials, appointed to ensure that the grain was "unadulterated, with no admixture of

earth or barley, untrodden and sifted"—Christopher Haas, *Alexandria in Late Antiquity: Topography and Social Conflict* (Baltimore: Johns Hopkins University Press, 1997), p. 42. The sacks in their thousands were then transported by canal to the harbor, where the grain fleet awaited them. From there the heavily laden ships fanned out to cities whose burgeoning populations had long outstripped the capacity of the surrounding countryside to support them. Alexandria was one of the key control points in the ancient world for bread and hence stability and hence power. Grain was not the sole commodity that Alexandria controlled; the city's merchants were famous for the trade in wine, linens, tapestries, glass, and—most interesting for our purposes— papyrus. The huge marshes near the city were particularly suitable for the cultivation of the reeds from which the best paper was made. All through the ancient world, from the time of the Caesars to the rule of the Frankish kings, "Alexandrian papyrus" was the preferred medium on which bureaucrats, philosophers, poets, priests, merchants, emperors, and scholars gave orders, recorded debts, and wrote down their thoughts.

87 **a determination to assemble:** Ptolemy III (246–221 BCE) is said to have sent messages to all the rulers of the known world, asking for books to copy. Officials were under order to confiscate from passing ships all the books that they had on board. Copies of these books were made and returned, but the originals went into the great library (where in the catalogue they were marked "from the ships"). Royal agents fanned out through the Mediterranean to buy or borrow more and more books. Lenders grew increasingly wary—borrowed books had a way of not coming back—and demanded large deposits. When, after intense cajoling, Athens agreed to lend Alexandria its precious authoritative texts of Aeschylus, Sophocles, and Euripides—texts that were zealously guarded in the city's records office—the city insisted on the enormous bond of 15 talents of gold. Ptolemy posted the bond, received the books, sent copies back to Athens, and, forfeiting the bond, deposited the originals in the Museum.

88 **was second in magnificence:** Ammianus Marcellinus, *History*, Loeb Classical Library, 315 (Cambridge, MA: Harvard University Press, 1940), 2:303. Cf. Rufinus: "The whole edifice is built of arches with enormous windows above each arch. The hidden inner chambers are separate from one another and provide for the enactment of various ritual acts and secret observances. Sitting courts and small chapels with images of the gods occupy the edge of the highest level. Lofty

houses rise up there in which the priests . . . are accustomed to live. Behind these buildings, a freestanding portico raised on columns and facing inward runs around the periphery. In the middle stands the temple, built on a large and magnificent scale with an exterior of marble and precious columns. Inside there was a statue of Serapis so vast that the right hand touched one wall and the left the other"—Cited in Haas, *Alexandria in Late Antiquity*, p. 148.

89 **The first blow came:** Alexandria was, as we have seen, a strategically important city, and it could not escape the conflicts that constantly tore at the fabric of Roman society. In 48 BCE, Julius Caesar pursued his rival Pompey to Alexandria. At the Egyptian king's command, Pompey was promptly murdered—his head was presented to Caesar who professed to be grief-stricken. But though he probably had no more than 4,000 troops, Caesar decided to remain and secure control of the city. At one point in the course of the nine-month struggle that followed, the gravely outnumbered Romans found themselves threatened by a royal fleet that had sailed into the harbor. Using resin-smeared pine torches with an undercoating of sulfur, Caesar's forces managed to set the ships on fire. The conflagration was intense, for the hulls were sealed with highly flammable pitch and the decks were caulked with wax. (Details of the firing of ancient fleets are from Lucan, *Pharsalia*, trans. Robert Graves [Baltimore: Penguin, 1957], p. 84, III:656–700). The fire leaped from the ships to the shore and then spread through the wharves to the library, or at least to storehouses that held some of the collections. The books themselves were not the object of attack; they were merely convenient combustible material. But burned books do not take into consideration the arsonist's intentions. Caesar left the conquered city in the hands of the deposed king's glamorous and resourceful sister, Cleopatra. Some portion of the library's losses may have been quickly restored—a few years later the besotted Mark Antony is said to have given Cleopatra some 200,000 books that he had looted from Pergamum. (Columns from Pergamum's library are still visible among the impressive ruins of that once great city on Turkey's Mediterranean coast.) Books randomly stolen from one library and dumped into another do not, however, make up for the destruction of a collection that has been painstakingly and intelligently assembled. No doubt the library staff worked feverishly to repair the losses, and the institution, with its scholars and its enormous resources, remained a celebrated one. But the point must have been painfully clear: Mars is an enemy of books.

89 **It was only a matter of time:** It was not until 407 that bishops in the empire were granted the legal authority to close or demolish temples—Haas, *Alexandria in Late Antiquity*, p. 160.

90 **"as though"**: Rufinus, cited in ibid., pp. 161–62.

91 **"Is it not true"**: *Greek Anthology*, p. 172.

92 **"If you decree"**: *The Letters of Synesius of Cyrene*, trans. Augustine Fitzgerald (Oxford: Oxford University Press, 1926), p. 253. Something in Hypatia's whole way of being evidently excited profound respect, not only from scholars but also from the great mass of her fellow citizens. A young man from Damascus who traveled to Alexandria to study philosophy some two generations later still heard stories of the admiration that Hypatia aroused: "The entire city naturally loved her and held her in exceptional esteem, while the powers-that-be paid their respects first to her"—Damascius, *The Philosophical History*, trans. Polymnia Athanassiadi (Athens: Apamea Cultural Association, 1999), p. 131. Cf. the poet Palladas' praise of Hypatia:

> Searching the zodiac, gazing on Virgo,
> Knowing your province is really the heavens,
> Finding your brilliance everywhere I look,
> I render you homage, revered Hypatia,
> Teaching's bright star, unblemished, undimmed . . .

Poems, trans. Tony Harrison (London: Anvil Press Poetry, 1975), no. 67.

92 **"Such was her self-possession"**: Socrates Scholasticus, *Ecclesiastical History* (London: Samuel Bagster & Sons, 1844), p. 482.

92 **Rumors began to circulate:** See *The Chronicle of John, Bishop of Nikiu* [c. CE 690], trans. R. H. Charles (London: Text and Translation Society, 1916): "she was devoted at all times to magic, astrolabes and instruments of music, and she beguiled many people through (her) Satanic wiles. And the governor of the city honoured her exceedingly; for she had beguiled him through her magic" (84:87–88), p. 100.

93 **the death knell:** More than two hundred years later, when the Arabs conquered Alexandria, they evidently found books on the shelves, but these were for the most part works of Christian theology, not pagan philosophy, mathematics, and astronomy. When Caliph Omar was asked what to do with this remnant, he is said to have sent a chilling reply: "If the content of the books is in accordance with the book of Allah, we may do without them, for in that case, the book of Allah

more than suffices. If, on the other hand, they contain matter not in accordance with the book of Allah there can be no need to preserve them. Proceed, then, and destroy them." Quoted in Roy MacLeod, ed., *The Library of Alexandria: Centre of Learning in the Ancient World* (London: I. B. Tauris, 2004), p. 10. If the story is to be believed, the papyrus rolls, parchments, and codices were distributed to the public baths and burned in the stoves that heated the water. This fuel supply, legend has it, lasted for some six months. See also Luciano Canfora, *The Vanished Library: A Wonder of the Ancient World*, trans. Martin Ryle (Berkeley: University of California Press, 1989), and Casson, *Libraries in the Ancient World*. On Hypatia, see Maria Dzielska, *Hypatia of Alexandria* (Cambridge, MA: Harvard University Press, 1995).

93 **"In place of the philosopher"**: Ammianus Marcellinus, *History*, trans. Rolfe, I: 47 (xiv.6.18).

94 **"I would fast"**: Jerome, *Select Letters of St. Jerome*, Loeb Classical Library, 2362 (Cambridge, MA: Harvard University Press, 1933), Letter XXII (to Eustochium), p. 125.

95 **"From the judicious precepts"**: "When I was a young man, though I was protected by the rampart of the lonely desert, I could not endure against the promptings of sin and the ardent heat of my nature. I tried to crush them by frequent fasting, but my mind was always in a turmoil of imagination. To subdue it I put myself in the hands of one of the brethren who had been a Hebrew before his conversion, and asked him to teach me his language. Thus, after having studied the pointed style of Quintilian, the fluency of Cicero, the weightiness of Fronto, and the gentleness of Pliny, I now began to learn the alphabet again and practice harsh and guttural words [*stridentia anhelantiaque verba*]"—Jerome, *Select Letters*, p. 419. In the same letter, Jerome advises a monk, "Twist lines too for catching fish, and copy out manuscripts, so that your hand may earn you food and your soul be satisfied with reading," p. 419. The copying of manuscripts in monastic communities, as we have already seen, turned out to be crucial to the survival of Lucretius and other pagan texts.

95 **"You lie"**: Jerome, *Select Letters*, p. 127.

96 **"O Lord, if ever"**: Ibid., p. 129.

96 **What he found so alluring:** "It is no small thing for a noble man, a man fluent of speech, a wealthy man, to avoid the accompaniment of the powerful in the streets, to mingle with the crowds, to cleave to the

poor, to associate with peasants." Ep. 66.6, in praise of Pammachius, cited in Robert A. Kaster, *Guardians of Language: The Grammarian and Society in Late Antiquity* (Berkeley: University of California Press, 1988), p. 81.

96 "What has Horace": Jerome, *Select Letters*, Letter XXII (to Eustochium), p. 125.

97 "He was born in the district": Pope Gregory I, *Dialogues*, trans. Odo John Zimmerman (Washington, DC: Catholic University of America Press, 1959), 2:55–56.

98 **Plato and Aristotle:** Not everyone agreed that Plato and Aristotle could be accommodated. Cf. Tertullian, "Against the Heretics," ch. 7:

> For philosophy is the material of the world's wisdom, the rash interpreter of the nature and dispensation of God. Indeed heresies are themselves instigated by philosophy. . . . What indeed has Athens to do with Jerusalem? What has the Academy to do with the Church? What have heretics to do with Christians? Our instruction comes from the porch of Solomon, who had himself taught that the Lord should be sought in simplicity of heart. Away with all attempts to produce a Stoic, Platonic, and dialectic Christianity! We want no curious disputation after possessing Christ Jesus, no inquisition after receiving the gospel! When we believe, we desire no further belief. For this is our first article of faith, that there is nothing which we ought to believe besides.

See *Ante-Nicene Fathers*, ed. Alexander Roberts and James Donaldson, 10 vols. (Grand Rapids: Wm. B. Eerdmans Publishing Co., 1951), 3:246. Conversely, as we will see, efforts were made in the fifteenth century and later to reconcile Christianity with a modified version of Epicureanism.

98 "figments of diseased imagination": Minucius Felix, *Octavius*, trans. T. R. Glover and Gerald H. Rendall, Loeb Classical Library, 250 (Cambridge, MA: Harvard University Press, 1931), p. 345 (mockery of Christians), p. 385 (mockery of pagans). See, similarly, in the same volume, Tertullian, *Apologeticus* ("Apology"), "I turn to your literature, by which you are trained in wisdom and the liberal arts; and what absurdities I find! I read how the gods on account of Trojans and Achaeans fell to it and fought it out themselves like so many pairs of gladiators . . . ," p. 75.

99 "What will be the use": Tertullian, *Concerning the Resurrection of the Flesh*, trans. A. Souter (London: SPCK, 1922), pp. 153–54.

100 **"Yes!" Tertullian addressed:** Ibid., p. 91.

101 **Though early Christians:** See James Campbell, "The Angry God: Epicureans, Lactantius, and Warfare," in Gordon and Suits, eds., *Epicurus: His Continuing Influence and Contemporary Relevance*. The shift in Christianity toward an angry God, Campbell observes, comes only in the fourth century, with the growth of power and prominence in the Roman world. Before then, Christianity was closer to the Epicururean attitude and more sympathetic to its doctrines. "Indeed Tertullian, Clement of Alexandria, and Athenagoras found so much to admire in Epicureanism that Richard Jungkuntz has warned that 'any generalizations about patristic antipathy to Epicureanism really need careful qualification to be valid.' The Epicurean practice of the social virtues, emphasis on forgiveness and mutual helpfulness, and suspicion of worldly values so closely paralleled similar Christian attitudes that . . . DeWitt has observed that it 'would have been singularly easy for an Epicurean to become a Christian'—and, one might suppose, a Christian to become an Epicurean," p. 47.

101 **"Let us not":** Then he added: "though indeed the gods have already in their wisdom destroyed their works, so that most of their books are no longer available"—Floridi on Sextus, p. 13. In addition to Epicureans, Julian wishes to exclude Pyrrhonians, that is, philosophical skeptics.

101 *apikoros,* **an Epicurean:** Strictly speaking, the term did not mean atheist. An *apikoros,* explained Maimonides, was a person who rejected revelation and insisted that God had no knowledge or interest in human affairs.

101 **If you grant Epicurus:** Tertullian, *Apologeticus,* 45:7 (Loeb, p. 197).

101 **"Epicurus utterly destroys":** See Lactantius, *De ira* ("A Treatise on the Anger of God"), in *Ante-Nicene Christian Fathers,* ed. Roberts and Donaldson, vol. 7, ch. 8.

102 **"not because it brings":** See Lactantius, *Divine Institutes,* 3–1.

103 **"He then noticed":** Pope Gregory I, *Dialogues,* 2:60.

103 **The infliction of pain:** Flagellation had widespread use as a punishment in antiquity, and not only in Rome: "If the guilty man is sentenced to be flogged," Deuteronomy (25:2) declares, "the judge shall cause him to lie down and be beaten in his presence." For the history

of flagellation, see Nicklaus Largier, *In Praise of the Whip: A Cultural History of Arousal*, trans. Graham Harman (New York: Zone Books, 2007).

104 **Violence was part of the fabric:** Public punishments did not, of course, end with paganism or die out in antiquity. Molinet reports that the citizens of Mons bought a bandit at a high price in order to enjoy the pleasure of seeing him quartered, "at which the people were happier than if a new sacred body had been revived"—(Molinet, in Jean Delumeau, *Sin and Fear: The Emergence of a Western Guilt Culture, 13th–18th Centuries*, trans. Eric Nicholson (New York: St. Martin's Press, 1990; orig. 1983), p. 107. The Swiss diarist Felix Platter remembered all his life something he had seen as a child:

> A criminal, having raped a seventy-year-old woman, was flayed alive with burning tongs. With mine own eyes I saw the thick smoke produced by his living flesh that had been subjected to the tongs. He was executed by Master Nicolas, executioner of Berne, who had come expressly for the event. The prisoner was a strong and vigorous man. On the bridge over the Rhine, just nearby, they tore out his breast; then he was led to the scaffold. By now, he was extremely feeble and blood was gushing from his hands. He could no longer remain standing, he fell down continually. Finally, he was decapitated. They drove a stake through his body, and then his corpse was thrown into a ditch. I myself was witness to his torture, my father holding me by the hand.

105 **but, with a few exceptions:** One of these exceptions was St. Anthony, who, according to his hagiographer, "possessed in a very high degree apatheia—perfect self-control, freedom from passion. . . . Christ, who was free from every emotional weakness and fault, is his model"—Athanasius [attr.], *Life of Anthony*, section 67, quoted in Peter Brown, "Asceticism: Pagan and Christian," in Averil Cameron and Peter Garnsey, eds., *Cambridge Ancient History: Late Empire, a.d. 337–425* (Cambridge: Cambridge University Press, 2008), 13: 616.

106 **By the year 600:** See Peter Brown, *The Rise of Western Christendom: Triumph and Diversity, a.d. 200–1000* (Oxford: Blackwell, 1996), p. 221; R. A. Markus, *The End of Ancient Christianity* (Cambridge: Cambridge University Press, 1990); and Marilyn Dunn, *The Emergence of Monasticism: From the Desert Fathers to the Early Middle Ages* (Oxford: Oxford University Press, 2000).

106 **The insistence that punishment:** Nothing is ever—quite—an innovation. The active pursuit of pain in emulation or imitation of the sufferings of a deity has precedents in the cults of Isis, Attis, and others.

107 **"The body has to be shaped"**: Cited, with much other evidence, in Largier, *In Praise of the Whip: A Cultural History of Arousal*, pp. 90, 188.

108 **"At Advent"**: Ibid., p. 36. Largier also rehearses the stories that follow, some of which at least should be treated with skepticism.

CHAPTER FIVE: BIRTH AND REBIRTH

111 **He had been born**: Ernst Walser, *Poggius Florentinus: Leben und Werke* (Hildesheim: Georg Olms, 1974).

112 **"each folder thick"**: Iris Origo, *The Merchant of Prato: Francesco di Marco Datini, 1335–1410* (Boston: David Godine; 1986, orig. 1957).

113 **"It is much sweeter"**: Lauro Martines, *The Social World of the Florentine Humanists, 1390–1460* (Princeton: Princeton University Press, 1963), p. 22.

113 **greatly increased the market for slaves**: "By the end of the fourteenth century there was hardly a well-to-do household in Tuscany without at least one slave: brides brought them as part of their dowry, doctors accepted them from their patients in lieu of fees—and it was not unusual to find them even in the service of a priest"—Origo, *Merchant of Prato*, pp. 90–91.

114 **"In the name of God"**: Ibid., p. 109.

114 **a vibrant international cloth industry**: Fine wool was purchased from Majorca, Catalonia, Provence, and the Cotswolds (the last being the most expensive and highest quality) and shipped across borders and through a tangle of rapacious tax authorities. The dyeing and finishing required further imports: alum from the Black Sea (to make mordant for fixing the dyes), oak gall-nuts (to make the highest quality purple-black ink), woad from Lombardy (for deep blue dyes and as a foundation for other colors); madder from the Low Countries (for bright red dyes or, combined with woad, for dark reds and purples). And these were only the routine imports. Rarer dyes, the kind displayed on the costly clothes proudly worn in aristocratic portraits from the period, included deep scarlet from murex shells in the eastern Mediterranean, carmine red known as *grana* from tiny cochineal insects, orange-red vermilion from a crystalline substance found on the shores of the Red Sea, and the extravagantly expensive and therefore much prized kermis red from the powdered remains of an oriental louse.

115 **"as though it had been designed"**: Martin Davis, "Humanism in

Script and Print," in *Cambridge Companion to Renaissance Humanism*, ed. Jill Kraye (Cambridge: Cambridge University Press, 1996), p. 48. The experience, Petrarch remarked, was more like looking at a painting than reading a book.

118 **curiosity had long been rigorously condemned:** Pious Christians were urged to suppress its impulses and to spurn its contaminated fruits. Though Dante's poetry confers a magnificent dignity on Ulysses' determination to sail beyond the Pillars of Hercules, the *Inferno* makes it clear that this determination is the expression of a fallen soul, condemned for eternity to reside near the innermost circle of Hell.

118 **Petrarch was a devout Christian:** See esp. Charles Trinkaus, *"In Our Image and Likeness": Humanity and Divinity in Italian Humanist Thought*, 2 vols. (Chicago: University of Chicago Press, 1970).

119 **"Gold, silver, jewels":** *"Aurum, argentum, gemmae, purpurea vestis, marmorea domus, cultus ager, pietae tabulae, phaleratus sonipes, caeteraque id genus mutam habent et superficiariam voluptatem: libri medullitus delectant, colloquuntur, consulunt, et viva quadam nobis atque arguta familiaritate junguntur."* Quoted in John Addington Symonds, *The Renaissance in Italy*, 7 vols. (New York: Georg Olms, 1971; orig. 1875–86), 2:53 (translated by SG).

119 **For his own present:** "Among the many subjects, I was especially interested in antiquity, inasmuch as I have always disliked my own age, so that, had not love of dear ones restrained me, I would always have wanted to be born in any other age. In order to forget my own time, I have always tried to place myself in spirit in other times." *Posteritati*, ed. P.G. Ricci, in Petrarch, *Prose*, p. 7, quoted in Ronald G. Witt, *In the Footsteps of the Ancients: The Origins of Humanism from Lovato to Bruni* (Leiden: Brill, 2000), p. 276.

122 **training that had the advantage:** The *Doctor utriusque juris (DUJ)* (the degree in both canon and civil law) took ten years.

123 **"I much prefer":** Witt, *In the Footsteps*, p. 263.

124 **"have become absorbed":** *Rerum fam.* XXII.2 in *Familiari*, 4:106, quoted in Witt, *In the Footsteps*, p. 62. The letter probably dates to 1359.

124 **"I have always believed":** Quoted in Martines, *Social World*, p. 25.

124 **To prove its worth:** For Petrarch, there were values that transcended mere style: "What good will it do if you immerse yourself wholly in the Ciceronian springs and know well the writings either of the Greeks or of the Romans? You will indeed be able to speak ornately, charmingly, sweetly, and sublimely; you certainly will not be able to speak seriously, austerely, judiciously, and, most importantly, uniformly"—*Rerum fam.* I.9, in Witt, *In the Footsteps*, p. 242.

124 **Salutati wanted:** Salutati was more complex than this brief account allows: in the early 1380s, at the urging of a friend, he wrote a massive defense of the monastic life, and he was ready, even in the midst of praising active engagement, to acknowledge the superiority, at least in principle, of contemplative withdrawal.

124 **It was here for Salutati:** See Salutati to Gaspare Squaro de' Broaspini in Verona, November 17, 1377: "In this noble city, the flower of Tuscany and the mirror of Italy, the match of that most glorious Rome from which it descends and whose ancient shadows it follows in the struggle for the salvation of Italy and the freedom of all, here in Florence I have undertaken a labor that is unstinting but for which I am exceptionally grateful." See Eugenio Garin, *La Cultura Filosofica del Renascimento Italiano: Ricerche e Documenti* (Florence: Sansuni, 1979), esp. pp. 3–27.

125 **"Will you always stand":** Witt, *In the Footsteps*, p. 308.

126 **"At the coming of Chrysolaras":** Symonds, *Renaissance in Italy*, pp. 80–81.

127 **Taxes were used in Florence:** "Just imagine," Niccoli wrote to the fiscal officials near the end of his life, "what sort of tax my poor goods can bear, with all the debts and pressing expenses I have. Which is why, begging your humanity and clemency, I pray that it will please you to treat me in such a way that current taxes will not force me in my old age to die far from my birthplace, where I have spent all I had." Quoted in Martines, *Social World*, p. 116.

127 **"Marriage gives an abundance":** Alberti, *The Family in Renaissance Florence (Libri della Famiglia)*, trans. Renée Neu Watkins (Columbia: University of South Carolina Press, 1969), 2:98. It is sometimes claimed that this vision of companionate marriage was only introduced by Protestantism, but there is considerable evidence of its existence much earlier.

128 "If he is rich": Origo, *Merchant of Prato*, p. 179.

129 "He had a housekeeper": Vespasiano da Bisticci, *The Vespasiano Memoirs: Lives of the Illustrious Men of the XV Century*, trans. William George and Emily Waters (London: Routledge, 1926), p. 402.

129 **Poggio could not possibly hope:** "One day, when Nicolao was leaving his house, he saw a boy who had around his neck a chalcedony engraved with a figure by the hand of Polycleitus, a beautiful work. He enquired of the boy his father's name, and having learnt this, sent to ask him if he would sell the stone; the father readily consented, like one who neither knew what it was nor valued it. Nicolao sent him five florins in exchange, and the good man to whom it had belonged deemed \that he had paid him more than double its value"—Ibid., p. 399. In this case at least, the expenditure proved a very good investment: "There was in Florence in the time of Pope Eugenius a certain Maestro Luigi, the Patriarch, who took great interest in such things as these, and he sent word to Nicolao, asking if he might see the chalcedony. Nicolao sent it to him, and it pleased him so greatly that he kept it, and sent to Nicolao two hundred golden ducats, and he urged him so much that Nicolao, not being a rich man, let him have it. After the death of this Patriarch it passed to Pope Paul, and then to Lorenzo de' Medici," ibid., p. 399. For a remarkable tracking of the movements through time of a single ancient cameo, see Luca Giuliani, *Ein Geschenk für den Kaiser: Das Geheimnis des grossen Kameo* (Munich: Beck, 2010).

131 **He specified that the books:** In reality, Niccoli's vision exceeded his means: he died massively in debt. But the debt was canceled by his friend Cosimo de' Medici, in exchange for the right to dispose of the collection. Half of the manuscripts went to the new Library of S. Marco, where they were housed in Michelozzi's magnificent structure; the other half formed the core of the city's great Laurentian Library. Though he was responsible for its creation, the idea of the public library was not Niccoli's alone. It had been called for by Salutati. Cf. Berthold L. Ullman and Philip A. Stadter, *The Public Library of Renaissance Florence: Niccolò Niccoli, Cosimo de' Medici, and the Library of San Marco* (Padua: Antenore, 1972), p. 6.

132 "In order to appear well read": Cino Rinuccini, *Invettiva contro a cierti calunniatori di Dante e di messer Francesco Petrarcha and di messer Giovanni Boccacio*, cited in Witt, *In the Footsteps*, p. 270. See Ronald Witt, "Cino

Rinuccini's *Risponsiva alla Invetirra di Messer Antonio Lusco,"* *Renaissance Quarterly* 23 (1970), pp. 133–49.

132 **"would not have recognized"**: Bruni, *Dialogus* 1, in Martines, *Social World*, p. 235.

133 **"While the literary legacy"**: Ibid.

133 **Poggio's "second self"**: Martines, *Social World*, p. 241.

133 **"He had a great gift"**: *Vespasiano Memoirs*, p. 353.

133 **"who with his labor"**: Martines, *Social World*, p. 265.

CHAPTER SIX: IN THE LIE FACTORY

137 **He knew himself**: See Poggio to Niccoli, February 12, 1421: "For I am not one of those perfect men, who are commanded to abandon father and mother and sell everything and give to the poor; that power belonged to very few people and only long ago, in an earlier age"— Gordan, *Two Renaissance Book Hunters*, p. 49.

137 **"I am determined"**: William Shepherd, *Life of Poggio Bracciolini* (Liverpool: Longman et al., 1837), p. 185.

138 **"I do not think"**: Gordan, *Two Renaissance Book Hunters*, p. 58.

138 **a peril deftly summed up**: Peter Partner, *The Pope's Men: The Papal Civil Service in the Renaissance* (Oxford: Clarendon Press, 1990), p. 115.

138 **"in which crime"**: Lapo da Castiglionchio, *On the Excellence and Dignity of the Roman Court*, in Christopher Celenza, *Renaissance Humanism and the Papal Curia: Lapo da Castiglionchio the Younger's De curiae commodis* (Ann Arbor: University of Michigan Press, 1999), p. 111.

139 **"What can be more alien"**: Ibid., p. 127.

139 **"the pope's domestic secretary"**: Ibid., p. 155.

140 **"mindlessness"**: Ibid., p. 205.

140 **took in some contemporaries**: See Celenza, *Renaissance Humanism and the Papal Curia*, pp. 25–26.

141 **"No one is spared"**: Ibid., p. 177.

142 **"Nobody was spared"**: Poggio, *The Facetiae, or Jocose Tales of Poggio*, 2 vols. (Paris: Isidore Liseux, 1879), Conclusion, p. 231. (References are to the volume in this Paris edition and to the number of the tale.) The

manuscript of the *Facetiae* did not appear until 1457, two years before Poggio's death, but Poggio represents the stories as circulating among the scriptors and secretaries many years earlier. Cf. Lionello Sozzi, "Le 'Facezie' e la loro fortuna Europea," in *Poggio Bracciolini 1380–1980: Nel VI centenario della nascità* (Florence: Sansoni, 1982), pp. 235–59.

142 "Now it is all right": Ibid., 1:16.

143 "At the end of the day": Ibid., 1:50.

143 There is the woman . . . and the stories that follow: Ibid., 1:5, 1:45, 1:123, 2:133.

144 "Per Sancta Dei Evangelia": Ibid., 2:161.

144 was on a list: Jesús Martínez de Bujanda, *Index des Livres Interdits*, 11 vols. (Sherbrooke, Quebec: Centre d'études de la Renaissance; Geneva: Droz; Montreal: Médiaspaul, 1984–2002), 11 (Rome):33.

144 "there is seldom room": Poggio, *Facetiae*, 1:23.

144 "of the inadequate men": Ibid., 1:113.

145 "At a meeting": Ibid., 2:187.

146 "Rightly I could have": John Monfasani, *George of Trebizond: A Biography and a Study of His Rhetoric and Logic* (Leiden: Brill, 1976), p. 110.

146 "they may be taken": Symonds, *The Revival of Learning* (New York: C. P. Putnam's Sons, 1960), p. 176. "In the fifteenth century scholarship was all-absorbing," p. 177.

148 "displays an excessive purity of life": "Aspira ad virtutem recta, non hac tortuosa ac fallaci via; fac, ut mens conveniat verbis, opera sint ostentationi similia; enitere ut spiritus paupertas vestium paupertatem excedat, tunc fugies simulatoris crimen; tunc tibi et reliquis proderis vera virtute. Sed dum te quantunvis hominem humilem et abiectum videro Curiam frequentantem, non solum hypocritam, sed pessimum hypocritam iudicabo." (17: p. 97). Poggio Bracciolini, *Opera omnia*, 4 vols. (Turin: Erasmo, 1964–69).

151 are "not congregations" . . . "a sink": Gordan, *Two Renaissance Book Hunters*, pp. 156, 158.

151 "I must try everything": Ibid., p. 54.

151 "to abandon": Ibid., p. 75.

151 "I do not know": Ibid., p. 66.

151 "My one ambition": Ibid., p. 68.

152 "some gleam of intellect": Ibid., pp. 22–24.

152 "I was upset and terrified": Ibid., p. 146.

152 "I found a book": Ibid.

152 "to be ruled in red": Ibid., p. 148.

153 "My country has not yet": Ibid., p. 164.

153 "Let us spend": Ibid., p. 166.

153 "I have already decided": Ibid., p. 173.

153 "Your Poggio": Ibid., p. 150.

154 sometime after 1410: The precise date of Poggio's appointment as apostolic secretary to John XXIII is unclear. In 1411 he was listed as the pope's scriptor and close associate (*familiaris*). But a papal bull of June 1, 1412, is signed by Poggio as *Secretarius* (as is a later bull, dating from the time of the General Council of Constance), and Poggio referred to himself during this period as *Poggius Secretarius apostolicus*. Cf. Walser, *Poggius Florentinus: Leben und Werke*, p. 25, n4.

CHAPTER SEVEN: A PIT TO CATCH FOXES

155 two rival claimants: For much of the fourteenth century the popes had resided at Avignon; only in 1377 did the French-born Gregory XI, supposedly inspired by the stirring words of St. Catherine of Siena, return the papal court to Rome. When Gregory died the next year, crowds of Romans, fearing that a new French pope would almost certainly be drawn back to the civilized pleasures and security of Avignon, encircled the conclave of cardinals and noisily demanded the election of an Italian. The Neapolitan Bartolomeo Prignano was duly elected and assumed the title Urban VI. Five months later the French faction of cardinals, claiming that they had been coerced by a howling mob and that the election was therefore invalid, held a new conclave in which they elected Robert of Geneva, who settled in Avignon and called himself Clement VII. There were now two rival popes.

The French faction had chosen a hard man for a hard time: Robert of Geneva had distinguished himself the year before, when as papal legate in charge of a company of Breton soldiers, he promised a complete amnesty to the rebellious citizens of Cesena if they would open their gates to him. When the gates were opened, he ordered a general massacre. "Kill them all," he was heard shouting. Urban VI, for his part, raised money to hire mercenaries, busied himself with the fantastically complicated alliances and betrayals of Italian politics, enriched his family, narrowly escaped traps set for him, ordered the torture and execution of his enemies, and repeatedly fled from and reentered Rome. Urban declared his French rival the antipope; Robert declared Urban the anti-Christ. The sordid details do not directly concern us—by the time Poggio came on the scene, both Robert of Geneva and Urban VI were dead and had been replaced by other equally problematical contenders for the papal see.

156 **Between these settlements:** See Poggio's melancholy observation in *De varietate fortunae*: "Survey the . . . hills of the city, the vacant space is interrupted only by ruins and gardens"—Quoted in Edward Gibbon, *The History of the Decline and Fall of the Roman Empire*, 6 vols. (New York: Knopf, 1910), 6:617.

157 **"This spectacle of the world"** . . . **"Cast your eyes":** Ibid., 6:302. Gibbon uses this passage as the climax of his vast *magnum opus*, the summary articulation of the disaster that had befallen Rome.

158 **"To be Pope":** Eustace J. Kitts, *In the Days of the Councils: A Sketch of the Life and Times of Baldassare Cossa (Afterward Pope John the Twenty-Third)* (London: Archibald Constable & Co., 1908), p. 152.

159 **people who desired:** Ibid., pp. 163–64.

162 **A citizen of Constance:** Ulrich Richental, *Chronik des Konstanzer Konzils 1414–1418* ("Richental's Chronicle of the Council of Constance"), in *The Council of Constance: The Unification of the Church*, ed. John Hine Mundy and Kennerly M. Woody, trans. Louise Ropes Loomis (New York: Columbia University Press, 1961), pp. 84–199.

162 **From other sources:** See, e.g., Remigio Sabbadini, *Le Scoperte dei Codici Latini e Greci ne Secoli XIV e XV* (Florence: Sansoni, 1905), 1:76–77.

164 **"some who lay in stables":** "Richental's Chronicle," p. 190.

164 **staging public executions:** "Some have said that a great crowd of persons were executed for robbery, murder, and other crimes, but that is not the truth. I could not learn from our magistrats at Constance that more than twenty-two had been put to death for any such cause"—"Richental's Chronicle," p. 157.

164 "Every fourteen days" . . . "There were also frogs": Ibid., pp. 91, 100.

166 "If he is manifestly sinful": Quoted in Gordon Leff, *Heresy, Philosophy and Religion in the Medieval West* (Aldershot, UK: Ashgate, 2002), p. 122.

167 a strange charge: Kitts, *In the Days of the Councils*, p. 335.

168 "When the Pope was to give": "Richental's Chronicle," p. 114.

170 "If His Holiness": Ibid., p. 116.

170 On March 20, 1415: This is Richental's account. Another contemporary observer, Guillaume Fillastre, has a different version of the event: "the Pope, realizing his situation, left the city by river during the night between Wednesday and Thursday, March 21, after midnight, under escort provided by Frederick, duke of Austria"—in *The Council of Constance*, p. 222.

170 "The members of the Curia": Fillastre in *The Council of Constance*, p. 236.

170 Seventy charges: E. H. Gillett, *The Life and Times of John Huss*, 2 vols. (Boston: Gould & Lincoln, 1863), 1:508.

171 At this point: Kitts, *In the Days of the Councils*, pp. 199–200.

172 "It was astonishing": Poggio's long letter about Jerome and Bruni's alarmed reply are quoted in William Shepherd, *The Life of Poggio Bracciolini* (Liverpool: Longman et al., 1837), pp. 78–90.

173 "He lived much longer": Richental's Chronicle," p. 135. Poggio, however, who claimed that he "was a witness of his end, and observed every particular of its process," told Bruni that "neither did Mutius suffer his hand to be burnt so patiently as Jerome endured the burning of his whole body; nor did Socrates drink the hemlock as cheerfully as Jerome submitted to the fire" (Shepherd, p. 88). Poggio's reference is to Mucius Scaevola, the legendary Roman hero who stoically thrust his hand into the flames and thus impressed Rome's enemy, the Etruscan Porsenna.

174 "Old women": This and the quotes to follow are from a letter to Niccoli, May 18, 1416, in Gordan, *Two Renaissance Book Hunters*, pp. 26–30.

176 an ancient commentary: L. D. Reynolds, *Texts and Transmission: A Survey of the Latin Classics* (Oxford: Clarendon Press, 1983), p. 158.

The commentary was by the fourth-century Roman grammarian Donatus.

176 **"These seven orations"**: Poggio's transcription of the Ciceronian speeches that he had discovered was identified in the Vatican Library [Vatican. lat. 11458 (X)] by A. Campana in 1948, with the following subscription: *Has septem M. Tulii orationes, que antea culpa temporum apud Italos deperdite erant, Poggius Florentinus, perquisitis plurimis Gallie Germanieque summo cum studio ac diligentia bibyothecis, cum latenetes comperisset in squalore et sordibus, in lucem solus extulit ac in pristinam dignitatem decoremque restituens Latinis musis dicavit* (p. 91).

178 **"He was sad"**: In the continuation of this description of the tattered manuscript, Poggio fantasizes that Quintilian's *Institutes* had been instrumental in saving the Roman Republic. Hence he imagines that the "imprisoned" Quintilian feels it "a disgrace that he who had once preserved the safety of the whole population by his influence and his eloquence could now not find one single advocate who would pity his misfortunes and take some trouble over his welfare and prevent his being dragged off to an undeserved punishment"—Letter to Niccoli, December 15, 1425, in Gordan, *Two Renaissance Book Hunters*, p. 105). In these words one may perhaps glimpse a twinge of Poggio's own guilty conscience at witnessing Jerome's condemnation and execution. Or rather, the rescue of the manuscript stands in for a failed rescue: saving a classical text from the clutches of the monks was a liberation that Poggio could not possibly have brought about for eloquent, doomed Jerome.

179 **"The one and only light"**: Ibid., Letter IV, p. 194.

180 **"If people, nations"**: Ibid., Letter IV, p. 197.

CHAPTER EIGHT: THE WAY THINGS ARE

185 **are among the foundations**: The key role played by Lucretius in early modern philosophy and natural science has been subtly explored by Catherine Wilson: *Epicureanism at the Origins of Modernity* (Oxford: Clarendon Press, 2008). See also W. R. Johnson, *Lucretius and the Modern World* (London: Duckworth, 2000); Dane R. Gordon and David B. Suits, *Epicurus: His Continuing Influence and Contemporary Relevance* (Rochester, NY: RIT Cary Graphic Arts Press, 2003); and Stuart Gillespie and Donald Mackenzie, "Lucretius and the Moderns," in *The Cambridge Companion to Lucretius*, ed. Stuart Gillespie and Philip Hardie (Cambridge: Cambridge University Press, 2007), pp. 306–24.

186 "the greatest thought": George Santayana, *Three Philosophical Poets: Lucretius, Dante, and Goethe* (Cambridge, MA: Harvard University Press, 1947), p. 23.

188 "But because throughout the universe": This is one of those innumerable moments in which Lucretius' dazzling verbal skills are inevitably lost in translation. Here in describing the innumerable combinations, he plays with similar words jostling one another: "sed quia multa modis multis mutata per omne."

188 The position of the elementary particles: In *The Logic of Sense*, trans. Mark Lester with Charles Stivale, ed. Constantin V. Boundas (New York: Columbia University Press, 1990), Gilles Deleuze explores the relationship between this minimal, indeterminate motion of atoms and modern physics.

189 if all of motion were one long: "If all movements are invariably interlinked, if new movement arises from the old in unalterable succession, if there is no atomic swerve [*declinando . . . primordia motus*] to initiate movement that can annul the decrees of destiny and prevent the existence of an endless chain of causation, what is the source of this free will possessed by living creatures all over the earth? What, I ask, is the source of this power of will wrested from destiny, which enables each of us to advance where pleasures leads us. . . ?" (2.251–58).

189 may deliberately hold himself back: Both willing oneself to go forward and willing oneself to remain stationary are only possible because everything is not strictly determined, that is, because of the subtle, unpredictable, free movements of matter. What keeps the mind from being crushed by inner necessity is "the minute swerve [*clinamen principiorum*] of the atoms at unpredictable places and times" (2.293–94).

189 Creatures whose combination: Just as there is no divine grace in any of this tangled history of development, there is no perfect or final form. Even the creatures that flourish are beset with flaws, evidence that their design is not the product of some sublime higher intelligence but of chance. Lucretius articulated, in effect, what human males, with chagrin, might call the principle of the prostate.

190 how a baby: Cf. Dryden's translation of these lines:

> Thus like a sailor by the tempest hurled
> Ashore, the babe is shipwrecked on the world:
> Naked he lies, and ready to expire;

> Helpless of all that human wants require:
> Exposed upon unhospitable earth,
> From the first moment of his hapless birth.

John Dryden, *Complete Poems*, ed. James Kinsley, 4 vols. (Oxford: Clarendon Press, 1958), 1:421. Here and elsewhere I have modernized Dryden's spelling and punctuation.

191 **that a calf recognizes its dam:** "For example, often before a god's gracefully ornamented shrine a calf falls a victim beside the incense-smoking altars, and with its last breath spurts a hot stream of blood from its breast. Meanwhile the bereaved mother ranges through green glades searching the ground for the imprint of those cloven hoofs. With her eyes she explores every place in the hope that she will be able to spy somewhere the young one she has lost. Now she halts and fills the leafy grove with her plaintive calls. Time after time she returns to the cowshed, her heart transfixed with longing for her calf" (2.352–60). This passage, of course, does more than make the point that a particular cow can identify its particular calf: it registers once again the destructiveness, the murderousness, of religion, this time from the perspective of the animal victim. The whole sacrificial cult, at once unnecessary and cruel, is set against something intensely natural, not only the capacity of a mother to identify her offspring but also the deep love that lies behind this identification. Animals are not material machines—they are not simply programmed, as we would say, to care for their young; they feel emotions. And one member of the species cannot simply substitute for another, as if individual creatures were interchangeable.

194 **or, less agreeably:** "Whose heart does not contract with dread of the gods, and who does not cower in fear, when the scorched earth shudders beneath the terrible stroke of the thunderbolt, and rumbles of thunder run across the vast heaven?" (5:1218–21).

196 **"It is comforting":** Hans Blumenberg, in his elegant short book on this passage, *Shipwreck with Spectator: Paradigm of a Metaphor for Existence*, trans. Steven Rendall (Cambridge, MA: MIT Press, 1997) shows that over the course of centuries of brooding and commenting on this passage, the spectator tended to lose his privileged position of distance: we are *on* the ship.

197 **"the finest description":** A. Norman Jeffares, *W. B. Yeats: Man and Poet*, 2nd. edn. (London: Routledge & Kegan Paul, 1962), p. 267, cited by

David Hopkins, "The English Voices of Lucretius from Lucy Hutchinson to John Mason Good," in *The Cambridge Companion to Lucretius*,
p. 266. Here is Dryden's translation of the passage:

> When Love its utmost vigor does imploy,
> Ev'n tben, 'tis but a restless wandring joy:
> Nor knows the Lover, in that wild excess,
> With hands or eyes, what first he would possess:
> But strains at all; and fast'ning where he strains,
> Too closely presses with his frantic pains;
> With biting kisses hurts the twining fair,
> Which shows his joys imperfect, unsincere. (1:414)

To modern ears, "unsincere" sounds strange, but it is a Latinism. *Sin-
cerus* in Latin can mean "pure," and Lucretius writes that the storm-
tossed violence arises from the fact that the lovers' pleasure is not
pure: *quia non est pura voluptas* (4:1081).

198 **the element of unsated appetite:** "Just like thirsty people who in
dreams desire to drink and, instead of obtaining water to quench
the fire that consumes their limbs, with vain effort pursue images of
water and remain thirsty, though they drink in the midst of a torrent
stream, so, in love, lovers are deluded by Venus with images: no matter how intently they gaze at the beloved body, they cannot sate their
eyes; nor can they remove anything from the velvety limbs that they
explore with roving, uncertain hands." (4.1097–1104).

198 **"when the youthful pair":** Here is Smith's more workmanlike prose
translation:

> At last, with limbs interlocked, they enjoy the flower of youth: the body has a
> presentiment of ecstasy, and Venus is on the point of sowing the woman's fields;
> they greedily press body to body and intermingle the salivas of their mouths,
> drawing deep breaths and crushing lips with teeth. But it is all in vain, since they
> cannot take away anything from their lover's body or wholly penetrate it and
> merge into it. At times they do indeed seem to be striving and struggling to do
> this: so eagerly do they remain fettered in the bonds of Venus, while their limbs
> are slackened and liquefied by the force of ecstasy.

201 **"Delight of humankind":** Smith's prose translation of the opening
lines reads:

> Mother of Aeneas' people, delight of human beings and the gods, Venus, power
> of life, it is you who beneath the sky's sliding stars inspirit the ship-bearing sea,
> inspirit the productive land. To you every kind of living creature owes its con-

ception and first glimpse of the sun's light. You goddess, at your coming hush the winds and scatter the clouds, for you the creative earth thrusts up fragrant flowers, for you the smooth stretches of the ocean smile, and the sky, tranquil now, is flooded with effulgent light.

Once the door to spring is flung open and Favonius' fertilizing breeze, released from imprisonment, is active, first, goddess, the birds of the air, pierced to the heart with your powerful shafts, signal your entry. Next wild creatures and cattle bound over rich pastures and swim rushing rivers: so surely are they all captivated by your charm and eagerly follow your lead. Then you inject seductive love into the heart of every creature that lives in the seas and mountains and river torrents and bird-haunted thickets and verdant plains, implanting in it the passionate urge to reproduce its kind.

CHAPTER NINE: THE RETURN

203 "The place is rather far away": Letter to Francesco Barbaro, in Gordan, *Two Renaissance Book Hunters*, Appendix: Letter VIII, p. 213.

203 the manuscript: The textual history of Lucretius has occupied scholars for many generations and was the object of the most famous of all philological reconstructions, that of the great German classicist Karl Lachmann (1793–1851). The lost scribal copy, made for Poggio, is known to textual scholars as the *Poggianus*. I have been greatly assisted in grasping the complexity of the textual issues by D. J. Butterfield of Cambridge University, to whom I am indebted.

207 "I have been relegated" . . . "plenty of men": Ibid., pp. 38, 46.

207 "I saw many monasteries" . . . "you had better": Ibid., pp. 46, 48.

208 "During my four years": Ibid., p. 74.

208 "I am hunting": Ibid., p. 65.

208 "I wanted the Lucretius" . . . "If you send me": Ibid., pp. 89, 92.

209 "Send me the Lucretius too": and the quotes that follow: Ibid., pp. 110, 154, 160.

209 Released from the confinement: The copies Niccoli made of a substantial number of ancient texts have survived and are in the San Marco collection to which he willed his library. These include, in addition to the Lucretius, works by Plautus, Cicero, Valerius Flaccus, Celsus, Aulus Gellius, Tertullian, Plutarch, and Chrysostom. Others—including the copy of Asconius Pedianus mentioned by

Poggio—are lost. See B. L. Ullman and Philip A. Stadter, *The Public Library of Renaissance Florence. Niccolò Niccoli, Cosimo de' Medici and the Library of San Marco* (Padua: Antenore, 1972), p. 88.

211 **"I fished out"** . . . **"when they arrive"**: Gordan, *Two Renaissance Book Hunters*, pp. 147, 166–67.

212 **a different form of cultural capital:** As Lauro Martines notes, power and wealth had shifted in the thirteenth century from the old feudal nobility to the merchant class, to families like the Albizzi, Medici, Rucellai, and Strozzi. But, though not any longer very wealthy, the bride's father was reasonably prosperous. "In 1427 Vaggia's father, Gino, claimed one large house with a courtyard and shop, two cottages, four farms, various land parcels, and some livestock. His remaining assets included an outstanding credit of 858 florins and government bonds with a market value of 118 florins. Altogether his gross capital came to 2424 florins. The debts on this estate amounted to 500 florins, and rental and subsistence deductions reduced Gino's taxable capital to 336 florins. Consequently, Poggio's match with Vaggia was hardly contracted with an eye (on his part) to forming an alliance with a moneyed family. Nevertheless, she brought him a dowry whose value, 600 florins, conformed with the dowries customarily given by the political families of medium stature, or by the distinguished old families (somewhat down at heel) whose major social virtue was their blood"—Lauro Martines, *The Social World of the Florentine Humanists, 1390–1460*, (Princeton: Princeton University Press, 1963), pp. 211–12.

214 **"become the protector of men":** William Shepherd, *Life of Poggio Bracciolini* (Liverpool: Longman et al., 1837), p. 394.

216 **"I am a witness":** Quoted in Charles Trinkaus, *In Our Image and Likeness: Humanity and Divinity in Italian Humanist Thought*, 2 vols. (Chicago: University of Chicago Press, 1970), 1:268.

CHAPTER TEN: SWERVES

220 **"Listen women":** Quoted in Alison Brown, *The Return of Lucretius to Renaissance Florence* (Cambridge, MA: Harvard University Press, 2010), p. 49. Cf. Girolamo Savonarola, *Prediche sopra Amos e Zacaria*, no. 3 (February 19, 1496), ed. Paolo Ghiglieri (Rome: A. Belardetti, 1971), 1:79–81. See also Peter Godman, *From Poliziano to Machiavelli: Florentine Humanism in the High Renaissance* (Princeton: Princeton University Press, 1998),

p. 140, and Jill Kraye, "The Revival of Hellenistic Philosophies," in *The Cambridge Companion to Renaissance Philosophy*, ed. James Hankins (Cambridge: Cambridge University Press, 2007), esp. pp. 102–6.

221 **Machiavelli's copy of Lucretius:** On Machiavelli's Lucretius manuscript, see Brown, *Return of Lucretius*, pp. 68–87, and Appendix, pp. 113–22.

221 **In his twenties, Ficino:** See James Hankins, "Ficino's Theology and the Critique of Lucretius," forthcoming in the proceedings of the conference on *Platonic Theology: Ancient, Medieval and Renaissance*, held at the Villa I Tatti and the Istituto Nazionale di Studi sul Rinascimento, Florence, April 26–27, 2007.

222 **a heretical adherence:** On the controversy, see Salvatore I. Camporeale, "Poggio Bracciolini contro Lorenzo Valla. Le 'Orationes in L. Vallam,'" in *Poggio Bracciolini, 1380–1980* (Florence: Sansoni, 1982), pp. 137–61. On the whole problem of orthodoxy in Valla (and Ficino as well), see Christopher S. Celenza's illuminating *The Lost Italian Renaissance: Humanists, Historians, and Latin's Legacy* (Baltimore: Johns Hopkins University Press, 2006), pp. 80–114.

222 **It is one thing to enjoy wine:** "Nunc sane video, cur in quodam tuo opusculo, in quo Epicureorum causam quantam datur tutaris, vinum tantopere laudasti . . . Bacchum compotatoresque adeo profuse laudans, ut epicureolum quendam ebrietatis assertorem te esse profitearis . . . Quid contra virginitatem insurgis, quod numquam fecit Epicurus? Tu prostitutas et prostibula laudas, quod ne gentiles quidem unquam fecerunt. Non verbis oris tui sacrilegi labes, sed igne est expurganda, quem spero te non evasurum." Cited in Don Cameron Allen, "The Rehabilitation of Epicurus and His Theory of Pleasure in the Early Renaissance," *Studies in Philology* 41 (1944), pp. 1–15.

222 **the manuscript of Lucretius' poem:** Valla directly quotes Lucretius, but only passages he could have found in Lactantius and other Christian texts.

222 **a spokesman for Epicureanism:** Indeed that spokesman, not a fictional character but the contemporary poet Maffeo Vegio, makes it clear that even he is not really an Epicurean, but that he is willing to play the role of a defender of pleasure in order to refute Stoical arguments for virtue as the highest good that, in his view, represent a far more serious threat to Christian orthodoxy.

223 **"When Antonio Raudense"**: Lorenzo Valla, *De vero falsoque bono/On Pleasure*, trans. A. Kent Hieatt and Maristella Lorch (New York: Abaris Books, 1977), p. 319. I will use the better known title, *De voluptate*, throughout.

The text of Valla's in question actually deploys several different strategies in addition to dialogical disavowal to protect its author from the charge of Epicureanism. Valla has good grounds then for indignantly rejecting Poggio's charge of Epicureanism. The Epicurean arguments that take up the entire second book of *De voluptate* and much of the first are carefully framed by proper Christian doctrines, doctrines that the narrator and the other interlocutors unanimously declare have carried the day.

223 **"It is plain"**: Valla, *De voluptate*, pp. 219–21.

223 **"Therefore"**: Ibid., p. 221.

224 **"If you were to see"**: Ibid., p. 295.

224 **an attempt to contain subversion**: Cf. Greenblatt, "Invisible Bullets: Renaissance Authority and Its Subversion," in *Glyph* 8 (1981), pp. 40–61.

225 **The question itself implies**: See Michele Marullo, *Inni Naturali* (Florence: Casa Editrice le Lettere, 1995); on Bruno and Epicureanism, see, among other works, Hans Blumenberg, *The Legitimacy of the Modern Age* (Cambridge, MA: MIT Press, 1983; orig. *Die Legitimität der Neuzeit*, 1966).

225 **"no more than a pine nut"**: "L'anima è sol . . . in un pan bianco caldo un pinocchiato"—Brown, *Return of Lucretius*, p. 11.

227 **"there are no people more Epicurean"**: Erasmus, "The Epicurean," in *The Colloquies of Erasmus*, trans. Craig R. Thompson (Chicago: University of Chicago Press, 1965), pp. 538, 542. On Erasmus's criticism of Marullo, see P. S. Allen, *Opus Epistolarum des. Erasmi Roterodami*, 12 vols. (Oxford: Oxford University Press, 1906–58), 2:187; 5:519, trans. in *Collected Works of Erasmus* (Toronto: University of Toronto Press, 1974–), 3:225; 10:344. *Contemporaries of Erasmus: A Biographical Register of the Renaissance and Reformation*, ed. P. G. Bietenholz and Thomas B. Deutscher (Toronto: University of Toronto Press, 2003), 2:398–99.

229 **"Since their life is so entirely given over"**: Cited in More, *Utopia*, ed. George M. Logan and Robert M. Adams (Cambridge: Cambridge University Press; rev. edn. 2002), p. 68.

229 **to convey a sense that was extremely difficult:** More plays a characteristically brilliant and self-conscious game in *Utopia* with the complex factors that led ancient texts to survive or perish, including the role of accident: "When about to go on the fourth voyage," Hythloday remarks, "I put on board, in place of wares to sell, a fairly large package of books, having made up my mind never to return rather than to come back soon. They received from me most of Plato's works, several of Aristotle's, as well as Theophrastus on plants, which I regret to say was mutilated in parts. During the voyage an ape found the book, left lying carelessly about, and in wanton sport tore out and destroyed several pages in various sections," p. 181.

231 **his own unjust society:** At the time I am writing this essay, in the United States one out of every nine African Americans aged twenty to thirty-five is incarcerated, while the United States has achieved the greatest disparity in wealth of any time in the past century.

234 **"that today at noon":** Ingrid D. Rowland, *Giordano Bruno: Philosopher/ Heretic* (New York: Farrar, Straus & Giroux, 2008), pp. 17–18, translating *Spaccio de la Bestia Trionfante*, 1, part 3, in *Dialoghi Italiani*, ed. Giovanni Gentile (Florence: Sansoni, 1958), pp. 633–37.

236 **"The fewer the better":** Walter L. Wakefield, "Some Unorthodox Popular Ideas of the Thirteenth Century," in *Medievalia et Humanistica*, p. 28.

236 **"When we were Jews":** John Edwards, "Religious Faith and Doubt in Late Medieval Spain: Soria circa 1450–1500," in *Past and Present* 120 (1988), p. 8.

237 **"The world is fine":** Giordano Bruno, *The Ash Wednesday Supper*, ed. and trans. Edward A. Gosselin and Lawrence S. Lerner (Hamden, CT: Archon Books, 1977), p. 91.

237 **"a delightful companion":** Jacopo Corbinelli, the Florentine secretary to Queen Mother Catherine de Medicis, cited in Rowland, *Giordano Bruno*, p. 193.

238 **"ordained by the gods":** *Ash Wednesday Supper*, p. 87.

238 **there were multiple worlds:** *De l'Infinito, Universo e Mondi*, Dialogue Quinto, in *Dialoghi Italiani*, pp. 532–33, citing *De rerum natura*, 2:1067–76.

239 **Thomas Harriot:** See J. W. Shirley, ed., *Thomas Harriot: Renaissance Scientist* (Oxford: Clarendon Press, 1974) and Shirley, *Thomas Harriot: A Biography*

(Oxford: Clarendon Press, 1983); J. Jacquot, "Thomas Harriot's Reputation for Impiety," *Notes and Records of the Royal Society* 9 (1951–2), pp. 164–87.

239 **"By the light of his senses":** *Ash Wednesday Supper*, p. 90.

CHAPTER ELEVEN: AFTERLIVES

242 **were only rarely called to investigate:** A famous exception was the inquisitorial investigation of Paolo Veronese for his 1573 depiction of the Last Supper, whose intense materiality—the swirling life, the food on the table, the dogs scratching and scrounging for scraps, and so forth—triggered accusations of irreverence and even heresy. Veronese avoided unpleasant consequences by renaming the work *The Feast in the House of Levi.*

243 **whose own signed copy:** Jonson wrote his name on the title page and, tiny as the book is—only 11 by 6 centimeters—he made many marks and jottings in the margins, evidence of an attentive and engaged reading. He seems to have been particularly struck by the passage in book 2 in which Lucretius denies that the gods have any interest in the behavior of mortals. At the foot of the page, he penned a translation of two of the lines:

> Far above grief & dangers, those blest powers,
> Rich in their active goods, need none of ours.

Cf. 2:649–50:

> Nam privata dolore omni, privata periclis,
> ipsa suis pollens opibus, nil indiga nostri.

Lucy Hutchinson translates the lines as follows:

> The devine nature doth it selfe possesse
> Eternally in peacefull quiettnesse,
> Nor is concernd in mortall mens affairs,
> Wholly exempt from dangers, griefes, and cares,
> Rich in it selfe, of us no want it hath.

244 **"I am not excessively fond":** *The Complete Essays of Montaigne*, trans. Donald M. Frame (Stanford: Stanford University Press, 1957), pp. 846, 240.

246 **"that imaginary kingship":** Ibid., p. 318.

246 **"Why shall a gosling":** Ibid., p. 397.

246 **"the quiver of pleasure":** Ibid., p. 310.

247 **sex and death:** The quotations that follow are from ibid., pp. 464, 634, and 664.

248 **"I want death":** Ibid., p. 62.

248 **"Go out of this world":** Ibid., p. 65.

249 **Scholars quickly confirmed:** M. A. Screech, *Montaigne's Annotated Copy of Lucretius: A Transcription and Study of the Manuscript, Notes, and Pen-Marks* (Geneva: Droz, 1998).

249 **"Since the movements of the atoms":** *"Ut sunt diuersi atomorum motus non incredibile est sic conuenisse olim atomos aut conuenturas ut alius nascatur montanus."*—Ibid., p. 11. I have altered Screech's translation: "Since the movements of the atoms are so varied, it is not unbelievable that the atoms once came together, or will together again in the future, so that another Montaigne be born."

250 **At a book sale in 1625:** Trevor Dadson, "Las bibliotecas de la nobleza: Dos inventarios y un librero, año de 1625," in Aurora Egido and José Enrique Laplana, eds., *Mecenazgo y Humanidades en tiempos de Lastanosa. Homenaje a la memoria de Domingo Ynduráin* (Zaragoza: Institución Fernando el Católico, 2008), p. 270. I am grateful to Professor Dadson's research into Spanish library inventories for all of the glimpses of Lucretius in post-Tridentine Spain.

250 **"Nothing comes from atoms":** Pietro Redondi, *Galileo Heretic*, trans. Raymond Rosenthal (Princeton: Princeton University Press, 1987; orig. Italian edn. 1983), "Documents," p. 340—*"Exercitatio de formis substantialibus et de qualitatibus physicis*, anonymous."

253 **"Faith must take first place":** Ibid., p. 132.

255 **the convicted scientist:** Redondi's core argument—that the attack on Galileo for heliocentrism served as a kind of cover for an underlying attack on his atomism—has been criticized by many historians of science. But there is no reason to think that the Church's motivation could only have been one or the other concern and not both.

256 **the text used by Montaigne:** "At Lucretius animorum immortalitatem oppugnat, deorum providentiam negat, religiones omneis tollit, summum bonum in voluptate ponit. Sed haec Epicuri, quem sequitur Lucretius, non Lucretii culpa est. Poema quidem ipsum propter senten-

tias a religione nostra alienas, nihilominus poema est. tantumne? Immo vero poema venustum, poema praeclarum, poema omnibus ingenii luminibus distinctum, insignitum, atque illustratum. Hasce autem Epicuri rationes insanas, ac furiosas, ut & illas absurdas de atomorum concursione fortuita, de mundis innumerabilibus, & ceteras, neque difficile nobis est refutare, neque vero necesse est: quippe cum ab ipsa veritatis voce vel tacentibus omnibus facillime refellantur" (Paris, 1563) f. ā3. I have used the translation of Ada Palmer, to whose unpublished essay, "Reading Atomism in the Renaissance," I am indebted.

257 **"had they not by misfortune"**: *Lucy Hutchinson's Translation of Lucretius: "De rerum natura,"* ed. Hugh de Quehen (Ann Arbor: University of Michigan Press, 1996), p. 139.

258 **"aspiring Muse"**: On the contrary, with a backward glance at John Evelyn, Hutchinson observed that a "masculine wit," presenting to the public only a single book of the difficult poem, "thought it worth printing his head in a laurel crown."

258 **"one great means"** . . . **"ridiculous, impious"**: *Lucy Hutchinson's Translation,* pp. 24–25.

258 **"out of youthful"**: Ibid., p. 23.

259 **"The little glory"**: Ibid., p. 26.

259 **"reaped some profit"**: Ibid.

259 **"I turned it"**: Ibid., p. 24.

261 **"In nature nothing"**: Francis Bacon, *Novum Organum,* II.ii.

261 **to retain a belief in God**: The most powerful philosophical expression of this view is in the works of the French priest, astronomer, and mathematician Pierre Gassendi (1592–1655).

261 **"That God in the Beginning"**: Isaac Newton, *Opticks,* Query 32 (London, 1718), cited in Monte Johnson and Catherine Wilson, "Lucretius and the History of Science," in *The Cambridge Companion to Lucretius,* pp. 141–42.

263 **"I [am] obliged"**: To William Short, October 31, 1819: "I consider the genuine (not the imputed) doctrines of Epicurus as containing everything rational in moral philosophy which Greece and Rome have left us." Cited in Charles A. Miller, *Jefferson and Nature: An Interpretation*

(Baltimore and London: Johns Hopkins University Press, 1988), p. 24.
John Quincy Adams, "Dinner with President Jefferson," from *Memoirs of John Quincy Adams, Comprising Portions of His Diary from 1795 to 1848*, ed. Charles Francis Adams (Philadelphia, 1874): November 3, 1807: "Mr. Jefferson said that the *Epicurean* philosophy came nearest to the truth, in his opinion, of any ancient system of philosophy. He wished the work of Gassendi concerning it had been translated. It was the only accurate account of it extant. I mentioned Lucretius. He said that was only a part—only the *natural* philosophy. But the *moral* philosophy was only to be found in Gassendi."

263 "I am," Jefferson wrote: Miller, *Jefferson and Nature*, p. 24.

SELECTED BIBLIOGRAPHY

Adams, H. P. *Karl Marx in His Earlier Writings*. London: G. Allen & Unwin, 1940.

Adams, John Quincy. "Dinner with President Jefferson," *Memoirs of John Quincy Adams, Comprising Portions of his Diary from 1795 to 1848*, ed. Charles Francis Adams. Philadelphia: J. B. Lippincott, 1874–77, pp. 60–61.

Alberti, Leon Battista. *The Family in Renaissance Florence*, trans. Renée Neu Watkins. Columbia, SC: University of South Carolina Press, 1969, pp. 92–245.

———. *Dinner Pieces*, trans. David Marsh. Binghamton, NY: Medieval and Renaissance Texts and Studies in Conjunction with the Renaissance Society of America, 1987.

———. *Intercenales*, ed. Franco Bacchelli and Luca D'Ascia. Bologna: Pendragon, 2003.

Albury, W. R. "Halley's Ode on the Principia of Newton and the Epicurean Revival in England," *Journal of the History of Ideas* 39 (1978), pp. 24–43.

Allen, Don Cameron. "The Rehabilitation of Epicurus and His Theory of Pleasure in the Early Renaissance," *Studies in Philology* 41 (1944), pp. 1–15.

Anon. "The Land of Cokaygne," in Angela M. Lucas, ed., *Anglo-Irish Poems of the Middle Ages: The Kildare Poems*. Dublin: Columbia Press, 1995.

Aquilecchia, Giovanni. "In Facie Prudentis Relucet Sapientia: Appunti Sulla Letteratura Metoposcopica tra Cinque e Seicento," *Giovan Battista della Porta nell'Europa del Suo Tempo*. Naples: Guida, 1990, pp. 199–228.

The Atomists: Leucippus and Democritus: Fragments, trans. and ed. C. C. W. Taylor. Toronto: University of Toronto Press, 1999.

Avrin, Leila. *Scribes, Script and Books: The Book Arts from Antiquity to the Renais-*

sance. Chicago and London: American Library Association and the British Library, 1991.

Bacci, P. *Cenni Biografici e Religiosità di Poggio Bracciolini*. Florence: Enrico Ariani e l'Arte della Stampa, 1963.

Bailey, Cyril. *The Greek Atomists and Epicurus: A Study*. Oxford: Clarendon Press, 1928.

Baker, Eric. *Atomism and the Sublime: On the Reception of Epicurus and Lucretius in the Aesthetics of Edmund Burke, Kant, and Schiller*. Baltimore: Johns Hopkins University Press, 2001.

Baldini, Umberto. *Primavera: The Restoration of Botticelli's Masterpiece*, trans. Mary Fitton. New York: H. N. Abrams, 1986.

Barba, Eugenio. "A Chosen Diaspora in the Guts of the Monster," *Tulane Drama Review* 46 (2002), pp. 147–53.

Barbour, Reid. *English Epicures and Stoics: Ancient Legacies in Early Stuart Culture*. Amherst, MA: University of Massachusetts Press, 1998.

Baron, Hans. *The Crisis of the Early Italian Renaissance: Civic Humanism and Republican Liberty in the Age of Classicism and Tyranny*. Princeton: Princeton University Press, 1955.

Bartsch, Shadi, and Thomas Bartscherer, eds. *Erotikon: Essays on Eros, Ancient and Modern*. Chicago: University of Chicago Press, 2005.

Beddie, James Stuart. *Libraries in the Twelfth Century: Their Catalogues and Contents*. Cambridge, MA: Houghton Mifflin, 1929.

———. "The Ancient Classics in the Medieval Libraries," *Speculum* 5 (1930), pp. 1–20.

Beer, Sir Gavin de. *Charles Darwin: Evolution by Natural Selection*. New York: Doubleday, 1964.

Benedict, St. *The Rule of Benedict*, trans. Monks of Glenstal Abbey. Dublin: Four Courts Press, 1994.

Bernard of Cluny. "De Notitia Signorum," in l'abbé Marquard Herrgott, ed., *Vetus Disciplina Monastica, Seu Collectio Auctorum Ordinis S. Benedicti*. Paris: C. Osmont, 1726, pp. 169–73.

Bernhard, Marianne. *Stifts-und Klosterbibliotheken*. Munich: Keyser, 1983.

Bernstein, John. *Shaftesbury, Rousseau, and Kant*. Rutherford, NJ: Fairleigh Dickinson University Press, 1980.

Berry, Jessica. "The Pyrrhonian Revival in Montaigne and Nietzsche," *Journal of the History of Ideas* 65 (2005), pp. 497–514.

Bertelli, Sergio. "Noterelle Machiavelliane," *Rivista Storica Italiana* 73 (1961), pp. 544–57.

Billanovich, Guido. "Veterum Vestigia Vatum: Nei Carmi dei Preumanisti Padovani," in Giuseppe Billanovich et al., eds., *Italia Medioevale e Umanistica*. Padua: Antenore, 1958.

Biow, Douglas. *Doctors, Ambassadors, Secretaries: Humanism and Professions in Renaissance Italy*. Chicago: University of Chicago Press, 2002.

Bischhoff, Bernhard. *Manuscripts and Libraries in the Age of Charlemagne*, trans. Michael M. Gorman. Cambridge: Cambridge University Press, 1994.

Bishop, Paul, ed. *Nietzsche and Antiquity: His Reaction and Response to the Classical Tradition*. Rochester, NY: Camden House, 2004.

Black, Robert. "The Renaissance and Humanism: Definitions and Origins," in Jonathan Woolfson, ed., *Palgrave Advances in Renaissance Historiography*. Houndmills, Basingstoke, UK, and New York: Palgrave Macmillan, 2005, pp. 97–117.

Blades, William. *The Enemies of Books*. London: Elliot Stock, 1896.

Blondel, Eric. *Nietzsche: The Body and Culture*, trans. Seán Hand. Stanford: Stanford University Press, 1991.

Boitani, Piero, and Anna Torti, eds. *Intellectuals and Writers in Fourteenth-Century Europe. The J. A. W. Bennett Memorial Lectures, Perugia, 1984*. Tübingen: Gunter Narr, 1986.

Bolgar, R. R., ed. *Classical Influences on European Culture, a.d. 1500–1700*. Cambridge: Cambridge University Press, 1976.

Bollack, Mayotte. *Le Jardin Romain: Epicurisme et Poésie à Rome*, ed. Annick Monet. Villeneuve d'Asq: Presses de l'Université Charles-de-Gaulle-Lille 3, 2003.

Benoît de Port-Valais, Saint. *Colophons de Manuscrits Occidentaux des Origines au XVIe Siècle/Benedictins du Bouveret*. Fribourg: Editions Universitaires, 1965.

Boyd, Clarence Eugene. *Public Libraries and Literary Culture in Ancient Rome*. Chicago: University of Chicago Press, 1915.

Bracciolini, Poggio. *The Facetiae, or Jocose Tales of Poggio*. Paris: Isidore Liseux, 1879.

———. "Epistolae—Liber Primus" in *Opera Omnia*, ed. Thomas de Tonelli. Turin: Bottega d'Erasmo, 1964.

———. *Two Renaissance Book Hunters: The Letters of Poggius Bracciolini to Nicolaus de Nicolis*, trans. Phyllis Walter Goodhart Gordan. New York: Columbia University Press, 1974.

———. *Lettere*, ed. Helene Harth. Florence: Leo S. Olschki, 1984.

———. *Un Vieux Doît-Il Se Marier?* trans. Véronique Bruez. Paris: Les Belles Lettres, 1998.

———. *La Vera Nobilità*. Rome: Salerno Editrice, 1999.

Brady, Thomas, Heiko A. Oberman, and James D. Tracy, eds. *Handbook of European History, 1400–1600: Late Middle Ages, Renaissance and Reformation*. Leiden: E. J. Brill, 1995.

Brant, Frithiof. *Thomas Hobbes' Mechanical Conception of Nature*, trans. Vaughan Maxwell and Anne I. Fansboll. Copenhagen: Levin & Munksgaard, 1928.

Bredekamp, Horst. *Botticelli: Primavera. Florenz als Garten der Venus.* Frankfurt am Main: Fischer Taschenbuch, 1988.

———. "Gazing Hands and Blind Spots: Galileo as Draftsman," in Jürgen Renn, ed., *Galileo in Context.* Cambridge: Cambridge University Press, 2001, pp. 153–92.

Bredvold, Louis. "Dryden, Hobbes, and the Royal Society," *Modern Philology* 25 (1928), pp. 417–38.

Brien, Kevin M. *Marx, Reason, and the Art of Freedom.* Philadelphia: Temple University Press, 1987.

Brody, Selma B. "Physics in Middlemarch: Gas Molecules and Ethereal Atoms," *Modern Philology* 85 (1987), pp. 42–53.

Brown, Alison. "Lucretius and the Epicureans in the Social and Political Context of Renaissance Florence," *I Tatti Studies: Essays in the Renaissance* 9 (2001), pp. 11–62.

———. *The Return of Lucretius to Renaissance Florence.* Cambridge, MA: Harvard University Press, 2010.

Brown, Peter. *Power and Persuasion in Late Antiquity: Towards a Christian Empire.* Madison: University of Wisconsin Press, 1992.

———. *The Rise of Western Christendom: Triumph and Diversity, a.d. 200–1000.* Oxford: Blackwell, 1996.

Bruckner, Gene A. *Renaissance Florence.* Berkeley: University of California Press, 1969, 1983.

Bull, Malcolm. *The Mirror of the Gods.* Oxford: Oxford University Press, 2005.

Bullough, D. A. *Carolingian Renewal: Sources and Heritage.* Manchester and New York: Manchester University Press, 1991.

Burns, Tony, and Ian Fraser, eds. *The Hegel-Marx Connection.* Basingstoke, UK: Macmillan Press, 2000.

Calvi, Gerolamo. *I Manoscritti di Leonardo da Vinci dal Punto di Vista Cronologico, Storico e Biografico.* Bologna: N. Zanichelli, 1925.

Campbell, Gordon. "Zoogony and Evolution in Plato's Timaeus, the Presocratics, Lucretius, and Darwin," in M. R. Wright, ed., *Reason and Necessity: Essays on Plato's Timaeus.* London: Duckworth, 2000.

———. *Lucretius on Creation and Evolution: A Commentary on De Rerum Natura, Book Five, Lines 772–1104.* Oxford: Oxford University Press, 2003.

Campbell, Keith. "Materialism," in Paul Edwards, ed., *The Encyclopedia of Philosophy.* New York: Macmillan Company and The Free Press, 1967, pp. 179–88.

Campbell, Stephen J. "Giorgione's Tempest, Studiolo Culture, and the Renaissance Lucretius," *Renaissance Quarterly* 56 (2003), pp. 299–332.

———. *The Cabinet of Eros: Renaissance Mythological Painting and the Studiolo of Isabella d'Este.* New Haven: Yale University Press, 2004.

Camporeale, Salvatore I. "Poggio Bracciolini versus Lorenzo Valla: The

Orationes in Laurentium Vallam," in Marino and Schlitt, eds. *Perspectives on Early Modern and Modern Intellectual History: Essays in Honor of Nancy S. Struever.* Rochester, NY: University of Rochester Press, 2000, pp. 27–48.

Canfora, Luciano. *The Vanished Library,* trans. Martin Ryle. Berkeley: University of California Press, 1990.

Cariou, Marie. *L'Atomisme; Trois Essais: Gassendi, Leibniz, Bergson et Lucrèce.* Paris: Aubier Montaigne, 1978.

Casini, Paolo. "Newton: The Classical Scholia," *History of Science* 22 (1984), pp. 1–58.

Casson, Lionel. *Libraries in the Ancient World.* New Haven: Yale University Press, 2002.

Castelli, Patrizia, ed. *Un Toscano del '400: Poggio Bracciolini, 1380–1459.* Terranuova Bracciolini: Amministrazione Comunale, 1980.

Castiglioni, Arturo. "Gerolamo Fracastoro e la Dottrina del *Contagium Vivum,*" *Gesnerus* 8 (1951), pp. 52–65.

Celenza, C. S. "Lorenzo Valla and the Traditions and Transmissions of Philosophy," *Journal of the History of Ideas* 66 (2005), pp. 24.

Chamberlin, E. R. *The World of the Italian Renaissance.* London: George Allen & Unwin, 1982.

Chambers, D. S. "Spas in the Italian Renaissance," in Mario A. Di Cesare, ed., *Reconsidering the Renaissance: Papers from the Twenty-first Annual Conference.* Binghamton, NY: Medieval and Renaissance Texts and Studies, 1992, pp. 3–27.

Chang, Kenneth. "In Explaining Life's Complexity, Darwinists and Doubters Clash," *The New York Times,* August 2, 2005.

Cheney, Liana. *Quattrocento Neoplatonism and Medici Humanism in Botticelli's Mythological Paintings.* Lanham, MD, and London: University Press of America, 1985.

Chiffoleau, Jacques. *La Comptabilité de l'Au-Delà: Les Hommes, la Mort et la Religion dans la Région d'Avignon à la Fin du Moyen Age (vers 1320–vers 1480).* Rome: Ecole Française de Rome, 1980.

Christie-Murray, David. *A History of Heresy.* London: New English Library, 1976.

Cicero. *The Speeches of Cicero,* trans. Louis E. Lord. Cambridge, MA: Harvard University Press, 1937.

———. *Tusculan Disputations,* trans. and ed. J. E. King. Cambridge, MA: Harvard University Press, 1960.

———. *De Natura Deorum; Academica,* trans. and ed. H. Rackham. Cambridge, MA: Harvard University Press, 1967.

———. *Cicero's Letters to His Friends,* trans. D. R. Shackleton Bailey. Harmondsworth, UK, and New York: Penguin Books, 1978.

Clanchy, M. T. *From Memory to Written Record: England, 1066–1307.* Cambridge, MA: Harvard University Press, 1979.

Clark, A. C. "The Literary Discoveries of Poggio," *Classical Review* 13 (1899), pp. 119–30.

Clark, Ronald William. *The Survival of Charles Darwin: A Biography of a Man and an Idea.* London: Weidenfeld & Nicolson, 1985.

Clay, Diskin. *Lucretius and Epicurus.* Ithaca, NY: Cornell University Press, 1983.

Cohen, Bernard. "Quantum in se Est: Newton's Concept of Inertia in Relation to Descartes and Lucretius," *Notes and Records of the Royal Society of London,* 19 (1964), pp. 131–55.

Cohen, Elizabeth S., and Thomas V. Cohen. *Daily Life in Renaissance Italy.* Westport, CT: Greenwood Press, 2001.

Cohn, Samuel, Jr., and Steven A. Epstein, eds. *Portraits of Medieval and Renaissance Living: Essays in Memory of David Herlihy.* Ann Arbor: University of Michigan Press, 1996.

Coleman, Francis. *The Harmony of Reason: A Study in Kant's Aesthetics.* Pittsburgh: University of Pittsburgh Press, 1974.

Connell, William J. "Gasparo and the Ladies: Coming of Age in Castiglione's *Book of the Courtier,*" *Quaderni d'Italianistica* 23 (2002), pp. 5–23.

———, ed. *Society and Individual in Renaissance Florence.* Berkeley and London: University of California Press, 2002.

———, and Andrea Zorzi, eds. *Florentine Tuscany: Structures and Practices of Power.* Cambridge: Cambridge University Press, 2000.

Contreni, John J. *Carolingian Learning, Masters and Manuscripts.* Aldershot, UK: Variorum, 1992.

Cranz, F. Edward. "The *Studia Humanitatis* and *Litterae* in Cicero and Leonardo Bruni," in Marino and Schlitt, eds., *Perspectives on Early Modern and Modern Intellectual History: Essays in Honor of Nancy S. Struever.* Rochester, NY: University of Rochester Press, 2001, pp. 3–26.

Crick, Julia, and Alexandra Walsham, eds. *The Uses of Script and Print, 1300–1700.* Cambridge: Cambridge University Press, 2004.

Cropper, Elizabeth. "Ancients and Moderns: Alessandro Tassoni, Francesco Scannelli, and the Experience of Modern Art," in Marino and Schlitt, eds., *Perspectives on Early Modern and Modern Intellectual History: Essays in Honor of Nancy S. Struever,* pp. 303–24.

Dampier, Sir William. *A History of Science and Its Relations with Philosophy and Religion.* Cambridge: Cambridge University Press, 1932.

Darwin, Erasmus. *The Letters of Erasmus Darwin,* ed. Desmond King-Hele. Cambridge: Cambridge University Press, 1981.

Daston, Lorraine, and Fernando Vidal, eds. *The Moral Authority of Nature.* Chicago: University of Chicago Press, 2004.

De Lacy, Phillip. "Distant Views: The Imagery of Lucretius," *The Classical Journal* 60 (1964), pp. 49–55.

De Quehen, H. "Lucretius and Swift's Tale of a Tub," *University of Toronto Quarterly* 63 (1993), pp. 287–307.

Dean, Cornelia. "Science of the Soul? 'I Think, Therefore I Am' Is Losing Force," *The New York Times*, June 26, 2007, p. D8.

Deimling, Barbara. "The High Ideal of Love," *Sandro Botticelli: 1444/45–1510.* Cologne: B. Taschen, 1993, pp. 38–55.

Deleuze, Gilles. *Logic du Sens.* Paris: Minuit, 1969.

———. *The Logic of Sense.* trans. Mark Lester with Charles Stivale. New York: Columbia University Press, 1990.

Delumeau, Jean. *Sin and Fear: The Emergence of a Western Guilt Culture, 13th–18th Centuries,* trans. Eric Nicholson. New York: St. Martin's Press, 1990.

Dempsey, Charles. "Mercurius Ver: The Sources of Botticelli's Primavera," *Journal of the Warburg and Courtauld Institutes* 31 (1968), pp. 251–73.

———. "Botticelli's Three Graces," *Journal of the Warburg and Courtauld Institutes* 34 (1971), pp. 326–30.

———. *The Portrayal of Love: Botticelli's Primavera and Humanist Culture at the Time of Lorenzo the Magnificent.* Princeton: Princeton University Press, 1992.

Depreux, Philippe. "Büchersuche und Büchertausch im Zeitalter der Karolingischen Renaissance am Beispiel des Briefwechsels des Lupus von Ferrières," *Archiv für Kulturgeschichte* 76 (1994).

Diano, Carlo. *Forma ed Evento: Principi per una Interpretazione del Mondo Greco.* Venice: Saggi Marsilio, 1993.

Didi-Huberman, Georges. "The Matter-Image: Dust, Garbage, Dirt, and Sculpture in the Sixteenth Century," *Common Knowledge* 6 (1997), pp. 79–96.

Diogenes. *The Epicurean Inscription [of Diogenes of Oinoanda],* ed. and trans. Martin Ferguson Smith. Naples: Bibliopolis, 1992.

Dionigi, Ivano. "Lucrezio," *Orazio: Enciclopedia Oraziana.* Rome: Istituto della Enciclopedia Italiana, 1996–98, pp. 15–22.

———. *Lucrezio: Le Parole e le Cose.* Bologna: Patròn Editore, 1988.

Diringer, David. *The Book Before Printing: Ancient, Medieval and Oriental.* New York: Dover Books, 1982.

Dottori, Riccardo, ed. "The Dialogue: Yearbook of Philosophical Hermeneutics," *The Legitimacy of Truth: Proceedings of the III Meeting.* Rome: Lit Verlag, 2001.

Downing, Eric. "Lucretius at the Camera: Ancient Atomism and Early Photographic Theory in Walter Benjamin's *Berliner Chronik,*" *The Germanic Review* 81 (2006), pp. 21–36.

Draper, Hal. *The Marx-Engels Glossary.* New York: Schocken Books, 1986.

Drogin, Marc. *Biblioclasm: The Mythical Origins, Magic Powers, and Perishability of the Written Word*. Savage, MD: Rowman & Littlefield, 1989.

Dryden, John. *Sylvae: or, the Second Part of Poetical Miscellanies*. London: Jacob Tonson, 1685.

Dunant, Sarah. *Birth of Venus*. New York: Random House, 2003.

Duncan, Stewart. "Hobbes's Materialism in the Early 1640s," *British Journal for the History of Philosophy* 13 (2005), pp. 437–48.

Dupont, Florence. *Daily Life in Ancient Rome*, trans. Christopher Woodall. Oxford and Cambridge, MA: Blackwell, 1993.

Dyson, Julia T. "Dido the Epicurean," *Classical Antiquity* 15 (1996), pp. 203–21.

Dzielska, Maria. *Hypatia of Alexandria*, trans. F. Lyra. Cambridge, MA: Harvard University Press, 1995.

Early Responses to Hobbes, ed. Gaj Rogers. London: Routledge, 1996.

Edwards, John. "Religious Faith and Doubt in Late Medieval Spain: Soria circa 1450–1500," *Past and Present* 120 (1988), pp. 3–25.

Englert, Walter G. *Epicurus on the Swerve and Voluntary Action*. Atlanta, GA: Scholars Press, 1987.

Epicurus. *The Epicurus Reader*, trans. and ed. Brad Inwood and L. P. Gerson. Indianapolis: Hackett, 1994.

Erwin, Douglas H. "Darwin Still Rules, But Some Biologists Dream of a Paradigm Shift," *The New York Times*, June 26, 2007, p. D2.

Faggen, Robert. *Robert Frost and the Challenge of Darwin*. Ann Arbor: University of Michigan Press, 1997.

Fara, Patricia. *Newton: The Making of a Genius*. New York: Columbia University Press, 2002.

———, and David Money. "Isaac Newton and Augustan Anglo-Latin Poetry," *Studies in History and Philosophy of Science* 35 (2004), pp. 549–71.

Fenves, Peter. *A Peculiar Fate: Metaphysics and World-History in Kant*. Ithaca, NY: Cornell University Press, 1991.

———. *Late Kant: Towards Another Law of the Earth*. New York: Routledge, 2003.

Ferrari, Mirella. "In Papia Conveniant ad Dungalum," *Italia Medioevale e Umanistica* 15 (1972), pp. 1–52.

Ferruolo, Arnolfo B. "Botticelli's Mythologies, Ficino's De Amore, Poliziano's Stanze per la Giostra: Their Circle of Love," *The Art Bulletin [College Art Association of America]* 37 (1955), pp. 17–25.

Ficino, Marsilio. *Platonic Theology*, ed. James Hankins with William Bowen; trans. Michael J. B. Allen and John Warden. Cambridge, MA, and London: Harvard University Press, 2004.

Finch, Chauncey E. "Machiavelli's Copy of Lucretius," *The Classical Journal* 56 (1960), pp. 29–32.

Findlen, Paula. "Possessing the Past: The Material World of the Italian Renaissance," *American Historical Review* 103 (1998), pp. 83–114.

Fleischmann, Wolfgang Bernard. "The Debt of the Enlightenment to Lucretius," *Studies on Voltaire and the Eighteenth Century* 29 (1963), pp. 631–43.
———. *Lucretius and English Literature, 1680–1740*. Paris: A. G. Nizet, 1964.
Flores, Enrico. *Le Scoperte di Poggio e il Testo di Lucrezio*. Naples: Liguori, 1980.
Floridi, Luciano. *Sextus Empiricus: The Transmission and Recovery of Pyrrhonism*. New York: Oxford University Press, 2002.
Foster, John Bellamy. *Marx's Ecology: Materialism and Nature*. New York: Monthly Review Press, 2000.
Fraisse, Simone. *L'Influence de Lucrèce en France au Seizième Siècle*. Paris: Librairie A. G. Nizet, 1962.
Frede, Michael, and Gisela Striker, eds. *Rationality in Greek Thought*. Oxford: Clarendon Press, 1996.
Fubini, Riccardo. "'Varietà: Un'Orazione di Poggio Bracciolini sui Vizi del Clero Scritta al Tempo del Concilio di Costanza,'" *Giornale Storico della Letteratura Italiana* 142 (1965), pp. 24–33.
———. *L'Umanesimo Italiano e I Suoi Storici*. Milan: Franco Angeli Storia, 2001.
———. *Humanism and Secularization: From Petrarch to Valla*, trans. Martha King. Durham, NC, and London: Duke University Press, 2003.
Fusil, C. A. "Lucrèce et les Philosophes du XVIIIe Siècle," *Revue d'Histoire Littéraire de la France* 35 (1928).
———. "Lucrèce et les Littérateurs, Poètes et Artistes du XVIIIe Siècle," *Revue d'Histoire Littéraire de la France* 37 (1930).
Gabotto, Ferdinando. "L'Epicureismo di Marsilio Ficino," *Rivista di Filosofia Scientifica* 10 (1891), pp. 428–42.
Gallagher, Mary. "Dryden's Translation of Lucretius," *Huntington Library Quarterly* 7 (1968), pp. 19–29.
Gallo, Italo. *Studi di Papirologia Ercolanese*. Naples: M. D'Auria, 2002.
Garaudy, Roger. *Marxism in the Twentieth Century*. New York: Charles Scribner's Sons, 1970.
Garin, Eugenio. *Ritratti di Umanisti*. Florence: Sansoni, 1967.
———. *La Cultura Filosofica del Rinascimento Italiano*. Florence: Sansoni, 1979.
Garrard, Mary D. "Leonardo da Vinci: Female Portraits, Female Nature," in Norma Broude and Mary Garrard, eds., *The Expanding Discourse: Feminism and Art History*. New York: HarperCollins, 1992, pp. 59–85.
Garzelli, Annarosa. *Miniatura Fiorentina del Rinascimento, 1440–1525*. Florence: Giunta Regionale Toscana: La Nuova Italia, 1985.
Ghiselin, Michael T. "Two Darwins: History versus Criticism," *Journal of the History of Biology* 9 (1976), pp. 121–32.
Gibbon, Edward. *The History of the Decline and Fall of the Roman Empire*, 6 vols. New York: Knopf, 1910.
Gigante, Marcello. "Ambrogio Traversari Interprete di Diogene Laerzio," in Gian Carlo Garfagnini, ed., *Ambrogio Traversari nel VI Centenario della Nascità*. Florence: Leo S. Olschki, 1988, pp. 367–459.

————. *Philodemus in Italy: The Books from Herculaneum*, trans. Dirk Obbink. Ann Arbor: University of Michigan Press, 1995.

Gildenhard, Ingo. "Confronting the Beast—From Virgil's Cacus to the Dragons of Cornelis van Haarlem," *Proceedings of the Virgil Society* 25 (2004), pp. 27–48.

Gillett, E. H. *The Life and Times of John Huss*. Boston: Gould & Lincoln, 1863.

Gleason, Maud. *Making Men: Sophists and Self-Presentation in Ancient Rome*. Princeton: Princeton University Press, 1995.

Goetschel, Willi. *Constituting Critique: Kant's Writing as Critical Praxis*, trans. Eric Schwab. Durham, NC: Duke University Press, 1994.

Goldberg, Jonathan. *The Seeds of Things: Theorizing Sexuality and Materiality in Renaissance Representations*. New York: Fordham University Press, 2009.

Goldsmith, M. M. *Hobbes' Science of Politics*. New York: Columbia University Press, 1966.

Golner, Johannes. *Bayerische Klosterbibliotheken*. Freilassing: Pannonia-Verlag, 1983.

Gombrich, Ernst H. "Botticelli's Mythologies: A Study in the Neoplatonic Symbolism of His Circle," *Journal of the Warburg and Courtauld Institutes* 8 (1945), pp. 7–60.

Gordon, Dane R., and David B. Suits, eds. *Epicurus: His Continuing Influence and Contemporary Relevance*. Rochester, NY: RIT Cary Graphic Arts Press, 2003.

Gordon, Pamela. "Phaeacian Dido: Lost Pleasures of an Epicurean Intertext," *Classical Antiquity* 17 (1998), pp. 188–211.

Grafton, Anthony. *Forgers and Critics: Creativity and Duplicity in Western Scholarship*. Princeton: Princeton University Press, 1990.

————. *Commerce with the Classics: Ancient Books and Renaissance Readers*. Ann Arbor: University of Michigan Press, 1997.

————, and Ann Blair, eds., *The Transmission of Culture in Early Modern Europe*. Philadelphia: University of Pennsylvania Press, 1990.

————, and Lisa Jardine, *From Humanism to the Humanities: Education and the Liberal Arts in Fifteenth- and Sixteenth-Century Europe*. Cambridge, MA: Harvard University Press, 1986.

Grant, Edward. "Bernhard Pabst: Atomtheorien des Lateinischen Mittelalters," *Isis* 87 (1996), pp. 345–46.

Greenblatt, Stephen. *Learning to Curse: Essays in Early Modern Culture*. New York and London: Routledge Classics, 2007.

Greenburg, Sidney Thomas. *The Infinite in Giordano Bruno*. New York: Octagon Books, 1978.

Greene, Thomas M. "Ceremonial Closure in Shakespeare's Plays," in Marino and Schlitt, eds., *Perspectives on Early Modern and Modern Intellectual History: Essays in Honor of Nancy S. Struever*. Rochester, NY: University of Rochester Press, 2000, pp. 208–19.

Greetham, David C. *Textual Scholarship: An Introduction*. New York: Garland, 1994.

———. *Textual Transgressions: Essays Toward the Construction of a Bibliography*. New York and London: Garland, 1998.

Gregory, Joshua. *A Short History of Atomism: From Democritus to Bohr*. London: A. C. Black, 1931.

Gregory I, Pope. *Dialogues*. Washington, DC: Catholic University of America Press, 1959.

———. *The Letters of Gregory the Great*, trans. John R. C. Martin. Toronto: Pontifical Institute of Medieval Studies, 2004.

Grieco, Allen J., Michael Rocke, and Fiorella Gioffredi Superbi, eds. *The Italian Renaissance in the Twentieth Century*. Florence: Leo S. Olschki, 1999.

Gruber, Howard E. *Darwin on Man: A Psychological Study of Scientific Creativity*. Chicago: University of Chicago Press, 1981, pp. 46–73.

Gruen, Erich S. *The Hellenistic World and the Coming of Rome*. Berkeley: University of California Press, 1984.

Guehenno, Jean. *Jean Jacques Rousseau*, trans. John Weightman and Doreen Weightman. London: Routledge & Kegan Paul, 1966.

Haas, Christopher. *Alexandria in Late Antiquity: Topography and Social Conflict*. Baltimore: Johns Hopkins University Press, 1997.

Hadot, Pierre. *What Is Ancient Philosophy?* trans. Michael Chase. Cambridge, MA: Harvard University Press, 2002.

Hadzsits, George D. *Lucretius and His Influence*. New York: Longmans, Green & Co., 1935.

Haines-Eitzen, Kim. *Guardians of Letters: Literacy, Power, and the Transmitters of Early Christian Literature*. Oxford: Oxford University Press, 2000.

Hale, John R., ed. *A Concise Encyclopaedia of the Italian Renaissance*. London: Thames & Hudson, 1981.

———. *The Civilization of Europe in the Renaissance*. London: HarperCollins, 1993.

Hall, Rupert. *Isaac Newton, Adventurer in Thought*. Oxford: Blackwell, 1992.

Hamman, A.-G. *L'Epopée du Livre: La Transmission des Textes Anciens, du Scribe a l'Imprimérie*. Paris: Libr. Académique Perrin, 1985.

Hankins, James. *Plato in the Italian Renaissance*. Leiden: E. J. Brill, 1990.

———. "Renaissance Philosophy Between God and the Devil," in Grieco et al., eds., *Italian Renaissance in the Twentieth Century*, pp. 269–93.

———. "Renaissance Humanism and Historiography Today," in Jonathan Woolfson, ed., *Palgrave Advances in Renaissance Historiography*. New York: Palgrave Macmillan, 2005, pp. 73–96.

———. "Religion and the Modernity of Renaissance Humanism," in Angelo Mazzocco, ed., *Interpretations of Renaissance Humanism*. Leiden: E. J. Brill, 2006, pp. 137–54.

———, and Ada Palmer. *The Recovery of Ancient Philosophy in the Renaissance: A Brief Guide*. Florence: Leo S. Olschki, 2008.

Hardie, Philip R. "Lucretius and the Aeneid," *Virgil's Aeneid: Cosmos and Imperium*. New York: Oxford University Press, 1986, pp. 157–240.

———. *Ovid's Poetics of Illusion*. Cambridge: Cambridge University Press, 2002.

Harris, Jonathan Gil. "Atomic Shakespeare," *Shakespeare Studies* 30 (2002), pp. 47–51.

Harris, William V. *Restraining Rage: The Ideology of Anger Control in Classical Antiquity*. Cambridge, MA: Harvard University Press, 2001.

Harrison, Charles T. *Bacon, Hobbes, Boyle, and the Ancient Atomists*. Cambridge, MA: Harvard University Press, 1933.

———. "The Ancient Atomists and English Literature of the Seventeenth Century," *Harvard Studies in Classical Philology* 45 (1934), pp. 1–79.

Harrison, Edward. "Newton and the Infinite Universe," *Physics Today* 39 (1986), pp. 24–32.

Hay, Denys. *The Italian Renaissance in Its Historical Background*. Cambridge: Cambridge University Press.

Heller, Agnes. *Renaissance Man*, trans. Richard E. Allen. London: Routledge & Kegan Paul, 1978 (orig. Hungarian 1967).

Herbert, Gary B. *The Unity of Scientific and Moral Wisdom*. Vancouver: University of British Columbia Press, 1989.

Himmelfarb, Gertrude. *Darwin and the Darwinian Revolution*. New York: W. W. Norton & Company, 1968.

Hine, William. "Inertia and Scientific Law in Sixteenth-Century Commentaries on Lucretius," *Renaissance Quarterly* 48 (1995), pp. 728–41.

Hinnant, Charles. *Thomas Hobbes*. Boston: Twayne Publishers, 1977.

Hirsch, David A. Hedrich. "Donne's Atomies and Anatomies: Deconstructed Bodies and the Resurrection of Atomic Theory," *Studies in English Literature, 1500–1900* 31 (1991), pp. 69–94.

Hobbes, Thomas. *Leviathan*. Cambridge: Cambridge University Press, 1991.

———. *The Elements of Law Natural and Politic: Human Nature, De Corpore Politico, Three Lives*. Oxford: Oxford University Press, 1994.

Hoffmann, Banesh. *Albert Einstein, Creator and Rebel*. New York: Viking Press, 1972.

Holzherr, George. *The Rule of Benedict: A Guide to Christian Living, with Commentary by George Holzherr, Abbot of Einsiedeln*. Dublin: Four Courts Press, 1994.

Horne, Herbert. *Alessandro Filipepi, Commonly Called Sandro Botticelli, Painter of Florence*. Princeton: Princeton University Press, 1980.

Hubbard, Elbert. *Journeys to Homes of Eminent Artists*. East Aurora, NY: Roycrafters, 1901.

Humanism and Liberty: Writings on Freedom from Fifteenth-Century Florence, trans. and ed. Renee Neu Watkins. Columbia, SC: University of South Carolina Press, 1978.

Hutcheon, Pat Duffy. *The Road to Reason: Landmarks in the Evolution of Humanist Thought*. Ottawa: Canadian Humanist Publications, 2001.

Hutchinson, Lucy. *Lucy Hutchinson's Translation of Lucretius: De rerum natura*, ed. Hugh de Quehen. Ann Arbor: University of Michigan Press, 1996.

Hyde, William de Witt. *From Epicurus to Christ: A Study in the Principles of Personality*. New York: Macmillan, 1908.

Impey, Chris. "Reacting to the Size and the Shape of the Universe," *Mercury* 30 (2001).

Isidore of Seville. *The Etymologies of Isidore of Seville*, ed. Stephen A. Barney et al. Cambridge: Cambridge University Press, 2006.

Jacquot, J. "Thomas Harriot's Reputation for Impiety," *Notes and Records of the Royal Society* 9 (1951–52), pp. 164–87.

Jayne, Sears. *John Colet and Marsilio Ficino*. Oxford: Oxford University Press, 1963.

Jefferson, Thomas. *Papers*. Princeton: Princeton University Press, 1950.

———. *Writings*. New York: Viking Press, 1984.

Jerome, St. *Select Letters of St. Jerome*, trans. F. A. Wright. London: William Heinemann, 1933.

———. *The Letters of St. Jerome*, trans. Charles Christopher Mierolo. Westminster, MD: Newman Press, 1963.

John, Bishop of Nikiu. *The Chronicle*, trans. R. H. Charles. London: Williams & Norgate, 1916.

John of Salisbury. *Entheticus, Maior and Minor*, ed. Jan van Laarhoven. Leiden: E. J. Brill, 1987.

Johnson, Elmer D. *History of Libraries in the Western World*. Metuchen, NJ: Scarecrow Press, 1970.

Johnson, W. R. *Lucretius and the Modern World*. London: Duckworth, 2000.

Jones, Howard. *The Epicurean Tradition*. London: Routledge, 1989.

Jordan, Constance. *Pulci's Morgante: Poetry and History in Fifteenth-Century Florence*. Washington, DC: Folger Shakespeare Library, 1986.

Joy, Lynn S. "Epicureanism in Renaissance Moral and Natural Philosophy," *Journal of the History of Ideas* 53 (1992), pp. 573–83.

Judd, John. *The Coming of Evolution: The Story of a Great Revolution in Science*. Cambridge: Cambridge University Press, 1910.

Kaczynski, Bernice M. *Greek in the Carolingian Age: The St. Gall Manuscripts*. Cambridge, MA: Medieval Academy of America, 1988.

Kain, Philip J. *Marx' Method, Epistemology and Humanism*. Dordrecht: D. Reidel, 1986.

Kamenka, Eugene. *The Ethical Foundations of Marxism*. London: Routledge & Kegan Paul, 1972.

Kantorowicz, Ernst H. "The Sovereignty of the Artist: A Note on Legal Maxims and Renaissance Theories of Art," in Millard Meiss, ed., *Essays in Honor of Erwin Panofsky*. New York: New York University Press, 1961, pp. 267–79.

Kargon, Robert Hugh. *Atomism in England from Hariot to Newton*. Oxford: Clarendon Press, 1966.

Kaster, Robert A. *Guardians of Language: The Grammarian and Society in Late Antiquity*. Berkeley: University of California Press, 1988.

Kemp, Martin. *Leonardo da Vinci, the Marvelous Works of Nature and Man*. Cambridge, MA: Harvard University Press, 1981.

———. *Leonardo*. Oxford: Oxford University Press, 2004.

Kemple, Thomas. *Reading Marx Writing: Melodrama, the Market, and the "Grundrisse."* Stanford: Stanford University Press, 1995.

Kenney, E. J. *Lucretius*. Oxford: Clarendon Press, 1977.

Kidwell, Carol. *Marullus: Soldier Poet of the Renaissance*. London: Duckworth, 1989.

Kitts, Eustace J. *In the Days of the Councils: A Sketch of the Life and Times of Baldassare Cossa (Afterward Pope John the Twenty-Third)*. London: Archibald Constable & Co., 1908.

———. *Pope John the Twenty-Third and Master John Hus of Bohemia*. London: Constable & Co., 1910.

Kivisto, Sari. *Creating Anti-Eloquence: Epistolae Obscurorum Virorum and the Humanist Polemics on Style*. Helsinki: Finnish Society of Sciences and Letters, 2002.

Kohl, Benjamin G. *Renaissance Humanism, 1300–1550: A Bibliography of Materials in English*. New York and London: Garland, 1985.

Kors, Alan Charles. "Theology and Atheism in Early Modern France," in Grafton and Blair, eds., *Transmission of Culture in Early Modern Europe*, pp. 238–75.

Korsch, Karl. *Karl Marx*. New York: John Wiley & Sons, 1938.

Koyré, Alexandre. *From the Closed World to the Infinite Universe*. Baltimore: Johns Hopkins Press, 1957.

Krause, Ernst. *Erasmus Darwin*, trans. W. S. Dallas. London: John Murray, 1879.

Krautheimer, Richard. *Rome: Profile of a City, 312–1308*. Princeton: Princeton University Press, 1980.

Kristeller, Paul Oskar. *Renaissance Thought: The Classic, Scholastic, and Humanist Strains*. New York: Harper, 1961.

———. *Renaissance Concepts of Man and Other Essays*. New York: Harper, 1972.

———. *Renaissance Thought and the Arts: Collected Essays*. Princeton: Princeton University Press, 1965, 1980.

———, and Philip P. Wiener, eds. *Renaissance Essays*. New York: Harper, 1968.

Kuehn, Manfred. *Kant: A Biography*. New York: Cambridge University Press, 2001.

Lachs, John. "The Difference God Makes," *Midwest Studies in Philosophy* 28 (2004), pp. 183–94.

Lactantius. "A Treatise on the Anger of God, Addressed to Donatus," in Rev. Alexander Roberts and James Donaldson, eds.; William Fletcher, trans., *The Works of Lactantius*. Vol. II. Edinburgh: T. & T. Clark, 1871, pp. 1–48.

Lange, Frederick Albert. *The History of Materialism: and Criticism of Its Present Importance*, trans. Ernest Chester Thomas, intro. Bertrand Russell. London: K. Paul, Trench, Trubner; New York: Harcourt, Brace, 1925.

Leff, Gordon. *Heresy, Philosophy and Religion in the Medieval West*. Aldershot, UK, and Burlington, VT: Ashgate, 2002.

Le Goff, Jacques. *The Medieval Imagination*, trans. Arthur Goldhammer. Chicago: University of Chicago Press, 1985.

Leonardo da Vinci. *The Notebooks*. New York: New American Library, 1960.

Leonardo da Vinci. *The Literary Works of Leonardo*, ed. Jean Paul Richter. Berkeley: University of California Press, 1977.

Leto, Pomponio. *Lucrezio*, ed. Giuseppe Solaro. Palermo: Sellerio, 1993.

Levine, Norman. *The Tragic Deception: Marx Contra Engels*. Oxford: Clio Books, 1975.

Lezra, Jacques. *Unspeakable Subjects: The Genealogy of the Event in Early Modern Europe*. Stanford: Stanford University Press, 1997.

Lightbrown, R. W. *Botticelli: Life and Work*. New York: Abbeville Press, 1989.

Löffler, Dr. Klemens. *Deutsche Klosterbibliotheken*. Cologne: J. P. Bachman, 1918.

Long, A. A. *Hellenistic Philosophy: Stoics, Epicureans, Sceptics*, 2nd edn. Berkeley: University of California Press, 1987.

———, and D. N. Sedley, *The Hellenistic Philosophers*, 2 vols. Cambridge: Cambridge University Press, 1987.

Longo, Susanna Gambino. *Lucrèce et Epicure à la Renaissance Italienne*. Paris: Honoré Champion, 2004.

Lucretius. *On the Nature of Things*, trans. W. H. D. Rouse, rev. Martin F. Smith. Cambridge, MA: Harvard University Press, 1924, rev. 1975.

———. *De Rerum Natura*, ed. Cyril Bailey. 3 vols. Oxford: Oxford University Press, 1963.

———. *The Nature of Things*, trans. Frank O. Copley. New York: W. W. Norton & Company, 1977.

———. *On the Nature of Things*, trans. Anthony M. Esolen. Baltimore: Johns Hopkins University Press, 1995.

———. *On the Nature of the Universe*, trans. Ronald Melville. Oxford: Oxford University Press, 1997.

———. *On the Nature of Things*, trans. Martin Ferguson Smith. London: Sphere Books, 1969; rev. trans. Indianapolis: Hackett, 2001.

———. *The Nature of Things*, trans. A. E. Stallings. London: Penguin, 2007.

————. *De Rerum Natura*, trans. David R. Slavitt. Berkeley: University of California Press, 2008.

Lund, Vonne, Raymond Anthony, and Helena Rocklinsberg. "The Ethical Contract as a Tool in Organic Animal Husbandry," *Journal of Agricultural and Environmental Ethics* 17 (2004), pp. 23–49.

Luper-Foy, Steven. "Annihilation," *Philosophical Quarterly* 37 (1987), pp. 233–52.

Macleod, Roy, ed. *The Library of Alexandria: Centre of Learning in the Ancient World*. London: I. B. Tauris, 2004.

MacPhail, Eric. "Montaigne's New Epicureanism," *Montaigne Studies* 12 (2000), pp. 91–103.

Madigan, Arthur. "Commentary on Politis," *Boston Area Colloquium in Ancient Philosophy* 18 (2002).

Maglo, Koffi. "Newton's Gravitational Theory by Huygens, Varignon, and Maupertuis: How Normal Science May Be Revolutionary," *Perspectives on Science*, 11 (2003), pp. 135–69.

Mah, Harold. *The End of Philosophy, the Origin of "Ideology."* Berkeley: University of California Press, 1987.

Maiorino, Giancarlo. *Leonardo da Vinci: The Daedalian Mythmaker*. University Park, PA: Pennsylvania State University Press, 1992.

Malcolm, Noel. *Aspects of Hobbes*. New York: Oxford University Press, 2002.

Marino, Joseph, and Melinda W. Schlitt, eds. *Perspectives on Early Modern and Modern Intellectual History: Essays in Honor of Nancy S. Struever*. Rochester, NY: University of Rochester Press, 2000.

Markus, R. A. *The End of Ancient Christianity*. Cambridge and New York: Cambridge University Press, 1990.

Marlowe, Christopher. *Christopher Marlowe: The Complete Poems and Translations*, ed. Stephen Orgel. Harmondsworth, UK, and Baltimore: Penguin Books, 1971.

Marsh, David. *The Quattrocento Dialogue*. Cambridge, MA, and London: Harvard University Press, 1980.

Martin, Alain, and Oliver Primavesi. *L'Empédocle de Strasbourg*. Berlin and New York: Walter de Gruyter; Bibliothèque Nationale et Universitaire de Strasbourg, 1999.

Martin, John Jeffries. *Myths of Renaissance Individualism*. Houndmills, Basingstoke, UK: Palgrave, 2004.

Martindale, Charles. *Latin Poetry and the Judgement of Taste*. Oxford: Oxford University Press, 2005.

Martines, Lauro. *The Social World of the Florentine Humanists, 1390–1460*. Princeton: Princeton University Press, 1963.

————. *Scourge and Fire: Savonarola and Renaissance Florence*. London: Jonathan Cape, 2006.

Marullo, Michele. *Inni Naturali*, trans. Doratella Coppini. Florence: Casa Editrice le Lettere, 1995.

Marx, Karl, and Frederick Engels. *Collected Works*, trans. Richard Dixon. New York: International Publishers, 1975.

———. *On Literature and Art*. Moscow: Progress Publishers, 1976.

Masters, Roger. *The Political Philosophy of Rousseau*. Princeton: Princeton University Press, 1968.

———. "Gradualism and Discontinuous Change," in Albert Somit and Steven Peterson, eds., *The Dynamics of Evolution*. Ithaca, NY: Cornell University Press, 1992.

Mayo, Thomas Franklin. *Epicurus in England (1650–1725)*. Dallas: Southwest Press, 1934.

McCarthy, George. *Marx and the Ancients: Classical Ethics, Social Justice, and Nineteenth-Century Political Economy*. Savage, MD: Rowman & Littlefield, 1990.

McDowell, Gary, and Sharon Noble, eds. *Reason and Republicanism: Thomas Jefferson's Legacy of Liberty*. Lanham, MD: Rowman & Littlefield, 1997.

McGuire, J. E., and P. M. Rattansi. "Newton and the Pipes of Pan," *Notes and Records of the Royal Society of London* 21 (1966), pp. 108–43.

McKitterick, Rosamond. "Manuscripts and Scriptoria in the Reign of Charles the Bald, 840–877," *Giovanni Scoto nel Suo Tempo*. Spoleto: Centro Italiano di Studi sull'Alto Medioevo, 1989, pp. 201–37.

———. "Le Role Culturel des Monastères dans les Royaumes Carolingiens du VIIIe au Xe Siècle," *Revue Benedictine* 103 (1993), pp. 117–30.

———. *Books, Scribes and Learning in the Frankish Kingdoms, 6th–9th Centuries*. Aldershot, UK: Variorum, 1994.

———, ed. *Carolingian Culture: Emulation and Innovation*. Cambridge: Cambridge University Press, 1994.

McKnight, Stephen A. *The Modern Age and the Recovery of Ancient Wisdom: A Reconsideration of Historical Consciousness, 1450–1650*. Columbia, MO: University of Missouri Press, 1991.

McLellan, David. *The Thought of Karl Marx*. New York: Harper & Row, 1971.

McNeil, Maureen. *Under the Banner of Science: Erasmus Darwin and His Age*. Manchester: Manchester University Press, 1987.

Meikle, Scott. *Essentialism in the Thought of Karl Marx*. London: Duckworth, 1985.

Melzer, Arthur M. *The Natural Goodness of Man: On the System of Rousseau's Thought*. Chicago: University of Chicago Press, 1990.

Merryweather, F. Somner. *Bibliomania in the Middle Ages*. London: Woodstock Press, 1933.

Michel, Paul-Henri. *The Cosmology of Giordano Bruno*, trans. R. E. W. Maddison. Paris: Hermann; Ithaca, NY: Cornell University Press, 1973.

Miller, Charles A. *Jefferson and Nature: An Interpretation*. Baltimore: Johns Hopkins University Press, 1988.

Moffitt, John F. "The *Evidentia* of Curling Waters and Whirling Winds: Leonardo's *Ekphraseis* of the Latin Weathermen," *Leonardo Studies* 4 (1991), pp. 11–33.

Molho, Anthony et al. "Genealogy and Marriage Alliance: Memories of Power in Late Medieval Florence," in Cohn and Epstein, eds., *Portraits of Medieval and Renaissance Living*, pp. 39–70.

Morel, Jean. "Recherches sur les Sources du Discours sur l'Inégalité," *Annales* 5 (1909), pp. 163–64.

Mortara, Elena. "The Light of Common Day: Romantic Poetry and the Everydayness of Human Existence," in Riccardo Dottori, ed., *The Legitimacy of Truth*. Rome: Lit Verlag, 2001.

Müller, Conradus. "De Codicum Lucretii Italicorum Origine," *Museum Helveticum: Revue Suisse pour l'Etude de l'Antiquité Classique* 30 (1973), pp. 166–78.

Mundy, John Hine, and Kennerly M. Woody, eds.; Louise Ropes Loomis, trans. *The Council of Constance: The Unification of the Church*. New York and London: Columbia University Press, 1961.

Murphy, Caroline P. *The Pope's Daughter*. London: Faber & Faber, 2004.

Murray, Alexander. "Piety and Impiety in Thirteenth-Century Italy," in C. J. Cuming and Derek Baker, eds., *Popular Belief and Practice*, Studies in Church History 8. London: Syndics of the Cambridge University Press, 1972, pp. 83–106.

———. "Confession as a Historical Source in the Thirteenth Century," in R. H. C. Davis and J. M. Wallace-Hadrill, eds., *The Writing of History in the Middle Ages: Essays Presented to Richard William Southern*. Oxford: Clarendon Press, 1981, pp. 275–322.

———. "The Epicureans," in Piero Boitani and Anna Torti, eds., *Intellectuals and Writers in Fourteenth-Century Europe*. Tübingen: Gunter Narr, 1986, pp. 138–63.

Nelson, Eric. *The Greek Tradition in Republican Thought*. Cambridge: Cambridge University Press, 2004.

Neugebauer, O. *The Exact Sciences in Antiquity*. Princeton: Princeton University Press, 1952.

Newton, Isaac. *Correspondence of Isaac Newton*, H. W. Turnbull et al., eds., 7 vols. Cambridge: Cambridge University Press, 1959–1984.

Nicholls, Mark. "Percy, Henry," *Oxford Dictionary of National Biography*, 2004–07.

Nichols, James. *Epicurean Political Philosophy: The De Rerum Natura of Lucretius*. Ithaca, NY: Cornell University Press, 1976.

Nussbaum, Martha. *The Therapy of Desire: Theory and Practice in Hellenistic Ethics*. Princeton: Princeton University Press, 2009, pp. 140–91.

Oberman, Heiko. *The Dawn of the Reformation*. Grand Rapids, MI: William Eerdmans Publishing Co., 1986.

Olsen, B. Munk. *L'Etude des Auteurs Classiques Latins aux XIe et XIIe Siècles*. Paris: Editions du Centre National de la Recherche Scientifique, 1985.

O'Malley, Charles, and J. B. Saunders. *Leonardo da Vinci on the Human Body: The Anatomical, Physiological, and Embryological Drawings of Leonardo da Vinci*. New York: Greenwich House, 1982.

O'Malley, John W., Thomas M. Izbicki, and Gerald Christianson, eds. *Humanity and Divinity in Renaissance and Reformation: Essays in Honor of Charles Trinkaus*. Leiden: E. J. Brill, 1993.

Ordine, Nuccio. *Bruno and the Philosophy of the Ass*, trans. Henryk Baraánski in collab. with Arielle Saiber. New Haven, CT: Yale University Press, 1996.

Origen. *Origen Against Celsus*, trans. Rev. Frederick Crombie, in *Anti-Nicene Christian Library: Translations of the Writings of the Fathers Down to A.D. 325*, ed. Rev. Alexander Roberts and James Donaldson, vol. 23. Edinburgh: T. & T. Clark, 1872.

Osborn, Henry Fairfield. *From the Greeks to Darwin: The Development of the Evolution Idea Through Twenty-Four Centuries*. New York: Charles Scribner's Sons, 1929.

Osler, Margaret. *Divine Will and the Mechanical Philosophy: Gassendi and Descartes on Contingency and Necessity in the Created World*. Cambridge: Cambridge University Press, 1994.

———, ed. *Atoms, Pneuma, and Tranquility: Epicurean and Stoic Themes in European Thought*. Cambridge: Cambridge University Press, 1991.

Osler, Sir William. "Illustrations of the Book-Worm," *Bodleian Quarterly Record*, 1 (1917), pp. 355–57.

Otte, James K. "Bernhard Pabst, *Atomtheorien des Lateinischen Mittelalters*," *Speculum* 71 (1996), pp. 747–49.

Overbye, Dennis. "Human DNA, the Ultimate Spot for Secret Messages (Are Some There Now?)," *The New York Times*, June 26, 2007, p. D4.

Overhoff, Jürgen. *Hobbes's Theory of the Will: Ideological Reasons and Historical Circumstances*. Lanham, MD: Rowman & Littlefield, 2000.

Pabst, Bernhard. *Atomtheorien des Lateinischen Mittelalters*. Darmstadt: Wissenschaftliche Buchgesellschaft, 1994.

Palladas. *Palladas: Poems*, trans. Tony Harrison. London: Anvil Press Poetry, 1975.

Panofsky, Erwin. *Renaissance and Renascences in Western Art*, 2 vols. Stockholm: Almqvist & Wiksell, 1960.

Parkes, M. B. *Scribes, Scripts and Readers: Studies in the Communication, Presentation and Dissemination of Medieval Texts*. London: Hambledon Press, 1991.

Parsons, Edward Alexander. *The Alexandrian Library, Glory of the Hellenic World: Its Rise, Antiquities, and Destructions*. New York: American Elsevier Publishing Co., 1952.

Partner, Peter. *Renaissance Rome, 1500–1559: A Portrait of a Society*. Berkeley: University of California Press, 1976.

———. *The Pope's Men: The Papal Civil Service in the Renaissance*. Oxford: Clarendon Press, 1990.

Paterson, Antoinette Mann. *The Infinite Worlds of Giordano Bruno*. Springfield, IL: Thomas, 1970.

Patschovsky, Alexander. *Quellen zur Böhmischen Inquisition im 14. Jahrhundert*. Weimar: Hermann Bohlaus Nachfolger, 1979.

Paulsen, Friedrich. *Immanuel Kant; His Life and Doctrine*, trans. J. E. Creighton and Albert Lefevre. New York: Frederick Ungar, 1963.

Payne, Robert. *Marx*. New York: Simon & Schuster, 1968.

Peter of Mldonovice. *John Hus at the Council of Constance*, trans. Matthew Spinka. New York: Columbia University Press, 1965.

Petrucci, Armando. *Writers and Readers in Medieval Italy: Studies in the History of Written Culture*, trans. Charles M. Kadding. New Haven and London: Yale University Press, 1995.

Pfeiffer, Rudolf. *History of Classical Scholarship from the Beginnings to the End of the Hellenistic Age*. Oxford: Clarendon Press, 1968.

Philippe, J. "Lucrèce dans la Théologie Chrétienne du IIIe au XIIIe Siècle et Spécialement dans les Ecoles Carolingiennes, " *Revue de l'Histoire des Religions* 33 (1896) pp. 125–62.

Philodemus. *On Choices and Avoidances*, trans. Giovanni Indelli and Voula Tsouna-McKirahan. Naples: Bibliopolis, 1995.

———[Filodemo]. *Mémoire Epicurée*. Naples: Bibliopolis, 1997.

———. *Acts of Love: Ancient Greek Poetry from Aphrodite's Garden*, trans. George Economou. New York: Modern Library, 2006.

———. *On Rhetoric: Books 1 and 2*, trans. Clive Chandler. New York: Routledge, 2006.

Poggio Bracciolini 1380–1980: Nel VI Centenario della Nascità. Florence: Sansoni, 1982.

Politis, Vasilis. "Aristotle on Aporia and Searching in Metaphysics," *Boston Area Colloquium in Ancient Philosophy* 18 (2002), pp. 145–74.

Porter, James. *Nietzsche and the Philology of the Future*. Stanford: Stanford University Press, 2000.

Primavesi, Oliver. "Empedocles: Physical and Mythical Divinity," in Patricia Curd and Daniel W. Graham, eds., *The Oxford Handbook of Presocratic Philosophy*. New York: Oxford University Press, 2008, pp. 250–83.

Prosperi, Adriano. *Tribunali della Coscienza: Inquisitori, Confessori, Missionari*. Turin: Giulio Einaudi, 1996.

Putnam, George Haven. *Books and Their Makers During the Middle Ages*. New York: G. P. Putnam's Sons, 1898.

Puyo, Jean. *Jan Hus: Un Drame au Coeur de l'Eglise*. Paris: Desclée de Brouwer, 1998.

Rattansi, Piyo. "Newton and the Wisdom of the Ancients," in John Fauvel, ed., *Let Newton Be!* Oxford: Oxford University Press, 1988.

Redshaw, Adrienne M. "Voltaire and Lucretius," *Studies on Voltaire and the Eighteenth Century* 189 (1980), pp. 19–43.

Reti, Ladislao. *The Library of Leonardo da Vinci*. Los Angeles: Zeitlin & Ver-Brugge, 1972.

Reynolds, L. D. *Texts and Transmission: A Survey of the Latin Classics*. Oxford: Clarendon Press, 1983.

———, and N. G. Wilson. *Scribes and Scholars: A Guide to the Transmission of Greek and Latin Literature*. London: Oxford University Press, 1968.

Reynolds, Susan. "Social Mentalities and the Case of Medieval Scepticism," *Transactions of the Royal Historical Society* 1 (1990), pp. 21–41.

Rich, Susanna. "De Undarum Natura: Lucretius and Woolf in *The Waves*," *Journal of Modern Literature* 23 (2000), pp. 249–57.

Richard, Carl. *The Founders and the Classics: Greece, Rome, and the American Enlightenment*. Cambridge, MA: Harvard University Press, 1994.

Riche, Pierre. *Education and Culture in the Barbarian West Sixth Through Eighth Centuries*, trans. John J. Cotren. Columbia, SC: University of South Carolina Press, 1976.

Richental, Ulrich von. *Chronik des Konstanzer Konzils 1414–1418*. Constance: F. Bahn, 1984.

Richter, J. P. *The Notebooks of Leonardo da Vinci*. New York: Dover Books, 1970.

Richter, Simon. *Laocoon's Body and the Aesthetics of Pain: Winckelmann, Lessing, Herder, Moritz, Goethe*. Detroit: Wayne State University Press, 1992.

Roche, J. J. "Thomas Harriot," *Oxford Dictionary of National Biography* (2004), p. 6.

Rochot, Bernard. *Les Travaux de Gassendi: Sur Epicure et sur l'Atomisme 1619–1658*. Paris: Librairie Philosophique J. Vrin, 1944.

Rosenbaum, Stephen. "How to Be Dead and Not Care," *American Philosophical Quarterly* 23 (1986).

———. "Epicurus and Annihilation," *Philosophical Quarterly* 39 (1989), pp. 81–90.

———. "The Symmetry Argument: Lucretius Against the Fear of Death," *Philosophy and Phenomenological Research* 50 (1989), pp. 353–73.

———. "Epicurus on Pleasure and the Complete Life," *The Monist*, 73 (1990), pp. 21–41.

Rösler, Wolfgang. "Hermann Diels und Albert Einstein: Die Lukrez-Ausgabe von 1923/24," *Hermann Diels (1848–1922) et la Science de l'Antiquité*. Geneva: Entretiens sur l'Antiquité Classique, 1998.

Rowland, Ingrid D. *Giordano Bruno: Philosopher/Heretic*. New York: Farrar, Straus & Giroux, 2008.

Ruggiero, Guido, ed. *A Companion to the Worlds of the Renaissance*. Oxford: Blackwell, 2002.

Ryan, Lawrence V. "Review of *On Pleasure* by Lorenzo Valla," *Renaissance Quarterly* 34 (1981), pp. 91–93.

Sabbadini, Remigio. *Le Scoperte dei Codici Latini e Greci ne' Secoli XIV e XV*. Florence: Sansoni, 1905.

Saiber, Arielle, and Stefano Ugo Baldassarri, eds. *Images of Quattrocento Florence: Selected Writings in Literature, History, and Art*. New Haven: Yale University Press, 2000.

Santayana, George. *Three Philosophical Poets: Lucretius, Dante, and Goethe*. Cambridge, MA: Harvard University Press, 1947.

Schmidt, Albert-Marie. *La Poésie Scientifique en France au Seizième Siècle*. Paris: Albin Michel, 1939.

Schofield, Malcolm, and Gisela Striker, eds. *The Norms of Nature: Studies in Hellenistic Ethics*. Paris: Maison des Sciences de l'Homme, 1986.

Schottenloher, Karl. *Books and the Western World: A Cultural History*, trans. William D. Boyd and Irmgard H. Wolfe. Jefferson, NC: McFarland & Co., 1989.

Sedley, David. *Lucretius and the Transformation of Greek Wisdom*. Cambridge: Cambridge University Press, 1998.

Segal, C. *Lucretius on Death and Anxiety: Poetry and Philosophy in De Rerum Natura*. Princeton: Princeton University Press, 1990.

Seznec, Jean. *The Survival of the Pagan Gods: The Mythological Tradition and Its Place in Renaissance Humanism and Art*, trans. Barbara F. Sessions. New York: Harper & Row, 1953.

Shapin, Steven, and Simon Schaffer. *Leviathan and the Air-Pump: Hobbes, Boyle, and the Experimental Life*. Princeton: Princeton University Press, 1985.

Shea, William. "Filled with Wonder: Kant's Cosmological Essay, the Universal Natural History and Theory of the Heavens," in Robert Butts, ed., *Kant's Philosophy of Physical Science*. Boston: Kluwer Academic Publishers, 1986.

Shell, Susan. *The Embodiment of Reason: Kant on Spirit, Generation, and Community*. Chicago: University of Chicago Press, 1996.

Shepherd, Wm. *Life of Poggio Bracciolini*. Liverpool: Longman et al., 1837.

Shirley, J. W. *Thomas Harriot: A Biography*. Oxford: Clarendon Press, 1983.

———, ed. *Thomas Harriot: Renaissance Scientist*. Oxford: Clarendon Press, 1974.

Sider, David. *The Library of the Villa dei Papiri at Herculaneum*. Los Angeles: J. Paul Getty Museum, 2005.

———, ed. and trans. *The Epigrams of Philodemos*. New York: Oxford University Press, 1997.

Sikes, E. E. *Lucretius, Poet and Philosopher*. New York: Russell & Russell, 1936.

Simonetta, Marcello. *Rinascimento Segreto: Il mondo del Segretario da Petrarca a Machiavelli*. Milan: Franco Angeli, 2004.

Simons, Patricia. "A Profile Portrait of a Renaissance Woman in the National Gallery of Victoria," *Art Bulletin of Victoria* [Australia] 28 (1987), pp. 34–52.

———. "Women in Frames: The Gaze, the Eye, the Profile in Renaissance Portraiture," *History Workshop Journal* 25 (1988), pp. 4–30.

Singer, Dorothea. *Giordano Bruno: His Life and Thought*. New York: H. Schuman, 1950.

Smahel, Frantisek, ed. *Häresie und Vorzeitige Reformation im Spätmittelalter*. Munich: R. Oldenbourg, 1998.

Smith, Christine, and Joseph F. O'Connor. "What Do Athens and Jerusalem Have to Do with Rome? Giannozzo Manetti on the Library of Nicholas V," in Marino and Schlitt, eds., *Perspectives on Early Modern and Modern Intellectual History: Essays in Honor of Nancy S. Struever*. Rochester, NY: University of Rochester Press, 2000, pp. 88–115.

Smith, Cyril. *Karl Marx and the Future of the Human*. Lanham, MD: Lexington Books, 2005.

Smith, John Holland. *The Great Schism, 1378*. London: Hamish Hamilton, 1970.

Smith, Julia M. H. *Europe After Rome: A New Cultural History, 500–1000*. Oxford: Oxford University Press, 2005.

Smuts, R. Malcolm, ed. *The Stuart Court and Europe: Essays in Politics and Political Culture*. Cambridge: Cambridge University Press, 1996.

Snow-Smith, Joanne. *The Primavera of Sandro Botticelli: A Neoplatonic Interpretation*. New York: Peter Lang, 1993.

Snyder, Jane McIntosh. "Lucretius and the Status of Women," *The Classical Bulletin* 53 (1976), pp. 17–19.

———. *Puns and Poetry in Lucretius' De Rerum Natura*. Amsterdam: B. R. Gruner, 1980.

Snyder, Jon R. *Writing the Scene of Speaking: Theories of Dialogue in the Late Italian Renaissance*. Stanford: Stanford University Press, 1989.

Spencer, T. J. B. "Lucretius and the Scientific Poem in English," in D. R. Dudley, ed., *Lucretius*. London: Routledge & Kegan Paul, 1965, pp. 131–64.

Spinka, Matthew. *John Hus and the Czech Reform*. Hamden, CT: Archon Books, 1966.

———. *John Hus: A Biography*. Princeton: Princeton University Press, 1968.

Stanley, John L. *Mainlining Marx*. New Brunswick, NJ: Transaction Publishers, 2002.

Stevenson, J. ed. *A New Eusebius: Documents Illustrating the History of the Church to ad 337*. London: SPCK, 1987.

Stinger, Charles L. *Humanism and the Church Fathers: Ambrogio Traversari (1386–*

1439) and Christian Antiquity in the Italian Renaissance. Albany: State University of New York Press, 1977.

———. *The Renaissance in Rome.* Bloomington: Indiana University Press, 1998.

Stites, Raymond. "Sources of Inspiration in the Science and Art of Leonardo da Vinci," *American Scientist* 56 (1968), pp. 222–43.

Strauss, Leo. *Natural Right and History.* Chicago: University of Chicago Press, 1953.

Struever, Nancy S. "Historical Priorities," *Journal of the History of Ideas* 66 (2005), p. 16.

Stump, Phillip H. *The Reforms of the Council of Constance (1414–1418).* Leiden: E. J. Brill, 1994.

Surtz, Edward L. "Epicurus in Utopia," *ELH: A Journal of English Literary History* 16 (1949), pp. 89–103.

———. *The Praise of Pleasure: Philosophy, Education, and Communism in More's Utopia.* Cambridge, MA: Harvard University Press, 1957.

Symonds, John Addington. *The Renaissance in Italy.* London: Smith, Elder & Co., 1875–86.

———. *Renaissance in Italy.* Vol. 3: *The Fine Arts.* London: Smith, Elder & Co., 1898.

Tafuri, Manfredo. *Interpreting the Renaissance: Princes, Cities, Architects,* trans. Daniel Sherer. New Haven: Yale University Press, 2006.

Teodoro, Francesco di, and Luciano Barbi. "Leonardo da Vinci: Del Riparo a' Terremoti," *Physis: Rivista Internazionale di Storia della Scienza* 25 (1983), pp. 5–39.

Tertullian. *The Writings of Quintus Sept. Flor. Tertullianus,* 3 vols. Edinburgh: T. & T. Clark, 1869–70.

———. *Concerning the Resurrection of the Flesh.* London: SPCK, 1922.

———. *Ante-Nicene Fathers,* ed. A. Roberts and J. Donaldson, vol. 4. Grand Rapids, MI: Wm. B. Eerdmans Publishing Co., 1951.

———. *Tertullian's Treatise on the Incarnation.* London: SPCK, 1956.

———. *Disciplinary, Moral and Ascetical Works,* trans. Rudolph Arbesmann, Sister Emily Joseph Daly, and Edwin A. Quain. New York: Fathers of the Church, 1959.

———. *Treatises on Penance,* trans. William P. Le Saint. Westminster, MD: Newman Press, 1959.

———. *Christian and Pagan in the Roman Empire: The Witness of Tertullian,* Robert D. Sider, ed. Washington, DC: Catholic University of America, 2001.

Tertulliano. *Contro gli Eretici.* Rome: Città Nuova, 2002.

Thatcher, David S. *Nietzsche in England 1890–1914.* Toronto: University of Toronto Press, 1970.

Thompson, James Westfall. *The Medieval Library.* Chicago: University of Chicago Press, 1939.

———. *Ancient Libraries.* Berkeley: University of California Press, 1940.

Tielsch, Elfriede Walesca. "The Secret Influence of the Ancient Atomistic Ideas and the Reaction of the Modern Scientist under Ideological Pressure," *History of European Ideas* 2 (1981), pp. 339–48.

Toynbee, Jocelyn, and John Ward Perkins. *The Shrine of St. Peter and the Vatican Excavations*. New York: Pantheon Books, 1957, pp. 109–17.

Trinkaus, Charles. *In Our Image and Likeness*. Chicago: University of Chicago Press, 1970.

———. "Machiavelli and the Humanist Anthropological Tradition," in Marino and Schlitt, eds., *Perspectives on Early Modern and Modern Intellectual History*. Rochester, NY: University of Rochester Press, 2000, pp. 66–87.

Tuma, Kathryn A. "Cézanne and Lucretius at the Red Rock," *Representations* 78 (2002), pp. 56–85.

Turberville, S. *Medieval Heresy and the Inquisition*. London and Hamden, CT: Archon Books, 1964.

Turner, Frank M. "Lucretius Among the Victorians," *Victorian Studies* 16 (1973), pp. 329–48.

Turner, Paul. "Shelley and Lucretius," *Review of English Studies* 10 (1959), pp. 269–82.

Tyndall, John. "The Belfast Address," *Fragments of Science: A Series of Detached Essays, Addresses and Reviews*. New York: D. Appleton & Co., 1880, pp. 472–523.

Ullman, B. L. *Studies in the Italian Renaissance*. Rome: Edizioni di Storia e Letteratura, 1955.

Vail, Amy, ed. "Albert Einstein's Introduction to Diels' Translation of Lucretius," *The Classical World* 82 (1989), pp. 435–36.

Valla, Lorenzo. *De vero falsoque bono*, trans. and ed., Maristella de Panizza Lorch. Bari: Adriatica, 1970.

———. *On Pleasure*, trans. A. Kent Hieatt and Maristella Lorch. New York: Abaris Books, 1977, pp. 48–325.

Vasari, Giorgio. *Lives of the Most Eminent Painters, Sculptors, and Architects*. London: Philip Lee Warner, 1912.

———. *The Lives of the Artists*, trans. Julia Conaway Bondanella and Peter Bondanella. Oxford: Oxford University Press, 1988.

Vespasiano. *The Vespasiano Memoirs: Lives of Illustrious Men of the XVth Century*, trans. William George and Emily Waters. New York: Harper & Row, 1963.

Virgil. *Virgil's Georgics*, trans. John Dryden. London: Euphorion Books, 1949.

Wade, Nicholas. "Humans Have Spread Globally, and Evolved Locally," *The New York Times*, June 26, 2007, p. D3.

Wakefield, Walter L. "Some Unorthodox Popular Ideas of the Thirteenth Century," *Medievalia et Humanistica* 4 (1973), pp. 25–35.

Walser, Ernst. *Poggius Florentinus: Leben und Werke*. Hildesheim: Georg Olms, 1974.

Warburg, Aby. *Sandro Botticellis Geburt der Venus und Frühling: Eine Untersuchung uber die Vorstellungen von der Antike in der Italienischen Frührenaissance.* Hamburg & Leipzig: Verlag von Leopold Voss, 1893.

———. *The Renewal of Pagan Antiquity: Contributions to the Cultural History of the European Renaissance,* trans. David Britt. Los Angeles: Getty Research Institute for the History of Art and the Humanities, 1999, pp. 88–156.

Ward, Henshaw. *Charles Darwin: The Man and His Warfare.* Indianapolis: Bobbs-Merrill, 1927.

Webb, Clement. *Kant's Philosophy of Religion.* Oxford: Clarendon Press, 1926.

Weiss, Harry B., and Ralph H. Carruthers. *Insect Enemies of Books.* New York: New York Public Library, 1937.

Weiss, Roberto. *Medieval and Humanist Greek.* Padua: Antenore, 1977.

Wenley, R. M. *Kant and His Philosophical Revolution.* Edinburgh: T. & T. Clark, 1910.

———. *The Spread of Italian Humanism.* London: Hutchinson University Library, 1964.

———. *The Renaissance Discovery of Classical Antiquity.* Oxford: Blackwell, 1969.

West, David. *The Imagery and Poetry of Lucretius.* Norman: University of Oklahoma Press, 1969.

Westfall, Richard. "The Foundations of Newton's Philosophy of Nature," *British Journal for the History of Science,* 1 (1962), pp. 171–82.

White, Michael. *Leonardo, the First Scientist.* New York: St. Martin's Press, 2000.

Whyte, Lancelot. *Essay on Atomism: From Democritus to 1960.* Middletown, CT: Wesleyan University Press, 1961.

Wilde, Lawrence. *Ethical Marxism and Its Radical Critics.* Houndmills, Basingstoke, UK: Macmillan Press, 1998.

Wilford, John Noble. "The Human Family Tree Has Become a Bush with Many Branches," *The New York Times,* June 26, 2007, pp. D3, D10.

Wind, Edgar. *Pagan Mysteries in the Renaissance.* Harmondsworth, UK: Penguin Books, 1967.

Witt, Ronald G. "The Humanist Movement," in Thomas A. Brady, Jr., Heiko A. Oberman, and James D. Tracy, eds., *Handbook of European History 1400–1600: Late Middle Ages, Renaissance and Reformation.* Leiden and New York: E. J. Brill, 1995, pp. 93–125.

———. *"In the Footsteps of the Ancients": The Origins of Humanism from Lovato to Bruni, Studies in Medieval and Reformation Thought,* ed. Heiko A. Oberman, vol. 74. Leiden: E. J. Brill, 2000.

Woolf, Greg, and Alan K. Bowman, eds. *Literacy and Power in the Ancient World.* Cambridge: Cambridge University Press, 1994.

Yarbrough, Jean. *American Virtues: Thomas Jefferson on the Character of a Free People*. Lawrence: University Press of Kansas, 1998.

Yashiro, Yukio. *Sandro Botticelli and the Florentine Renaissance*. Boston: Hale, Cushman, & Flint, 1929.

Yates, Frances A. *Giordano Bruno and the Hermetic Tradition*. Chicago: University of Chicago Press, 1964.

Yatromanolakis, Dimitrios, and Panagiotis Roilos. *Towards a Ritual Poetics*. Athens: Foundation of the Hellenic World, 2003.

Yoon, Carol Kaesuk. "From a Few Genes, Life's Myriad Shapes," *The New York Times*, June 26, 2007, pp. D1, D4–D5.

Zimmer, Carl. "Fast-Reproducing Microbes Provide a Window on Natural Selection," *The New York Times*, June 26, 2007, pp. D6–D7.

Zorzi, Andrea, and William J. Connell, eds. *Lo Stato Territoriale Fiorentino (Secoli XIV–XV): Ricerche, Linguaggi, Confronti*. Pisa: Pacini, 2001.

Zwijnenberg, Robert. *The Writings and Drawings of Leonardo da Vinci: Order and Chaos in Early Modern Thought*, trans. Caroline A. van Eck. New York: Cambridge University Press, 1999.

PHOTOGRAPH CREDITS

Portrait of young Poggio. *Biblioteca Medicea Laurenziana, Florence, Ms. Strozzi 50, 1 recto. By permission of the Ministero per i Beni e le Attività Culturali with all rights reserved*

Poggio's transcription of Cicero. *Biblioteca Medicea Laurenziana, Florence, Ms. Laur.Plut.48.22, 121 recto. By permission of the Ministero per i Beni e le Attività Culturali with all rights reserved*

Seated Hermes. *Alinari / Art Resource, NY*

Resting Hermes. *Erich Lessing / Art Resource, NY*

Bust of Epicurus. *By courtesy of the Museo Archeologico Nazionale di Napoli / Soprintendenza Speciale per i Beni Archeologici di Napoli e Pompei*

The Flagellation of Christ, Michael Pacher. *The Bridgeman Art Library International*

Heretic Hus, burned at the stake. *By courtesy of the Constance Rosgartenmuseum*

Portrait of elderly Poggio. *© 2011 Biblioteca Apostolica Vaticana, Ms. lat.224, 2 recto*

Niccoli's transcription of *On the Nature of Things. Biblioteca Medicea Laurenziana, Florence, Ms. Laur.Plut.35.30, 164 verso. By permission of the Ministero per i Beni e le Attività Culturali with all rights reserved*

La Primavera, Sandro Botticelli. *Erich Lessing / Art Resource, NY*

Montaigne's edition of Lucretius. *Reproduced by kind permission of the Syndics of Cambridge University Library*

Ettore Ferrari's statue of Giordano Bruno. *Photograph by Isaac Vita Kohn*

INDEX

Eden Haile